THE CAVALRY
THAT BROKE
NAPOLEON

THE CAVALRY THAT BROKE NAPOLEON

THE KING'S DRAGOON GUARDS AT WATERLOO

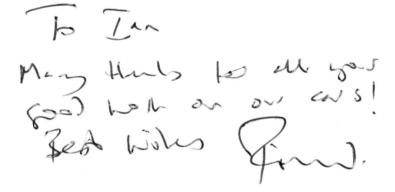

To Ian

Many thanks to all your
good luck on our cars!
Best wishes [signature].

RICHARD GOLDSBROUGH

FOREWORD BY HRH PRINCE CHARLES

The
History
Press

For all the officers and men of the 1st or King's Dragoon Guards who fought at Waterloo and for my father Harold (Bill) Goldsbrough. You were all great men and will be remembered.

★★★

'I often shed tears for the loss of my Brave Comrades, I could never imagine that men could fight as they did, they seem to have the strength and courage of lions rather than of men.'

RSM Barlow KDG

Cover illustration: The Charge of the King's Dragoon Guards at Waterloo (© Peter Archer).

First published 2016
This paperback edition published 2019

The History Press
97 St George's Place
Cheltenham, GL50 3QB
www.thehistorypress.co.uk

© Richard Goldsbrough, 2016, 2019

The right of Richard Goldsbrough to be identified as the Author of this work has been asserted in accordance with the Copyright, Designs and Patents Act 1988.

British Library Cataloguing in Publication Data.
A catalogue record for this book is available from the British Library.

ISBN 978 0 7509 9210 7

Typesetting and origination by The History Press
Printed and bound in Great Britain by TJ International Ltd

MIX
Paper from
responsible sources
FSC® C013056

CONTENTS

This book chronicles the contribution, and the fate, of a single Regiment, 1st The King's Dragoon Guards (KDG), during the Battle of Waterloo, that epic struggle that defined European politics for almost a century. On 18th June 1815, the charge of the Household Brigade, of which the KDG represented almost half the formation sabre strength, threw back the French 1st Cuirassiers around La Haye Saint Farm. Remarkably, this was the same Regiment that the KDG had previously faced at the battles of Oudenarde (1708), Malplaquet (1709), and Fontenoy (1742). It was one of the pivotal actions of a momentous day, one that was filled with drama, danger, daring and death, and upon which the destiny of millions hung. In stopping the French cavalry in their tracks, the KDG bought for Wellington more precious time in which the Allied Army could hold the Waterloo ridgeline, in which the Prussians could close, inexorably, on Napoleon's right flank and, ultimately, in which Napoleon's ambitions to dominate Europe could be finally extinguished.

The KDG success was not without cost, and the Regiment suffered more casualties, both killed and wounded, than the whole of the Light Brigade in their famous charge at Balaclava. So few officers remained alive or unscathed at the close of the day that the Regimental Sergeant Major, WO1 Barlow, invited them to share a spartan meal with himself and the surviving senior ranks, a tradition that persists to the present day in their descendent Regiment, 1st The Queen's Dragoon Guards (QDG).

I have been proud to be the Colonel-in-Chief of The Queen's Dragoon Guards for the last 13 years, as was my Grandmother, Queen Elizabeth, The Queen Mother, before me. The current Regiment has served honourably in almost every conflict and campaign the British Army has taken part in since their formation in 1959: Malaya, Aden, Northern Ireland, Bosnia, Kosovo, Iraq and Afghanistan. They continue to display all the verve, loyalty, courage, resilience and steadfastness of their predecessors, and they continue to draw strength and inspiration from the example of 1st The King's Dragoon Guards, and their remarkable heroism and sacrifice, on that extraordinary day in June 1815.

ACKNOWLEDGEMENTS

My first thanks go to HRH Prince Charles, Prince of Wales, for kindly writing the foreword to this book, which concerns the antecedent regiment to the Queen's Dragoon Guards (QDG), of which he is the colonel-in-chief.

There are three people without whom this book would not have been published who must next be thanked. There is my friend and military historian Peter Caddick-Adams, who thoughtfully encouraged me. It was his introduction to Tim Newark, another accomplished historian and also a journalist, that ensured this book was commissioned; Tim promoted it in such a way that it was accepted by The History Press. The last of this trio to whom my thanks must go is Chrissy McMorris, the managing editor of that publisher, who has been responsible for ensuring my book went to print.

Special thanks must go to Philip Haythornthwaite, who, on the death of the 7th Marquess of Anglesey, must now be considered as the doyen of historians of the British cavalry of the Regency Period. Philip was tireless in his kind help in ensuring the finer details of the King's Dragoon Guard's (KDG) uniform and tactics were correctly described, as well as providing images and useful quotations. Another who has helped me produce this study of the KDG was Clive Morris, the curator of 1st The Queen's Dragoon Guards Heritage Trust. His painstaking work of reproducing the service records of every KDG who fought at Waterloo would make a book in itself. On the basis of his work, much of the analysis of the KDG officers' and soldiers' origins and fates have been made. Another Cardiff-based supporter has been Gareth Glover, whose production of the *Waterloo Archive* series has underpinned an unbeatable knowledge of primary sources related to the battle. He has kindly pointed me in the right direction in my quest for information relating to the KDG and Waterloo. My old regiment, 1st The Queen's Dragoon Guards, has been generous in its support of this book from the top down. My thanks go to the Colonel of the Regiment, Lt-Gen. Sir Simon Mayall KBE, Lt-Col Dan Duff, the commanding officer, and the officers and men, many of whom helped in some way with my demands for photographs of the regiment's artwork. Thanks also must go to the Regimental Secretary, Lt-Col Richard (Basher) Brace, who has helped with this book and put up with me since I was the disorganised 4th Troop leader in A Squadron, of which he was the squadron sergeant-major. Also thanks must go to Jono Beatson-Hird and my fellow trustees of 1st The Queen's Dragoon Guards Heritage Trust, who have supported me in this endeavour and in my desire to commemorate all the KDGs who fought during its finest hour on 18 June 1815.

Many other kind people have helped me in so many different ways. I list them below in no particular order and I apologise if I have mistakenly omitted anyone deserving of my thanks from this list: Mark Adkin, Anthony D'Arcy Irvine, Peter Archer, Rodney Atwood, Andrew Bamford, Professor Alessandro Barbero, Becs Barrett, Professor Ian Beckett, Jill Birtwistle, Viscount Brookeborough, Siobhan Brooks, Lady Frances Carter, Andrew Cormack, Raven Cozens-Hardy (photographs), Etienne Claude, Peter Dance of H. Tempest Ltd, Tricia Datené, Paul Dawson, Peter and Sylvia Derry, the Hon. Julia Elton, Andrew Field, Callum Graham (maps), Canon Anthony Hawley, John Lee, Robert Lowry, Elizabeth Mann, James Morrow, Rebecca Newton, John Julius Norwich, Ronald Pawly, Harry Pilcher, John Quicke, Col Alan Richmond, Andrew Roberts, Michael Russell, Agata Rutkowska, John Shead, Gen. Sir Rupert Smith, Elizabeth Vickers (photographs), Gen. Sir Christopher Wallace (who has sadly now passed away), Lt-Gen. Sir Barney White-Spunner, Pierre de Wit.

Last, and by no means the least, I pass on my thanks to my family for their backing. Thanks go to my ever-patient mother Audrey, my understanding children Jack, Emily and Hugh, who have seen little of their father whilst this was written, and to my supportive wife Gina, who has tolerated this enterprise.

INTRODUCTION

Every 18 June we Queen's Dragoon Guards subalterns used to squeeze into our mess kits and proceed to the Sergeants' Mess. En route we had to be alert to the other officers' attempts at spur theft. The price for not being correctly dressed with one's mess wellingtons properly appointed was a bottle of Gosset, the then regimental champagne. We were later joined by the more senior regimental officers in the anteroom of the Warrant Officers' and Sergeants' Mess. Dinner was a jovial, alcohol-fuelled affair which ended in mess rugby, which involved a competition between the officers and sergeants of moving a package between the two ends of the anteroom. Invariably we returned to the Officers' Mess tired, bruised and a little unsteady on our feet, which those spurs did not help.

Yet there was a purpose to this ritual, and that was to remember our biggest and best battle honour, Waterloo. The tradition of the officers dining with the sergeants originated on the night of 18 June 1815, when the King's Dragoon Guards's 540-odd sabres had been reduced to thirteen and the two remaining officers ate with their men. From that day on, every 18 June the officers and sergeants of the KDG dined together. The KDG were amalgamated with the Queen's Bays in 1959 to form the QDG, and their Waterloo dinner tradition has continued with that regiment. Notwithstanding over 300 years of existence and a regimental standard festooned with battle honours, the one awarded for 18 June 1815, when Wellington and Blücher defeated Napoleon, is paramount. However, at Waterloo the KDG met its own Waterloo, as the regiment lost more men than perished in the whole of the Light Brigade in its fabled charge at Balaclava some thirty-nine years later.

I have long since left the QDG but still take an active interest in its illustrious past as one of its regimental heritage trustees. Having just experienced the Waterloo bicentennial celebrations in 2015, I was disappointed to see or hear little mention of the KDG. One particular cavalry regiment with immaculate PR seemed to charge at one from every angle, but there was very little air time for the rest of the British heavy brigades, nor for its largest component, the KDG. As fate would have it, I was offered the chance to write just the book to highlight this almost forgotten regiment and its Waterloo exploits. On the award of the contract from The History Press, I decided to pledge my proceeds to be put towards a memorial to the KDG. Hopefully this will be at or near La Haye Sainte, the site of their first and battle-saving charge on 18 June 1815.

I have been lucky to have been taken on a fascinating journey in researching this book. It is not only a military history but also a social one, which revealed much about Regency society in Britain and Ireland. From reading Captain James Naylor's diary, one really can imagine the KDG officers in a Jane Austen novel. This may actually have been the case, as 4th Troop's Captain John Sweny's brother Mark served under and was a great friend of Jane Austen's brother Francis. Mark met Jane on several occasions when she lived in Alton. The links are very tenuous and this is mere conjecture, but was it just coincidence that she created characters in her novels with the same or similar names as KDG officers such as William Elton (Philip Elton in *Emma*), William D'Arcy-Irvine (Fitzwilliam Darcy in *Pride and Prejudice*) and the Hon. Henry Bernard, son of the Earl of Bandon (Colonel Brandon in *Sense and Sensibility*)? Whilst there is no record of Jane having inter-acted with the KDG, the Sweny brothers were very close, so there may have been a connection. One of the most powerful experiences has been the contact with descendants of those KDGs who charged, many of whom left such graphic first-hand accounts of their and the regiment's actions in this battle. The power of the Internet has put me in touch with nine of the direct descendants and close relatives, which represented almost a third of the regimental officers. I have also been in touch with Sergeant John Stubbing's direct descendants and Private John Derry's great-great-grandson.[1] What is amazing is that some of the officers' families are still living in the same place that they were located at the time of Waterloo. The Eltons are still seated at Clevedon Court in Somerset; the Bernards remain in a house on their estate at Bandon, notwithstanding having been burned out of Castle Bernard by the IRA in 1921; the Quickes still live in Newton St Cyres; and the Brookes are still seated at Colebrooke in County Fermanagh.

What has also been fascinating is that I walk in the footsteps of so many of the KDGs who fought at Waterloo. I live in the village of Kingsclere in Hampshire, and this one village attracted the largest number of recruits amongst the Waterloo men, with forty-three having lived within 20 miles of it and twenty-one from within 15 miles. Their ghosts are everywhere. I live yards away from the house in which Private Joseph Long's brothers were born at Nutkin's Farm. Troop Sergeant-Major (TSM) David Benwell's uncle's house, Long Cross Farm, is still standing opposite Cheam, my children's school. And I worship at a church in which six of these men were christened, all but one falling at Waterloo.[2] The coincidences have continued on my KDG Waterloo research odyssey, with Captain George Battersby's Waterloo medal having been donated to the QDG regimental museum by an old friend from Jamaica's godmother Dorothy Michelin, who had been a Battersby and the sister-in-law of a great friend of my father's. I have also experienced great kindness from the many experts I have consulted and whose insights on their respective subjects have been fascinating and duly recognised in the acknowledgements.

There was one source for this book which was especially helpful and deserves a special mention – Bishop Michael Mann's book *And They Rode On*, published in 1984. This pithy account of the KDG at the battle focused on the canvas of Waterloo. My book has been an attempt to provide a background and to add some colour to those who fought. I hope that this book, which was intended to get the reader as close as possible to both the men and the regiment, will reveal the KDG as they really were and highlight what they contributed to probably the most significant battle ever fought by the British Army. This book is my pietas to the magnificent men of the 1st or King's Dragoon Guards who served at Waterloo. Let their names live on.

1

CUIRASSIERS MENACE

They knew the French were out there somewhere, and they needed to know where, and fast. Yet the Allied horsemen were blindfolded by the clouds of spent gunpowder that hung low over the battlefield in a black and white veil. The moisture in the air, produced by the heavy rain of the night before, caused the smoke from the hundreds of cannons to linger. They could do nothing in this miasma but wait and hope for a window in the smog through which they could see and discover the location of the main French assault.

Some moments later, a buzzing alerted them to their opponent's whereabouts. Many later likened that sound to the murmur of a swarm of bees. This droning was overlaid by the steady and ominous drumbeat of the *pas de charge* that some of these cavalrymen, as veterans of the Peninsular War, knew only too well. The hum was interrupted intermittently by the jarring reports coming from what must have been a great concentration of guns some way to the south-east. As they moved to the forward edge of the ridge, the breeze freshened and blew a gap in the haze. The revelation was the sight of a dark mass of infantry, the 16,000 men of Count d'Erlon's I Corps of Napoleon's *Grande Armée*, which, at that moment, was poised to shatter the centre of Wellington's army around the farm of La Haye Sainte.

So how did matters get to this point, where the future of an independent Europe hung on such a slim thread around this Brabantine farmhouse? Napoleon had returned from exile on Elba and, at this stage of the proceedings, only the Duke of Wellington could stop him on the field of Waterloo with his Anglo-Allied army. His ally, Marshal Blücher, was also in the vicinity on 18 June to help with his Prussian army, but he was still some miles away from Waterloo. And it was not known whether he would reach the Allies in time to save them from the impending French assault. The opposing armies first met at the indecisive battle fought at Quatre Bras on 16 June, but this action did not decide the matter. The following

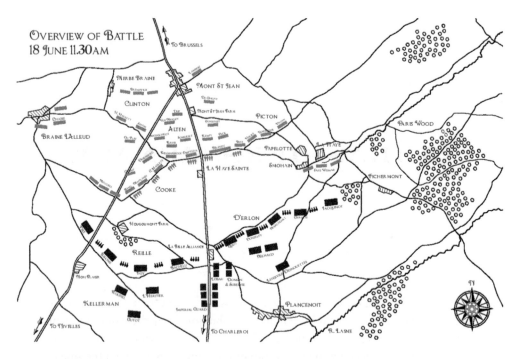

Overview of the Battle of Waterloo, 18 June, 11.30 a.m. (Gareth Glover)

evening, the antagonists lined up opposite each other in the rolling fields just south of Brussels. That place was referred to as Waterloo by Wellington in his dispatches. However, this area was on the Mont St Jean plateau, somewhat to the south of the village of Waterloo where the Duke had established his headquarters.

There had been a foul night on 17 June, with a torrential downpour of rain which soaked the battlefield into a morass. Between 11.30 and 11.45 a.m. on 18 June, Napoleon had started the battle. The French initiation of the action had been delayed by their need to wait for the sodden ground to harden somewhat before their artillery could be deployed successfully, and the late arrival of some of Durette's soldiers and elements of the French Imperial Guard. Hostilities began with the French bombardment in the area of the château of Hougoumont. After this softening-up process had been completed, the 6th Division of Reille's II Corps, under Napoleon's brother Jerôme, had assaulted this château in a feint attack. This did not meet with the immediate success that had been hoped for and had now become a battle of attrition. The French objective for the assault on Hougoumont was principally to neutralise this fortified farm complex that threatened the left flank of Reille's II Corps, which was to march in echelon to d'Erlon's I Corps. It was also hoped that an attack on Hougoumont would suck in many of Wellington's reserves to his right flank in order to expose the Allied centre to Napoleon's main attack, which was to be the *coup de main* by d'Erlon's Corps.

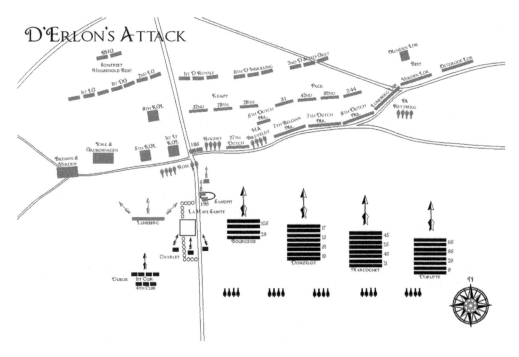

D'Erlon's attack. (Gareth Glover)

However, the results so far were having the opposite effect, as the château was consuming more in numbers of French rather than Allied reserves. In spite of this setback, Napoleon continued with his plans to attack the Allied centre at 1 p.m. with a 30-minute bombardment of that area by the guns of the French Grand Battery, which was located to the south-east of La Haye Sainte. When the guns fell silent at around 1.30 p.m., d'Erlon's men had advanced north to the assault in the direction of the Allied line on the forward edge of the Mont St Jean plateau. The French attacked in four columns, with the divisions of Quiot, Donzelot, Marcognet and Durutte, and a frontage of 600 yards. Allied round shot had torn into their ranks, yet they had still come on relentlessly and rigidly stuck to their axis of attack. The left of that line led directly to the whitewashed farm of La Haye Sainte.

Whilst the rapidly approaching masses of French infantry engrossed this clutch of British cavalry officers on the plateau, there was a simultaneous and closer threat of hundreds of French cuirassiers gathering in the fields below them. These steel-encased horsemen were the forward elements of Brigadier-General Baron Dubois's 1st Cavalry Brigade. Although one of these regiments had the subsidiary task to take some of the Allied guns, it seemed that these cuirassiers' main mission was to protect the left or western flank of d'Erlon's corps in its assault and to probe the lines of Allied infantry on the ridge just to the north-west of La Haye Sainte. The farm was now barely visible amid the blue tide that was swamping it. The French cavalry had moved to a few hundred yards from where the British observers and their horses were huddled. At a closer glance, most of this small group would have been just about distinguishable, notwithstanding their mud-spattered uniforms. The brown busbies would have only indicated they were hussars. However, it was their dark blue dolmans, brown fur-trimmed pelisses and their just-about-visible, double gold-striped trousers that would have identified most of them as being officers of the British 7th Hussars.[1]

These men were now witnessing the French emperor's gambit at Waterloo, his key opening move which had been concealed by the feint attack on the Château of Hougoumont over to their west. He had based his battle plan on his tactical principles of fast and aggressive action concentrated on a decisive point. Napoleon's plan that day was so simple, and he was confident in its success. The job in hand would be 'nothing more serious than eating one's breakfast', as he famously reassured his agitated Chief of Staff, Marshal Soult, on the night before the battle.[2]

Napoleon's intention appeared to have been to use some of his cuirassiers to cover Quiot's 1st Division in d'Erlon's I Corps, as well as to provide protection to the right flank of Reille's II Corps. They could also have been deployed in a speculative attempt to create a hole in Wellington's centre around the Mont St Jean crossroads, just north of La Haye Sainte farm. If Napoleon's cavalry had managed to rupture that decisive point, his infantrymen could have followed the cuirassiers and flooded through any resultant gap, thereby splitting Wellington's forces in half. The French could then have rolled up the flanks of the Allied army, which would likely have resulted in its defeat. It was not so much the taking of ground but the destruction of Wellington's army that was Napoleon's strategy. His intention had been to separate and destroy each of the Allied armies piecemeal in order to negotiate a peace with them that would allow his resumption of the emperorship of the French on terms favourable to himself.

The hussars rode westwards along the edge of the low plateau of Mont St Jean ridge on the muddy track known locally as the *Chemin d'Ohain*. This road ran from the village of Braine l'Alleud in the south-west of Wellington's position and continued north-east to the village of Ohain. Much of it marked the Allied front line. Almost halfway along the Allied positions, the horsemen arrived at the crossroads where the Ohain road crossed the main road that ran south from Brussels to Charleroi. The crossroads itself was a significant place and was later named the Elm Tree, or Wellington's, Crossroads, as it was here, under a tree, that the Duke spent some time during the battle.

Almost opposite them and to the left was one of the two major Allied strongpoints, La Haye Sainte, where the 2nd Light Battalion of the King's German Legion (KGL), under Major Baring, was holding out against the surging French columns. They could recognise but not see these German troops in the farm buildings, as well as the 95th Rifles, holed up in a sandpit next to the farm, by the distinctive cracks of their Baker rifles, that sounded so different to the lower-pitched report of the muskets carried by most of the other infantry on the battlefield. Nearby them, on their right, were Ompteda's King's German Legionaries. The hussar officers were aware that the British heavy cavalry, 'the heavies', were nearby and behind them, out of sight on the reverse slope of the Allied position. The Household Brigade was on the west side of the Brussels–Charleroi road behind Ompteda's brigade, and the Union Brigade was to the east of this road behind Pack's brigade.

Having reined in their horses, to the right, they could spy Kielmansegge's Hanoverians and Halkett's British brigade stretching down in a line to the west. Moments later, the wind had started to swirl and once more the shrouds of smoke parted to allow the hussars to observe the ground in the valley to their south. To their astonishment, through this window in the clouds they saw yet more French in the drenched fields of rye in the valley below them. This time they were not the dark columns of infantry, they were the steel-clad ranks of hundreds of cuirassiers. Major Thornhill was the first to notice this new threat from this group, who were ADCs to Henry Paget, 2nd Earl of Uxbridge, himself still a 7th Hussar as the regimental colonel[3], and the general commanding the British cavalry. Uxbridge and his entourage had just been positioning two cavalry brigades in the area of Hougoumont in response to the French attacks there. They were in the process of riding east along the Allied front line when they had spotted the French cuirassiers.

Uxbridge was described by Baron Stockmar in his diaries as, 'A tall, well-made man; wild, martial face, high forehead, with a large hawk's nose', and he had 'a great ease of manner'. He was no stranger to Napoleon's armies, having faced them in the Peninsular War, where, when under the command of Sir John Moore, he had been one of the most successful leaders of cavalry, achieving great successes at the battles of Sahagún and Benavente (1808). Not only a great commander, he had also introduced much-needed reforms to British cavalry training methods in 1797–98. But in 1810, his adulterous affair with Wellington's younger brother Henry's wife, Lady Charlotte Wellesley, put his illustrious career on hold. His romantic preferences, along with his seniority to Wellington, stopped him from being employed in the Duke's Peninsular campaign. Wellington was not happy when Uxbridge was foisted on him as his sole commander of cavalry in April 1815.

In *One Leg*, Uxbridge's biography, his descendant, the 7th Marquess of Anglesey, wrote, 'Wellington, always sceptical of "clever" men, much preferred the sound and solid to the brilliant and imaginative. Wellington felt safer with officers who bore in mind his own advice to Combermere, "that cavalry should be always held well in hand".'[4] Uxbridge was certainly not the Duke's first choice to lead the cavalry in the upcoming Flanders campaign in 1815, given they had not previously served together and because the Earl was 'clever'. Wellington's first choice for the job had been his old cavalry chief in the Peninsular, Lord Combermere. Uxbridge's biographer appears to have thought he was more of a 'yes-man', with whom Wellington had served since 1799 during his India days. At the very least, he would have tolerated the appointment of Uxbridge alongside Combermere as the co-commander.

This was revealed in the commander-in-chief's secretary, Major-General Sir Henry Torrens's, letter to the Earl of Bathurst, in which Sir Henry expressed his desire for a deal that might 'eventually be made for the employment both of Lords Uxbridge and Combermere. Upon this point the Duke has been perfectly fair and reasonable.'[5] However, the Prince Regent, the Duke of York, and some senior officers at Horse Guards ensured there was to be only one commander of the cavalry, and that was to be Uxbridge. In spite of their families' antagonism and their professional differences, the two men got on at a personal level.[6]

However, Uxbridge, as will be discovered later, still had a point to prove to his chief that day, and may also have been smarting at his put-down by the Duke earlier that morning. As second-in-command, just in case anything should happen to his boss, Uxbridge quite reasonably wished to know what Wellington's plans were for the battle. The Duke replied with the question, 'Who will attack first tomorrow, I or Buonaparte?', to which Uxbridge replied, 'Buonaparte.' Upon which Wellington caustically replied, 'Buonaparte has not given me any idea of his projects; and as my plans will depend upon his, how can you expect me to tell you what mine are?'[7]

It was now 2 p.m. and the sight of the French cuirassiers spurred Uxbridge into action. However, the cavalry commander and his retinue were still unaware that the cuirassiers were reorganising, exhausted and elated, having just all but destroyed the Lüneburg Light Battalion. This unit had suffered 50 per cent casualties, including its commanding officer, Lieutenant-Colonel Klencke, who had been seriously wounded; and its colour was taken. The unfortunate Hanoverians had been ordered to leave the safety of their square and rush the 200 yards or so to relieve the pressure on La Haye Sainte, where Major Baring and his 400 King's German Legionnaires looked like they were about to be overwhelmed by the forward elements of d'Erlon's infantry. These French troops were from Colonel Charlet's brigade. The Hanoverians and some of Baring's men were caught in the open by the cuirassiers and did not stand a chance. They suffered rather like the French infantry were to later in the day during the subsequent charges by the British 'heavies'. The contest of cavalry against infantry that was broken and in the open was always going to be a one-sided affair.

After the assault on the Lüneburgers, the cuirassier commander, Colonel Ordener, knew that he had to get his men to regroup in order to focus on the job with which Marshal Ney had personally tasked him. This was the 'capture and removal of an English battery placed near to the farm of Mont St Jean, which was inflicting too much harm on our line'.[8] He probably then intended to probe north, with the hope of cutting the Allied line in the area of the squares belonging to Kielmansegge's Hanoverians and Ompteda's KGL. This point was just west of the Elm Tree Crossroads. It was also just a couple of hundred yards distant from the

1st, or King's Dragoon Guards, which regiment was located in the centre of the Household Cavalry Brigade's holding area on the Mont St Jean plateau.

The men of the KDG spent a miserable night on 17 June. They had bivouacked as best they could in a muddy morass of a field and the rain had bucketed down throughout the night. TSM James Page, a native of Merton, and an old sweat of fifteen years' service with the regiment, described the KDG's night and their actions in the early hours of the day of the battle: 'We began to get dry, and as the rain ceased we wrung out our clothes, put them on again, and very few of them have been pulled off since.'[9] Page thought the men were in a bad physical state, as the 3rd Troop sergeant-major continued his description of their conditions in his letter:

> We remained in this situation the whole of the night halfway up to our knees in mud. Firing commenced the next morning, viz the 18th at daybreak which made the third day. What seemed worst of all during these three days, we could draw no rations, consequently we were without anything to eat or drink.[10]

Page's comments were supported by one of the KDG officers, Captain James Naylor, the commander of 6th Troop, whose diary entry for 18 June mentioned that, 'We continued our retreat until we took position in front of Waterloo for the night, where we bivouacked during an incessant rain and without any refreshment or forage.'[10] Naylor had joined the regiment around the same time as Page, and was the second most senior captain in the regiment after Michael Turner.[11]

Regimental Sergeant-Major (RSM) Thomas Barlow had a particularly frustrating night but was cheered up by a kind gesture from Naylor, as he described in a letter home to his wife Betsy:

> [We] then retired to a strong position near Waterloo and Bivouacked for the night, on very wet ground and inclement weather and without covering we remained all night, the wet ground our bed, the canopy of heaven our curtain, no sooner had I dismounted and taken off my valise when my horse and my servants ran away, you may judge my situation when I inform you that my Cloak and Blue Great Coat were on my horse and could not be found. Capt Naylor gave me a cigar to smoke which was all the comfort I had that night. The next morning I sent men in search of my horse who were so fortunate as to find him and the cloak but the coat was gone.[12]

Barlow was the most senior non-commissioned officer (NCO) in the regiment. At that time he was 30 years old and younger than Page. Barlow had progressed swiftly through the ranks, having only served for fourteen years since he enlisted at the age of 16. He wrote a series of letters to his wife in the Yorkshire town of Bradford during the Flanders campaign and the occupation of Paris. Another useful source of information on the KDG at Waterloo was from the pen of Captain William Elton, who commanded 1st Troop. Straight after the battle, he wrote a letter to his fellow KDG troop captain John Bringhurst's former boss, General Sir Henry Fane. This was to inform the general of his friend's death at Waterloo. In this letter, Elton mentioned the men's condition that morning was such that, 'notwithstanding the bivouac that night in such weather, they were next day quite fit for service'.[13]

At first light, the KDG began to prepare itself for battle. Horses and men were turned out the best they could be in the conditions, and weapons were cleaned. At around 6 a.m., the four regiments were concentrated into a brigade formation and then moved south a short distance in the direction of the enemy, to take up position as a second line behind the infantry on the forward edges of the Mont St Jean plateau.[14] The KDG's final location before the first charge was in the middle of the Household Brigade's concentration area. This was at the bottom of a reverse slope, 'with its left near to the Brussels–Charleroi main road, or *chaussée*, about 250 yards in front of the farm at Mont Saint Jean'.[15] Mont St Jean was to the north of their location. Directly to their south, and between them and the French, was Ompteda's 2nd KGL Brigade of Alten's 3rd British Division.

Further out, to their south-east, and directly east of Ompteda's men, was Picton's 5th Infantry Division on the Allied left flank. To their south-east were the farms of Papelotte and La Haye and the Château of Frichermont. The village of Plancenoit, just to the north of which the centre of the French Army was arrayed, was around 2 miles almost directly to their south. This village lay just east of the Brussels– Charelroi road that ran down to the south in their immediate east, past the farm of La Haye Sainte. To the Household Brigade's front and west was the Allied right flank, protected, amongst other units, by the Guards brigades of Maitland and Byng. These were located just to the north of the Château of Hougoumont, which lay 1½ miles to the south-west of the 1st Cavalry Brigade's location.

Naylor commented in his diary how the soldiers, although having been put on alert at daybreak, did very little until 11 a.m., when the KDG was formed into squadrons. 'Having formed up the first incident of significance for the regiment was the bombardment from the French cannons.'[16] However, those members of the regiment who recorded the events of mid-to-late morning that day all seem to have different recollections as to when they started suffering from incoming French cannon fire. Elton thought it had started earlier than the other observers:

At ten o'clock the regiment began to suffer before they were mounted & in columns, from the shot which missed the English batteries 200 yards in our front. Major Bringhurst recommended the colonel to move nearer to the battery, which was done with good effect; the shot passing over us & killing the Belgian cavalry who took our ground during the time they staid [*sic*] in the field; and previous to their running away and plundering our baggage.[17]

Private Thomas Hasker, a 26-year-old former framework knitter from Birmingham, reckoned the bombardment started around the time the regiment was formed into squadrons. He wrote, 'About eleven o'clock, the balls came whistling over the hills, occasionally striking one or other of our men or horses.'[18] Naylor reckoned the first salvoes came over an hour later, writing, 'At 12 a general cannonade commenced by which we experienced some loss.'[19] The inconsistency in timings is seen amongst many of the observers to this battle.[20] Page gave more detail on the bombardment in one of his letters:

> The men were ordered to dismount and lie on the ground beside their horses so as to avoid the worst of the cannon fire. We lost many men and horses by the cannon of the enemy. While covering the infantry we were sometimes dismounted in order to rest our horses, also when we were in the low ground, so that the shot from the French might fly over our heads. Whilst in this situation I stood leaning with my arm over my mare's neck when a large shot struck a horse by the side of mine[,] killed him on the spot and knocked me and my mare nearly down, but it did us no injury.[21]

Elton's commentary on the events that morning continued, 'Lord E. Somerset thinking we were still too much in line of the batteries, deployed into line on one side & in rear of the infantry.'[22]

Lord Edward Somerset was the general commanding the 1st British Cavalry Brigade to which the KDG belonged. He was a historically fitting choice of British commander, given the opponents that day. As a Plantagenet, he was a direct descendant of King Edward III, the victor of Crécy and Poitiers; be it as it might from the wrong side of the 3rd Duke of Somerset's blanket. Anyway, he was a good officer who earned promotion as fast as regulation would permit. He proved himself a talented cavalry commander in the Peninsular War, having been present at the Battle of Vitoria and commanded his regiment at Talavera and Bussaco. He gained particular recognition for his actions at the Battle of Orthez. Significantly, he had taken part in the famous charge of Le Marchant's heavy cavalry at Salamanca, for which success he was promoted to major-general and given command of the Hussar Brigade.

During the Hundred Days campaign in 1815, Wellington numbered the cavalry brigades in a sequence of one to seven. The first two were designated heavy. As the 1st Heavy Cavalry Brigade, along with the KDG, contained the Household troops of the 1st and 2nd Life Guards and the Royal Horse Guards (Blues), it was referred to as the Household Brigade. The 2nd British Cavalry Brigade contained an English, a Scottish and an Irish regiment and was thus called the Union Brigade. The latter regiments were the 1st Royal Dragoons (Royals), the 2nd, Royal North British Dragoons (Greys) and the 6th, Inniskilling Dragoons. It was commanded by Major-General Sir William Ponsonby.

The rest of the Allied cavalry consisted of light dragoons and hussars. The 3rd Brigade was an Allied composite and comprised 1st and 2nd Light Dragoons of the KGL and the British 23rd Light Dragoons, and was commanded by Major-General Sir William Dornberg. Major-General Sir John Vandeleur commanded the 4th Cavalry Brigade, which comprised the 11th, 12th and 16th Light Dragoons. The regiments of the 5th Brigade, under Major-General Sir Colquhoun Grant, that were present at Waterloo were the 7th and 15th Hussars and the 13th Light Dragoons, attached from the 7th Cavalry Brigade. The 6th Brigade was another Allied composite, which comprised the 10th and 18th Hussars as well as the 1st Hussars of the KGL, commanded by Major-General Sir Hussey Vivian. The 7th Cavalry Brigade, under Sir Frederick Arentschildt, consisted of just the 13th Light Dragoons and the 3rd KGL Hussars. As the latter had only arrived at Waterloo on the morning of 18 June, the 13th Light Dragoons had been attached to Grant's 5th Cavalry Brigade and the 3rd KGL Hussars, with seven troops present, had stood on their own at the Battle of Waterloo in the rear of the centre.[23]

Meanwhile, back on the battlefield of Waterloo, the commander of cavalry was not happy. Uxbridge realised that he had to snuff out the French threat as quickly as possible or the day would be lost. This meant he probably had to throw in the nearest cavalry unit he had to hand. This was the Household Cavalry Brigade, located just a couple of hundred yards away from where Uxbridge and his retinue had halted. He then galloped east along the Mont St Jean ridge to the 1st Cavalry Brigade's concentration area some 330 yards north of the Elm Tree Crossroads, at the junction of the Ohain and Brussels–Genappe roads, just north of La Haye Sainte. It was now around about 2.10 p.m.

2

UXBRIDGE 'PUTS THE WHOLE IN MOTION'

Just prior to Uxbridge's arrival at the Household Brigade's location, Somerset's observers had returned from their reconnaissance. Earlier in the day he had sent a subaltern from each of the four Household Brigade regiments to the forward edge of the Mont St Jean ridge to observe the enemy's dispositions. They now returned with news of the cuirassiers approaching from the west and pointed out the French infantry massing to the east of La Haye Sainte. With the benefit of this intelligence, Somerset anticipated his chief's orders to charge and had given orders for his brigade to form up. To the west of the Household Brigade was the Dutch-Belgian Heavy Brigade commanded by Major-General Trip, and just to the east of the Brussels road was the Dutch-Belgian 2nd Light Brigade, under Major-General van Merlen; both brigades were part of the Netherlands Cavalry Division. The Duke of Cumberland's Hussars of the Hanoverian Cavalry Brigade, under Lieutenant-Colonel Hake, were positioned in the rear of the Household Brigade. As they had not been ordered to dismount, they suffered heavily from the French artillery fire.

Private Thomas Playford of the 2nd Life Guards described the commander of the cavalry's arrival at the Household Brigade's concentration area:

> The Earl of Uxbridge rode forward to gain a full view of the conflict and to watch the progress of events, that he might bring our brigade of a thousand powerful swordsmen into action under the most favourable circumstances and at a moment when a charge of heavy cavalry was particularly wanted. [1]

Uxbridge, once he observed the cuirassiers reform and attack the infantry squares of the Hanoverians and the KGL, realised the extreme precariousness of the Allied situation and decided at that point to send in the Household Brigade to save the situation. Playford was also aware of this threat, as he 'naturally concluded a powerful attempt was being made to force the centre of the British army; and as there were no troops in our rear, we viewed ourselves as a last resource to defeat this project'.[2]

There has been some debate as to who decided to launch the heavy cavalry at Waterloo.[3] In a letter dated 18 October 1842, published in Siborne's book *Waterloo Letters*, the Marquis of Anglesey (as Uxbridge was by then styled) made it unequivocal that he made the decision to launch the two heavy cavalry brigades for their first, and shrewdly timed, charges when he wrote:

> I received no order from the Duke of Wellington to make the first charge or any other during the day. I will in a moment explain to you the footing upon which he placed me upon my arrival in Brussels. The Duke said, 'I place the whole of the Cavalry and Light Artillery of the United Army under your command.'

He finished the letter by stating, 'I felt that he [Wellington] had given me *carte blanche*, and I never bothered him with a single question respecting the movements it might be necessary to make.'[4] The Duke was still alive when this letter was published, and thus could easily have challenged Anglesey's assertions had they been a lie. So it is safe to assume, as Uxbridge had alluded to in his letter, that Wellington had shrewdly delegated the decision on when and where to deploy his horsemen to his competent commander of the cavalry.

Having arrived at his decision to launch the 1st Cavalry Brigade, Uxbridge then, to use his own words, 'ordered the Household Brigade to prepare to form line'.[5] He went on to give Lord Edward Somerset his orders. These were for the Household Brigade to charge Dubois's 1st and 4th Regiments of Cuirassiers that were only a few hundred yards to their front in a southerly direction. Like the French cuirassiers, their opponents in this particular tournament, these British cavalry were big men on big horses of over 15 hands, wielding the 1796-pattern heavy cavalry broadswords. As can be seen from contemporary illustrations in this book and from the comments made by British cavalrymen who fought at Waterloo, the 'heavies' did not slash their enemies with their sabres but killed them with the point. Luckily for them, a recent British Army directive had been issued whereby the fairly useless hatchet points of these swords were instructed to be filed down to a spear point. This made body-piercing an altogether easier task that day for the heavy brigades, who were faced with armoured opponents often impervious to the edge of their blades.

By this time, the French general Bourgeois's 2nd Brigade of Quiot's 1st Division was smashing into Kempt's 8th Brigade. The British infantry replied with volley fire and a charge that pushed the French back down the ridge. However, on their left, the infantry of Marcognet's 3rd Division and Donzelot's 2nd Division were making real headway against Pack's and van Bijlandt's men. The latter's Dutch-Belgian brigade, already severely tried at Quatre Bras, was so shaken up that it was subsequently broken, having been driven backwards by the massed French infantry.[6] The majority of this brigade retreated to the rear, which left a hole in the Allied front line, through which the forward elements of the French infantry stormed on to the top of the Mont St Jean plateau. However, some of the Dutch-Belgians maintained their position and many of that brigade returned in pursuit of the French once the latter's attack had been repulsed. As his troops poured on to the top of the ridge, Napoleon was about to make the incision in the Allied line right where he had wanted it; victory was within his grasp. Yet the thin red line stood firm. Picton's men suddenly stood up from their reverse slope positions and volley-fired into the faces of their assailants. The French then wavered. Having reacted to the immediate threat of the French cuirassiers, Uxbridge had galloped on eastwards to the Union Brigade to assess the situation to the east of the Brussels–Charleroi road. It was now 2.20 p.m. and he decided that this was the moment to act again. He could see the plight of the Hanoverian soldiers to the east of La Haye Sainte and the more grave threat from the sudden retreat of van Bijlandt's men. He knew he had to launch a counter-strike now, as there were no more Allied troops behind Kempt's wavering lines.[7] In addition to unleashing the Household Brigade, he would order the Union Brigade to charge as well to stop this infantry threat. Without a moment's hesitation, Uxbridge commanded Ponsonby to order the Union Brigade to charge d'Erlon's infantry as soon as they saw the Household Brigade starting to advance south.

For Uxbridge, this was the moment of truth. For him, this was not just a simple contest of the Allies versus the French; or, for that matter, between himself and the Duke on a personal and professional basis. The very honour of the British cavalry was at stake. Up until this point, the Duke of Wellington had made clear 'that cavalry should always be held well in hand; that your men and horses should not be used up in wild and useless charges, but put forward when you are sure that their onset will have a decisive effect'.[8] He was even reported to have said, 'I will say, the cavalry of other European armies have won victories for their generals, but mine have invariably got me into scrapes.'[9]

Wellington expressed his belief that the British cavalry trooper was more than a match for his French counterpart, but that French cavalry discipline was superior to that of the British:

> I consider our cavalry so inferior to the French from want of order, although I consider one squadron a match for two French squadrons, that I should not have liked to see four British against four French; and, as the numbers increased, and

our order became more necessary, I was more unwilling to risk our cavalry without having superiority of numbers ... Mine would gallop, but could not preserve
their order, and therefore I could not use them till our admirable infantry had
moved the French cavalry from their ground.[10]

His prejudice against the British cavalry arose from his first experience of battle in
the Peninsular War at Vimeiro (1808). During this action, the 20th Light Dragoons
had continued too far after a successful charge, and were only saved by the bayonets
of the 50th Regiment. Wellington's initial poor impression of the British cavalry
was reinforced by their actions in two further battles in the Peninsular War. These
were during the battles of Campo Mayor (1811) and Maguilla (1812). In the first
action, the 13th Light Dragoons charged and broke the French, but then threw
away their success with a wild pursuit of the enemy. General Beresford, commanding the cavalry, lost touch with the 13th Light Dragoons and, in the mistaken belief
that they had been captured, called off the action. His decision allowed the French
infantry to escape unmolested.

    This debacle led to Wellington firing off his famous Waterloo Dispatch, which
was his 1811 letter to Beresford. This was his severe rebuke of the 13th Light
Dragoons, whose conduct he described as 'that of a rabble, galloping as fast as
their horses could carry them across a plain, after an enemy to whom they could
do no mischief when they were broken ... If the 13th [Light] Dragoons are again
guilty of this conduct I shall take their horses from them.'[11] The Battle of Maguilla
was the third major event on which Wellington based his mistrust of the British
cavalry. Here, a French cavalry brigade, under the command of Brigade-General
Lallemand, routed a similar-sized British brigade under Brigadier-General Slade.
Slade's cavalry, having routed the French cavalry, galloped wildly after them. Failing
to reform, they were taken in the flank and the rear by the French cavalry reserve.

    After this battle, Wellington was prompted to write the condemnation that
tainted the name of British cavalry officers for many years thereafter. This rebuke
was contained in a letter to one of his generals, Lord Hill, dated 18 June 1812, in
which he wrote, 'I entirely concur with you in the necessity of inquiring into it
(the cavalry action at Maguilla). It is occasioned entirely by a trick of our officers
of cavalry have acquired of galloping at everything, and then galloping back as fast
as they gallop on the enemy.' However, Wellington's dispatch to Beresford did not
seem to be a fair assessment of what actually took place.[12]

    During the morning of 18 June 1815, it was likely that he was still apprehensive
of the performance of his mounted arm. However, Uxbridge intended to set the
record straight that day and prove the Duke wrong in his views on the cavalry.
Wellington's cavalry maxim, contained in the aforementioned letter of his to Lord
Hill after Maguilla, was that, 'All cavalry should charge in two lines, of which one
should be in reserve.' The commander of cavalry followed that axiom to the letter

in his orders to his heavy brigade commanders by arranging their forces to charge with one regiment in reserve. Uxbridge placed the Union Brigade on the start line for the first charge as follows: in the east on the left, three squadrons of the Inniskillings, under Lieutenant-Colonel Muter; on the right to the west, with the right-hand squadron touching the Brussels–Charleroi road, three squadrons of the Royals, under Lieutenant-Colonel Clinton; and in reserve three squadrons of Scots Greys, under Lieutenant-Colonel Hamilton.

The Household Brigade's formation was larger, with three regiments up and one in reserve. It was located to the right of the Union Brigade and just to the west of the Brussels–Charleroi road. Uxbridge placed them as follows: to the extreme east, on the left, and within sight of the Royals, two squadrons of 2nd Life Guards, under Lieutenant-Colonel the Honourable Edward Lygon; in the centre, four squadrons of the KDG, commanded by Lieutenant-Colonel Fuller; in the west, on the extreme right, two squadrons of the 1st Life Guards, under the command of Lieutenant-Colonel Ferrior; and in reserve two squadrons of the Blues, under Lieutenant-Colonel Sir Robert Hill. The axis of the left-hand squadron of the left-hand regiment of the Household Brigade, the 2nd Life Guards, was to be just to the right of the Brussels–Charleroi road. Likewise the axis for the right-hand squadron of the Royals was to abut the right or east of that road, making it the boundary between the two heavy cavalry brigades. It was hoped that these squadrons could be in contact to ensure the cohesion of the 1st and 2nd Cavalry Brigades during the first charge of the 'heavies'.

There has been some uncertainty of how many squadrons of KDG charged that day. Many accounts and representations in maps, like that in Siborne's *Waterloo Letters*, recorded them to have fielded only three squadrons. However, Sir Henry Torrens, the military secretary to the Duke of York, made it clear there were four squadrons in his letter to the Duke of Wellington on 21 April 1815, 'In reference to what I said to you respecting the inefficiency in numbers of the Household Cavalry Brigade, four squadrons of the 1st Dragoon Guards have been ordered to be attached to it.'[13]

It can also be shown that there were four squadrons on the basis of anecdotes made by two of the KDG squadron commanders. Elton mentioned, 'the right squadron & mine paired off'. So clearly there were two squadrons to the west on the right of the KDG line; the one nearest the centre commanded by Elton and the most westerly right-hand squadron most likely to have been commanded by Graham, as the most senior KDG officer after Fuller, who, as commanding officer, would not have commanded a squadron. And yet there must have been two further KDG squadrons, as Captain Waymouth of the 2nd Life Guards reported, 'He [Naylor] distinctly remembers that he commanded the centre Squadron of the King's.'[14] So if Naylor commanded the centre squadron, then there must have been another to his left in the east, which would have been a fourth squadron, presumably commanded by the KDG's senior captain, Michael Turner.

A possible explanation for the popular perception that the KDG was a three-squadron regiment at Waterloo was that the four KDG squadrons were arranged in three blocks on the start line before the first charge. Elton's and Naylor's comments that they commanded centre squadrons could have meant their units were lumped together in a two-squadron bloc behind their brigade commander for greater control. The fact that the KDG had four squadrons at the battle was also substantiated by Page's statement that there were eight KDG troops at Waterloo, as each squadron comprised two troops.[15]

At around 2.15 p.m., the regiment shook out for its first charge as a regiment in twenty-one years. Barlow described the events leading up to this charge:

> The Regiment formed in close Columns of Squadrons ready to commence the attack, the enemy then began to cannonade to which our column was very much exposed, we lost several men and horses at this time and after remaining in this situation and much exposed for about an hour we deployed into line.[16]

Captain Naylor gave some indications of the timing of these events in his diaries, 'We deployed and (I think) about 2 o'clock a charge was made by the Heavy Brigades.'[17] Uxbridge stated that having given Ponsonby his orders, 'I instantly returned to the Household Brigade, and put the whole in motion.'[18]

At around this time, the Household Brigade was undergoing the same unusual experience as Uxbridge and his aides had experienced on arriving at the Elm Tree Crossroads. They could hear, smell and feel the battle but could see nothing, as Playford, who was located on the KDG's left, described this experience:

> [T]here was a tremendous thunder of cannon which drowned every other sound, immediately in front of us; but the rising ground before us concealed from our view what was taking place. The conflict was raging violently beyond the rising ground in front of us, and the roar of artillery with the report of small arms was incessant, yet we could not see what was taking place.[19]

Private John Derry KDG from Leicester, a 23-year-old former apprentice winder to a framework knitter, in 8th Troop was recorded as remembering that at that moment, 'how he mounted ready for battle, was fearful and besought divine deliverance in prayer'.[20] The brave man that he was, Uxbridge placed himself in the front rank of the left-hand squadron of the 2nd Life Guards just west of the Brussels–Charleroi road, effectively having positioned himself at the front and in the centre of his two heavy brigades for the first charge.[21] This was a decision he was later to rue.

Just before the order for the charge was given, the KDG was made aware of just how close the enemy cavalry were. Barlow mentioned in one of his letters, 'I had no sooner moved into the Ranks after having been employed to mark the ground when the enemy cavalry charged our Infantry in the centre; we were ordered to charge[;] this was an important moment.'[22] Elton reinforced the point that the Household Brigade's charge was launched just in time to meet the immediate threat of the French cuirassiers as they forced the infantry of Ompteda's KGL and Kielmansegge's Hanoverians to form square:

> The enemy after several attacks upon the Duke's position, the brow of a hill wherein he was repulsed, seemed likely to succeed opposite our brigade by the increased fire of the artillery and musquestry [sic], 200 yards in our front. The infantry suddenly broke out of their line into solid squares & we saw the crests of the cuirassiers.[23]

With the appearance of the distinctive outlines of the cuirassiers' helmets, the stage was now set for Uxbridge, not only to save the day for the Allies but to reclaim the honour of the British cavalry and to prove both their and his effectiveness to his doubting master. The situation was now critical to the Allies. A counter-stroke was vital to prevent the French cavalry from supporting d'Erlon's infantry in overrunning Wellington's centre. To achieve this, Uxbridge's 'heavies' had to do the job, where the stakes did not get any higher than that of the future of Europe itself. As almost a quarter of this number were from the KDG, they were easily the biggest regimental presence in the British heavy cavalry that was poised to stop Napoleon.

Fiction cannot compete with the facts of the drama that was about to unfold. The time was now 2.25 p.m. on Sunday 18 June 1815, as Somerset's duty trumpeter, the 16-year-old Private John Edwards of the 1st Life Guards, raised his instrument to sound the 'charge'. However, as the shrill notes were sounded, the Household Brigade still waited until, as Sergeant-Major Page later wrote, 'the word "charge" was given for our Brigade by Colonel Fuller'.[24] The commanding officer of the King's Dragoon Guards was quoted to have then shouted joyously to his men, 'On to Paris!'[25]

★★★

This is the story of The Cavalry that Broke Napoleon: The 1st, or King's Dragoon Guards. It is an account of a regiment, the men it comprised and the epic feat of arms they achieved on 18 June 1815.

3

GLORIOUS PAST

The 1st, or King's Dragoon Guards was founded in 1685 at the same time as all but one of the seven original British dragoon guard regiments. The KDG was the senior British cavalry regiment of the line. The order of precedence within arms in the British Army was usually dictated by the age of the regiment, with the oldest being the most senior. Although there were two mounted regiments that were founded before the KDG, they ranked as its juniors. This was because in 1685 these regiments were not line cavalry but were designated dragoons, or mounted infantry. Hence the KDG were, outside the Household regiments of the Life Guards and the Royal Horse Guards, the oldest regiment of horse in the British Army, and therefore ranked first in terms of precedence in the British cavalry of the line.

The line cavalry was born in 1685, when King James II was able to convince Parliament to expand the existing standing army to meet the threat of the Duke of Monmouth, who had landed in Lyme Regis on 11 June of that year. Parliament duly gave dispensation for the immediate raising of six regiments of horse and two of dragoons. With the exception of the 7th Dragoon Guards, raised three years later as the Duke of Shrewsbury's Horse, these six regiments of horse were to become the dragoon guards regiments and were numbered from one to seven. The King's Dragoon Guards was the first to be founded, on 6 June 1685, by a royal charter commanding Sir John Lanier to raise the Queen's Regiment of Horse, so named after King James II's wife Queen Mary of Modena. It was numbered the Second Regiment of Horse, as the previously established Royal Horse Guards was ranked as the First Regiment of Horse.

The founding father of the regiment was Sir John Lanier, an experienced and respected professional soldier who had fought for much of his life on the Continent. He served in a troop of English auxiliaries under Sir Henry Jones in France, where he lost an eye. He then was promoted to be a lieutenant-colonel in Monmouth's Horse in the French Army. In terms of the officers' backgrounds, with the exception of a couple of young courtiers, seven of the nine troop commanders were veterans who had joined from other mounted regiments. The majority had served in the three troops of Horse Guards and Horse Grenadiers (Life Guards). Of the young courtiers who became troop leaders in the new regiment, one was to be the second colonel of the regiment after the death of Sir John Lanier, who was killed at the Battle of Steenkirk in 1692. In his teens he had been known as 'the beau', and he was the Honourable Henry Lumley.[1] Lumley was the younger brother of Richard, Earl of Scarborough, who had been one of the 'Immortal Seven' influential Englishmen who were signatories of the letter that invited William of Orange to take the throne of England in the Glorious Revolution of 1688. During this upheaval, Lanier, with his regiment, remained loyal to King James II until 'he forsook the throne',[2] and then he gave his allegiance to William of Orange.

Lumley was the man who really shaped the Queen's Horse, from his assumption of command in 1692 until he retired a quarter of a century later in 1717. He commanded the Queen's Horse in its initial actions. The first was the successful suppression of a mutinous Scots regiment at Sleaford in Lincolnshire, for which the regiment was awarded its first battle honour. This event was followed by its first actual feat of arms when it was sent to Scotland. Here it helped to suppress the rising by Jacobite Highland clan chiefs under the Duke of Gordon.

After a brief respite, the Jacobite threat resurfaced, this time in Ireland. On 1 July 1690, at the Battle of the Boyne, King William III seized the moment by launching himself at the Irish horsemen in a massed charge with most of his cavalry. The Queen's Horse, which numbered a total of 360 men, took part in this attack.[3] The Williamite cavalry then proceeded to take the Irish infantry in their right flank, which broke and led to a general Jacobite retreat. The Queen's Horse was recognised for its contribution to the King's victory, winning its second battle honour for the Boyne. It then took part in the final and decisive Battle of Aughrim on 12 July 1691. The Queen's Horse was part of Ruvigny's Brigade which 'bored down all before it with astounding "impetuosity" [and] decided the fate of the day'.[4] This battle ended the Jacobite threat to Ireland.

The next conflict that involved Britain was the Nine Years War (1688–97), and the recurring theme of containing the French had begun. The first major action on the Continent in which the Queen's Horse had participated ended in a defeat of the British and their allies some 20 miles south-east of Brussels, near the villages of Neerlanden and Neerwinden. However, the bravery of successive charges by the Queen's Horse had ensured the Allied infantry were able to retreat without being massacred by the French. After a brief peace, another European conflagration started, the War of the Spanish Succession (1701–14). Once again it was fear of French domination, through a tie-up of the thrones of Spain and France, that galvanised the other major European states (except Bavaria) to re-form the Grand Alliance in 1701 as a bulwark against this threat.

It was not until July 1704 that the regiment was involved in its first major battle of the war, which was the storming of the hilltop fortress of the Schellenberg. The Queen's Horse arrived in the area of this enemy castle having just taken part in the epic march of the Duke of Marlborough's army, which covered around 300 miles in five weeks from the Netherlands to the Bavarian border near Donauwörth. On 2 July, at around 6 p.m., Marlborough threw in his infantry, which failed. The Queen's Horse was part of Wood's Brigade in the cavalry contingent of thirty squadrons commanded by Lieutenant-General Lumley, which were kept behind the infantry. On the repulse of the second assault, the Bavarian Grenadiers broke the Allied infantry and were about to turn their failed assault into a rout but were stopped by some guardsmen and dismounted cavalrymen from the Queen's Horse. The regiment then took part in the pursuit of the enemy and won a fifth battle honour for its contribution to this victory.

The next engagement in which the Queen's Horse was involved was one of the most important victories for the British Army since its inception. This was the Battle of Blenheim, fought on 13 August 1704. The regiment had been part of the British cavalry under the Queen's Horse's own colonel, Lieutenant-General Lumley, and had been held in reserve directly behind General Cutts's infantry. At this battle, the regiment had mustered 480 sabres, which was around twice that of the other British cavalry regiments at the time. Its large size was still a characteristic of the regiment in 1815, as it was even then one of the largest mounted units in the British Army. When the Allied infantry was buckling under repeated French attacks at Blenheim, Lumley was ordered by Marlborough to bring the British cavalry regiments forward as part of a general advance over the River Nebel to meet the enemy.

The regiment was part of this deployment that took it over the boggy ground around the Nebel. The French then charged and pushed Lumley's horse back to the river they had just crossed. The Queen's Horse was particularly hard hit, having been charged by the enemy's horse, whilst being peppered with musket and cannonballs. On forming up, the regiment was charged and dispersed by enemy cavalry, but the French were held off by volley fire from the Queen's Horse's compatriots in the foot regiments nearby. The two opposing cavalry formations fought it out until the French broke. It was at around 4.30 p.m. that all the Allied cavalry regiments combined to drive all thirty squadrons of the French west and off the field of battle. Subsequently, Blenheim came to be the earliest battle honour to have been emblazoned on the KDG's standard.[5]

Marlborough had to wait two years until he was able to bring the French and their allies to a proper battle again at Ramillies in 1706. Whilst this was more of a victory for Britain's Dutch allies, the Queen's Horse had, in conjunction with the

Scots Greys, taken prisoner the whole of the French *Régiment du Roi*. The regiment also might have taken a set of French kettledrums during the enemy's retreat at the end of the battle, which was commemorated in a painting by Robert Alexander Hillingford. The Queen's Horse and the other British cavalry on the extreme right of the Allied line then took part in harrying the fleeing enemy.

The next action in which the regiment was involved was at Oudenarde in July 1708. During this battle, the Queen's Horse and the rest of the cavalry remained in a static position as spectators of the fighting that raged in front of them. The battle ended as another resounding victory for Marlborough's and his ally Prince Eugene of Savoy's armies. Notwithstanding its lack of action, the Queen's Horse was still awarded a battle honour for Oudenarde. This action was followed by the Battle of Malplaquet in September 1709. The Queen's Horse was located with the rest of the British cavalry on the right wing of the first line of Marlborough's army. This had been a pyrrhic victory for the British and their allies, who lost around 20,000 men to the French losses of 14,000. The regiment lost fifty-five officers and men. Victory and another battle honour had come to the Queen's Horse for a heavy price at Malplaquet.

In 1714, just after the accession of King George I to the throne, the Queen's Horse's name was changed to the King's Own Regiment of Horse. This was because the new king did not then have a Queen Consort. The name change was also granted in recognition of the regiment's services in Marlborough's campaigns. Sometime after the change in name, there came a new colour of regimental facing, with the yellow of the Stuart livery having been replaced by the dark blue of the Hanoverians.[6] This remains as the facing colour of the KDG's descendant regiment, the QDG, to this day.

Another sea change for the regiment took place in 1714, when one of its two founding fathers, General Henry Lumley, resigned and sold his colonelcy of the regiment to Lord Irwin. Although Sir John Lanier, the first commanding officer, had established and led the regiment through its first seven years, Lumley had forged it into being one of Europe's cavalry elite during Marlborough's hard-fought campaigns. Lumley had been with the regiment for thirty-two years from its inception and was instrumental in helping it to win those half-dozen dazzling battle honours, from the Schellenberg to Malplaquet.

There then followed a period of twenty-nine years of peacetime activities for the regiment in the form of home duties. It moved around the country, being stationed principally in the Midlands, the West Country, the London area and southern England. Few events of significance took place in this period, apart from the odd royal review and the brief regimental service of William Pitt the Elder, who had joined the King's Horse as a cornet in 1731. However, the future prime minister did not remain long with the regiment, having been forced to resign his commission for his maiden speech in the House of Commons in which he opposed the Excise Bill.

The next major European conflict was the War of the Austrian Succession (1740–48). The first action that involved the King's Horse was the Battle of Dettingen, which took place in June 1743 on the east bank of the River Main near Frankfurt in what is now Germany. The regiment endured several hours of defilade fire from the French batteries on the south bank of the river. The French commander, Gramont, attacked the Allied left wing with his elite French household cavalry regiments of the *Maison du Roi* and the *Gens d'Armes*. The King's Horse was moved from the right and counter-attacked the *Gens d'Armes* with Ligonier's Horse, but they were pushed back by their armoured French opponents. The French artillery then stopped their cannonade and their infantry enveloped the regiment's left flank.

It was a desperate fight and the King's Horse nearly lost its standard when Cornet Allcroft, who was carrying it, was killed, but the flag was saved. The regimental historian, Richard Cannon, described this event: 'In the middle of this action the King's Own Regiment of Horse was moved to the left of the line to drive back a portion of the enemy's cavalry which was endeavouring to turn that flank, which service it performed with great gallantry.'[7] The King's Horse, along with some other British regiments, rallied and drove back the French. Although Dettingen had ended in triumph and another battle honour, the regiment had suffered forty-five soldiers killed, which was the third highest casualties of the British cavalry on the day.[8]

The Battle of Fontenoy followed, which was somewhat of an anti-climax after Dettingen, with the cavalry inactive for much of the first part of the battle. The reason was that their commander, General Campbell, had been mortally wounded and had not communicated any of his plans to his subordinates; so the cavalry just remained behind the infantry for most of the conflict.[9] Although not in contact with the enemy, the King's Horse and British cavalry suffered from the French cannons throughout the day. At the end of the battle, the British cavalry attacked the enemy and provided a vital screen to allow the retreat of their defeated infantry. However, as the battle had been a defeat for the Allies, no battle honour was awarded to the regiment for this action.

After Fontenoy, the Jacobite threat was snuffed out at the Battle of Culloden, as a result of which the government had been keen to cut costs. This resulted in an overhaul of the British cavalry. Two troops of Life Guards were disbanded and the three senior regiments of horse were converted into dragoon guards, thereby reducing the pay scales of their soldiers (but not those of the officers) to those of dragoons. The King's Warrant of 9 January 1747 read, 'Our regiment of Dragoons now under the command of General Sir Philip Honeywood shall bear the title of Our First Regiment of Dragoon Guards.' However, the regiment's more usual name was now the King's Dragoon Guards.

The next series of battles the regiment was to fight was in the Seven Years War (1754–63). This was a global war which partially involved Britain's and France's colonies, and affected Britain in Europe in 1758 with the French invasion of Hanover. As a result, Britain sent a force under Charles, 3rd Duke of Marlborough to reclaim the Electorate of Hanover from the French. After the inactivity of guard duties, the first major action the regiment was to see was the Battle of Minden, exactly a year after having landed on the Continent. At this battle, the KDG was deployed in the first line of the right-hand column, under the commander of the cavalry, Lord George Sackville. Like Fontenoy, this was another frustrating battle for the British cavalry due to its not having been employed. This time the cavalry's inaction was as a result of the inertia of Sackville, who repeatedly refused orders to charge the enemy until it was too late for the cavalry to get involved.

One of the KDG's most significant and little-discussed actions was at the Battle of Corbach in Northern Hesse, a German electorate north of Frankfurt, where the Allies under Karl-Wilhelm, the Hereditary Prince of Brunswick, attacked the French forces under St Germain. The combination of the heavy French bombardment and charges by their cavalry threw the Allied retreat into a rout. A contemporary historian recorded, 'In this desperate situation, the prince [Prince Ferdinand of Brunswick] put himself at the head of Bland's [as the KDG were then known] and Howard's dragoons, who perfectly seconded the ardour of this young hero. They soon checked the career of the French cavalry, covered the retreat of the Germans, and thus saved the army.'[10] However, Major Mills's squadron of KDG, which had taken part in this charge, paid the price for its bravery in saving the army, as only twenty-four men returned from that squadron. The regiment lost forty-seven killed and one officer and seven men wounded.

After the Battle of Corbach, Karl-Wilhelm targeted an isolated French corps located outside the town of Warburg. The KDG was positioned behind the Marquess of Granby at the right of the first line of British cavalry. At the crucial moment in this battle, Ferdinand threw in the British cavalry under Granby to save the situation. This charge was made epic by Granby's loss of his wig at the outset, and apparently caused huge amusement in the British ranks and led to the expression of 'going at it bald-headed'.[11]

After rebutting a charge by the French horse, the British cavalry wheeled on the enemy infantry and took them in the rear and from the side. However, the three squadrons of KDG out on the extreme right took the full impact of a French counter-attack from three squadrons from the Bourbon Brigade. The KDG was overthrown and only saved by two squadrons of the Blues. The regiment recovered, re-formed and rejoined the action largely intact. The French infantry were then broken by the British cavalry charges, and the KDG comprised part of the force of ten squadrons that Granby led in pursuit of the broken enemy, who were chased across the River Diemel.

In 1763, at the end of the Seven Years War, the KDG was recalled to England. There ensued another cycle of peacetime soldiering that lasted for around thirty years. The regiment's activities were pretty much the same list of home duties and moving around the country. One remarkable officer joined in this period; the flamboyant but extremely effective Banastre Tarleton, who was commissioned into the regiment in 1775 and went on to achieve many successes in the American War of Independence (1775–83), where he was a commander of Loyalist light cavalry. The villain in Mel Gibson's film *The Patriot*, Colonel William Tavington, was based on Tarleton, but the latter was not responsible for the atrocities as Gibson portrayed. Tarleton went on to become a general and narrowly missed out to Wellington for command of the British forces in the Peninsular War.

The last action the KDG was to see before Waterloo was some twenty years previously in the Flanders campaign of the French Revolutionary War. The regiment was part of a force which helped defeat the enemy in the Battle of Villers-en-Cauchies in northern France on 24 April 1794.[12] Yet its contribution to this victory cannot have been that great, as it was not awarded a battle honour for it.[13] The KDG went on to fight at Beaumont-en-Cambrésis later that month. Frederick, Duke of York, who commanded the British troops, feinted to the French front and then sent his cavalry in from the right flank. The KDG was in the third line of Allied cavalry which charged around 20,000 French infantry obliquely from the north whilst they were facing to the east and caused great slaughter. This was a legendary cavalry action and the battle was described by the historian of the British Army, Fortescue, as 'the greatest day in the annals of the British horse'.[14] The regiment only suffered seven men killed and picked up a £500 bounty from the Duke of York as well as a battle honour.

In the period between the KDG's departure from Flanders in 1795 until its return to that region in 1815, it spent its service on home duties. It was initially based in the south of England, before being posted to York in 1808 and then on to Scotland, where it remained for a couple of years. In 1810, it was moved to Ireland and ended up in Clonmel in 1812. It was from this southern Irish garrison town that the KDG was moved to Flanders via England in 1814. There were few significant events recorded in the *The Digest of Services*[15] during this period, save the arrival in 1805 of the man who was to command the KDG at Waterloo, William Fuller.

Prior to his arrival from the 10th Dragoons, the regiment had suffered several years of mismanagement at the hands of a dishonest commanding officer, Lieutenant-Colonel Elliott, who was convicted of fraudulent behaviour and dismissed from the service. To compound the regiment's problems, Elliott's replacement, Lieutenant-Colonel Fane, had been an absentee commanding officer who only spent four months with his regiment. Fuller probably managed to tackle this breakdown in regimental discipline by ruling with a firm hand, as, according to one KDG officer, Hibbert, just prior to Waterloo he was in line for his generalship.[16] The other event of significance was in 1813, when on Lord Heathfield's death, Lieutenant-General Sir David Dundas took over the colonelcy of the KDG.

★★★

That was the broad background to the KDG as a regiment from its inception in 1685 until its last long posting before Waterloo in Clonmel in 1812. The regiment's story will be resumed in chapter nine, with its move from Clonmel to England for the winter of 1814 and its subsequent move to Flanders at the end of April 1815. Yet what was the background of the officers and men who comprised this regiment and fought at Waterloo?

4

WHO WERE THE MEN?

In the early years of the nineteenth century, KDG recruiting policy was directed from above at the British cavalry's headquarters at Horse Guards. As was to be expected, the numbers to be recruited, retained and lost were dictated by the external threats of Napoleon and the internal ones of civil unrest in Ireland and in the working-class districts of the industrialised towns. A good example was the surge in KDG recruiting in the years 1804–06 which was a direct and lagged response to fears of an invasion by the French between 1803 and 1805. The KDG was an English cavalry regiment. Although there were a few Irish, Scots and Welsh in its ranks, 96 per cent of the men and 88 per cent of the officers who fought at Waterloo were English.

The county of origin of the rank and file, in descending order, were: Leicestershire (16 per cent), Lancashire (12 per cent) and Hampshire (10 per cent), which together accounted for well over a third of the recruits. The two other counties where most recruiting took place were Yorkshire and then Nottinghamshire.[1] The vast majority of these recruits had been either textile workers or agricultural labourers. The next largest original occupation of KDG recruits was of miners from the Lancashire pits. Thus, with the exception of those from agricultural backgrounds, most recruits would have been unfamiliar with horses and had to be trained from scratch. There was little in the way of a continuation of using old skills, apart from the farriers, many of whom had formerly been blacksmiths.

According to army regulations of 1807, cavalry regiments in the early nineteenth century could recruit wherever in Britain they liked. Presumably the KDG chose to recruit in areas with a large pool of better quality potential recruits. On occasions recruiting took place near to where the regiment was based. Over the fifteen years leading up to Waterloo, during which time the bulk of the men who fought at Waterloo had joined the regiment, the KDG actively recruited in three counties. Leicestershire was visited the most by the KDG recruiting teams, followed by Lancashire and then Hampshire. For most of the men who arrived at the regiment in this period, their motivation for joining was the push factor of the bad conditions in the textiles industries and agriculture in the early years of the nineteenth century. Private Thomas Hasker of 3rd Troop KDG was a good example of such a man.

Hasker was born and brought up in the turbulent urban city centre of Birmingham. He was one of four children of a non-conformist minister who had championed the cause of the rebellious dissenters who were seeking to improve the lot of the poor. Sadly, father Hasker had hit the bottle as a result of his failed business ventures. This led to an unstable upbringing for young Hasker, who consequently became a bit of a rebel and left school at the age of 13. He tried and failed to stick at a multitude of different careers. Given his inability to hold down a job, he embarked on a peripatetic life in order to find work, moving from Birmingham to Bosworth, to Leicester and thence to Ashby-de-la-Zouch and Lichfield. When he reached his 16th birthday, life could not have been worse, as his mother died and he moved, jobless and destitute, to Nottingham. In the words of his biographer:

> All other doors closed, he deliberated, went to the barracks, looked about, decided that he was incapable of taking care of himself, and that nobody else cared for him. Within an hour he had enlisted in His Majesty's 1st (or King's) Regiment of Dragoon Guards.[2]

Hasker's last job was as a framework knitter, which was the majority occupation of the recruits from the Midlands. The French wars and the fickleness of fashion, with the switch from stockings to trousers, meant that the hosiery industry was in decline at the beginning of the nineteenth century. Employment prospects for the framework knitters were diminished by increasing mechanisation, which resulted in the Luddite riots.

It was the same story for the Lancashire cotton workers and those in the Yorkshire wool industry. The rising cost of living which resulted from the state of the economy, shortages caused by the war with France, mechanisation and deteriorating working conditions, induced many to heed the KDG recruiting call when its teams targeted the major towns in their areas in the period 1800–14. The job descriptions recorded show the regional differentiation of the type of textile work done previous to enlisting. Over 67 per cent of those joining from Lancashire had been working in the cotton industry.

By town, the most recruiting trips took place in Leicester, with thirteen out of fifteen visits between 1799 and 1814. Nottingham was the next most visited town, with eight visits over a longer period starting in 1792. Lancaster had nine visits from 1792 to 1814. The reason for this was probably the relatively higher availability of labour in those counties. In Leicestershire and Nottinghamshire, although the majority of recruits had been working in textiles, the numbers were lower, as 38 and 47 per cent respectively had been farm labourers prior to enlistment. The type of textiles work in which they had been employed varied by region. Many had been framework knitters, which was the basis of the hosiery industry peculiar to Birmingham and the East Midlands. Similar to the East Midlands, Yorkshire recruits were split, 36 per cent having been woollen workers and 23 per cent farm labourers.

In comparing the county of origin for the other ranks of the KDG with the other cavalry regiments at Waterloo, there seems to be a pattern of all of them recruiting from the industrial areas of the Midlands, Lancashire and Yorkshire. Whilst there were regiments stationed in Ireland, the South West and on the South Coast, these midland/northern counties were the areas where the majority of the British cavalry were stationed in the first fourteen years of the eighteenth century. They were based in the urban regions to control civil unrest. These were well populated regions, so a rich source of supply of potential recruits. Hence the bulk of the cavalrymen of Waterloo came from those areas. So, with the exception of Hampshire, the KDG recruited in much the same counties as her sister regiments. And whilst there is evidence that other cavalry regiments, like the 15th Light Dragoons, also recruited in Hampshire, it seems that the KDG would have been the most likely candidate as that county's cavalry regiment.

Hampshire was the anomaly of the big five KDG recruiting counties, as it was the only one with an economy which was based almost entirely on agriculture, with 84 per cent of the recruits previously having been employed on the land. What is interesting is that Hampshire was neither harder hit in terms of an agricultural depression than any of the other larger counties with rural-based economies, nor was it a KDG garrison county over the period of recruitment in question of 1800–15. The recruiting teams tended to have 'fixed stations' from where they conducted their business. A regular visit was made to Basingstoke, but Winchester, Andover and Southampton were also targeted. Whilst there are examples of recruiting trips to small population centres, for example Dalston, Staffordshire, in 1801 and Ham in Surrey in 1808, it was unusual to recruit outside the larger towns.

The commanding officer had the discretion to choose one of the trips to fairs or markets if it was felt there would be a good chance of hiring the right men. The 1813 visit to the relatively tiny community of Kingsclere in north Hampshire stands out as one such one-off trip. This was probably prompted by the commanding officer, Fuller, having appreciated and trusted Sergeant-Major Benwell's strong connections in Kingsclere, the village of his birth and life before joining the regiment. His uncle Thomas, as a yeoman farmer, was a man of standing in the local community who lived and worked at Long Cross Farm. As a result of these strong local connections, it was probably Benwell who was the senior NCO used for this recruiting visit to the Parish of Kingsclere in February 1813. On this visit, four local men were recruited, privates George Long, Samuel Tucker, Jeremiah Hill and John Picton.

Like the farm labourers of Leicestershire, those of Hampshire were attracted to the perceived better quality of life in the army. For the last two decades of the eighteenth century up to Waterloo, the English rural population had been under pressure from bad harvests, changing demographics and a creaking poor relief system. A number of factors had made life more uncomfortable for English agricultural workers. The structural changes of the Enclosure Acts meant that farm workers were no longer retained for the whole year during which the labourer used to live with his employer and receive cash and payment in kind in the form of his subsistence. The new norm was for employment on cash-only, short-term contracts, and jobs were seasonal. The agricultural worker's standard of living was further threatened by having been squeezed by the price rises brought on by the shortages caused by the Napoleonic Wars.

To make matters worse, mechanisation, such as the introduction of threshing machines, had reduced the work available and added to the problem of the seasonal nature of the men's employment. Another potential setback for the rural labourer was that rapid progress to enclose the land meant subsistence for the unemployed became increasingly difficult for the rural poor as they lost the ability to pasture their animals on and to collect wood from common land which had been enclosed. Not only were rural times hard, but the pay differential between the soldier and the farm labourer had widened in favour of the soldier so as to make a career in the services relatively more attractive.[3] A private in the KDG could expect to earn twice as much as a farm labourer in the years leading up to Waterloo. Whilst the average weekly wage in the south of England for an agricultural labourer in 1805 was around 9s,[4] a private in the KDG could expect to earn 18s 1d when his wages were added to his allowances for additional expenses, as set out below.[5]

Rates of pay in the cavalry were better than those in the infantry. Cavalry sergeants and corporals made around 40 per cent more per annum than their counterparts in the infantry; as did cavalry trumpeters over infantry drummers. The differential between privates in the two arms was less, at around a quarter more for dragoons. The Household Cavalry were paid better than the line cavalry. Overall, soldiers in the Royal Horse Guards (Blues) made more; and the Life Guards made the most, with their privates being paid over half as much again as dragoons, at 1s 11¼d a day versus the KDG private on 1s 3d. In addition to this pay, dragoons were paid a daily subsistence allowance for a horse of 9d a day[6] and additional allowances of 1s 4d a day (which included 1d for small beer) net of deductions.

The additional allowances were for the following items: 5s 1d for messing; 2s 7½d for necessaries; and 1s 7½d for laundry, pipe and general cleaning of appointments.[7] When moving between quarters, privates received 9d, of which 6d from his pay and a penny from his beer money were paid to the owner of the lodgings or inn where he was staying on a daily basis for accommodation and three meals. When in quarters, food was paid for by the troop captain and the soldier only had to pay the owner of the hostelry 2d for his bed, five pints of cider or small beer, vinegar, salt and to cover the rental cost of using his host's cooking utensils. There was a small cash allowance when in camp of ¾d a day as soldiers were provided with bread at cheap prices, their living accommodation and cooking utensils, coal and candles, and five pints of beer a day.[8]

However, it was not just the push factors of economic hardship; then, as is the case now, there were many young men seeking adventure in serving their country. A KDG recruiting poster from this period posted in the Angel Inn, Honiton, and shown in the plates, advertised for:

> Any YOUNG MAN who is desirous to make a Figure in Life, and wishes to quit a dull laborious Retirement in the Country, has now an Opportunity of entering at once into that glorious State of Ease and Independence, which he cannot fail to enjoy in the KING'S DRAGOON GUARDS.

Probably the greatest incentive to join, however, was the offer of a bounty £23 17s 6d paid in 1812 for recruits who enlisted for life, and £18 or so for those enlisting for five years. These limited service periods could be extended on two occasions by a further seven years, but most recruits signed on for life.[9] In the case of the KDG of this generation, most left either as a result of the wounds they sustained at Waterloo or from reduction when the regimental establishment was slimmed down on several occasions.

The new soldiers were sought by the voluntary enlistment of men by the regimental recruiting team visits to various targeted towns. The army regulations of 1807 were quite specific about what sort of person the KDG needed to recruit:

> In the heavy cavalry, men shall not be enlisted over twenty five years of age; their height shall not be less than five feet seven inches; growing lads, under eighteen years of age, may be taken as low as five feet six inches, provided they are in every other respect strictly eligible.

The KDG pretty much respected these rules, as there were only a handful of soldiers at Waterloo who were below the minimum height for heavy cavalry. However, the average height of the KDG soldier had fallen from 5ft 10in in 1798[10] to 5ft 7in at Waterloo.[11] Yet the KDG other ranks' average height at Waterloo was exactly the same as the average height recorded for its sister regiment, the 2nd Dragoon Guards, as measured in 1813.[12] These heavy cavalrymen were still relatively tall in terms of the British Army, when the height restrictions for general service in 1806 was as low as 5ft 4in.

The recruiting process was set out in detail in the Regulations and Instructions for carrying on the Recruiting Service of His Majesty's Forces in the United Kingdom of Great Britain and Ireland, dated 28 October 1806. The recruiting officer from the regiment was obliged to first report to the field officers of districts responsible for recruiting parties. There were fifteen recruiting districts in England, and the ones that concerned the KDG were principally Manchester for the North West, Nottingham and Birmingham for the Midlands and Southampton for Hampshire. The recruiting teams would normally set up shop in a tavern, like the Angel Inn at Honiton, and there sell the life of a KDG to anyone who would satisfy the army's and the regiment's requirements.

In addition to the age and height restrictions, there were other requirements based on the individual's physical and moral state. His declaration included the statement that he was not an already enrolled soldier and that 'he had no Rupture, and was not troubled with Fits, and was in no way disabled by Lameness, Deafness, or otherwise, but had the perfect Use of his Limbs and Hearing, and was not an Apprentice'. From 1806, he was also not to demonstrate symptoms of scurvy, sore legs and 'scald head', which was to have scurf on his scalp.[13]

As well as having to pass a medical, the men had to be attested by a magistrate within four days on enlistment.[14] They also had to read or be read *The Articles of War*. This document set out the grounds for the death penalty if a soldier was either involved in mutiny or failed to report such an event. The other compulsory act of the recruitment process was the necessity for the recruit to swear an Oath of Allegiance to the sovereign that he would 'defend Him in his Person, Crown and dignity against all his enemies'.

★★★

To be a KDG officer, one had a slightly less high but similar caché to that of officers in the Household Cavalry and the regiments of Foot Guards. To have gained a place in the regiment, the officers would have had to have been at least 16 years old, to have found someone of influence to have recommended them and to have made an application to the commander-in-chief of the army via the military secretary. There were four routes by which an individual could become commissioned into the regiment. The most unusual way of receiving a commission was one granted 'without purchase', which was the method by which Lieutenant Thomas Brander became an officer in the KDG in 1811. These 'without purchase' vacancies arose on the death of an officer, with the transfer of an officer to a post on the staff and when the size of the officer corps had been expanded.

The second method of entry, by which the vast majority of the KDG officers who served at Waterloo had entered the army and the regiment, was through the 'purchase system'. They were men of means who, when they joined the army, had sufficient funds to purchase their cornetcy. This was the most junior of the commissioned ranks and equivalent to a second lieutenant today. Around the time of Waterloo, the cost of buying a cornetcy was almost twice as much for the cavalry, at £735, than as it was for in the infantry, at £400. The cost for the same rank in the Life Guards and the Royal Horse Guards was respectively £1,600 and £1,050.[15] Clearly the higher costs for the cavalry meant the KDG officers need to have some sort of private income to afford this initial outlay and the requirement they had to buy their own kit.

However, purchase could trump seniority. An example of this in the KDG was a comparison of the speeds of promotion of lieutenants George Quicke and John Hibbert. Although Hibbert joined the regiment some nine months after Quicke, the former was to become a lieutenant a good year-and-a-half before Quicke, as Hibbert explained in one of his letters home on 11 June 1815:

> It was the most lucky thing in the world that I purchased the lieutenancy for Quicke, who refused the purchase, has had no less than nine Lieutenants put over him, so that he is now in a worse situation than when he joined, for as we are upon the war establishment we have twenty-four lieutenants and he is at the bottom of all these, and consequently will get reduced when we return home to a certainty, for the promotion can never be so quick as to get him out of the break. I have not seen an army list lately, but I rather think I am the thirteenth lieutenant, consequently not safe, but it is odd if there is not a single promotion in the regiment before we return, for one would get me completely out of the scrape.[16]

Essentially what Hibbert had done was to pay the difference between his rank of cornet and that of lieutenant, and thus leapfrogged Quicke. The same must have been the case with the wealthy Lieutenant Joseph Greaves (later to assume the name of Elmsall in 1817, no doubt on the inheritance of yet more wealth). Greaves joined the regiment a few weeks after Quicke but was promoted to lieutenant eight months before him.

Somewhat confusingly, officers could have two different seniority dates or different ranks, based on their length of service in the army and for their time in the KDG. Their army seniority dated from when they had initially bought a cornetcy in the first regiment that they had joined, whilst their seniority within the KDG dated from when they had first joined the regiment. Examples in the KDG of officers holding different ranks in army and regiment were Henry Graham and John Bringhurst, who were brevet majors in the KDG but their army rank was that of captains.

Another way into the KDG was by a transfer from another regiment by purchasing a rank that was up for sale by a serving KDG officer who was looking to either retire or transfer into another regiment, or by filling a 'non-purchase' vacancy.

The two officers who had taken that route to joining the KDG were the commanding officer, William Fuller, who had joined from the 10th Dragoons in 1805, and George Battersby, who had moved to the KDG from the 23rd Light Dragoons in the year before Waterloo. By the time of Waterloo, the purchase system was becoming a far less important determinant of promotion and regimental seniority was the main criterion for advancement. Apart from purchase and seniority, officers could be promoted on merit.

The fourth method by which men were commissioned into the regiment was by coming up through the ranks. Prior to serving in the KDG, the commander of 4th Troop, John Sweny, had served as a sergeant-major in the 4th Dragoon Guards. He had gained a captaincy in the KDG by purchase in 1805 and his first job was as regimental adjutant. The adjutant at Waterloo was Lieutenant Thomas Shelver, who had been promoted on merit, having previously been a troop sergeant-major in the regiment. The third ex-ranker present at Waterloo was the Quartermaster John Brown, who had been commissioned a few days before the battle, having been a KDG troop sergeant-major. He was the second longest-serving KDG, having joined the regiment the year after Major Graham in 1795.

On achieving a new rank, all officers had to pay a commission fee, which increased the higher the rank. In dragoon guards regiments like the KDG, this ranged from £6 6d for cornets up to £10 3s 6d for promotion to lieutenant-colonel. As with soldiers' pay and in the prices of commissions, officers' pay reflected similar differentials between Household and line cavalry and infantry. The Life Guards officers were the highest paid, then line cavalry officers, and the lowest paid were the infantry officers. With the exception of subalterns, mounted officers had higher rates of pay, and Foot Guards officers were paid more than their counterparts in the line cavalry. In 1810, the KDG officers' annual pay was as follows: lieutenant-colonel, £404 15s; majors, £351 6s 3d; captains, £266 2s 11d; lieutenants, £164 5s; and cornets, £146.[17]

There were various deductions from the officers' annual pay: income tax of around 5 per cent; poundage of 5 per cent, to pay the regimental agent; 'agency' fees of 2½ per cent, which helped cover the costs of running the regiment; a day's pay to go to Chelsea Hospital; and the vast majority of his pay went to cover his food and drink. By deducting these expenses from a cornet's salary, it is easy to see why a private income was necessary for KDG officers, as all he would have left over from his pay would have been around 2s 6d per day. Most officers had a servant, who would have cost at least a shilling a day, so the KDG cornet would have had a disposable income of only 1s 6d a day.[18]

The social backgrounds of the KDG officers who fought at Waterloo were slightly higher than those in other cavalry regiments. There was one son of a peer, the Hon. Henry Bernard, who was the son of Viscount Bandon, and there were also three sons of baronets – William Elton, Francis Brooke and William Stirling – which was a relatively high tally for a British cavalry regiment at Waterloo, which on average boasted one of each.[19] The commanding officer, William Fuller, had a slightly different background to his fellow officers in that he came from a wealthy family of merchant bankers, based in the City of London. He had been brought up in Dorking, Surrey, and had joined the fashionable 10th Dragoons as a cornet in 1792. He was promoted to major in 1800 and transferred to the KDG as its commanding officer in 1805. The remaining officers were mostly, judging by their home addresses, sons of country gentlemen from all over England. Outside of England, there were five Anglo-Irish officers: Captain George Battersby, lieutenants William Irvine and Ralph Babington and cornets Francis Brooke and the Hon. Henry Bernard. There was one officer from Scotland, William Stirling from Castlemilk near Glasgow.

In sharp contrast to their battle-hardened opponents on 18 June 1815, only two officers appear to have had any experience of fighting prior to Waterloo. Bringhurst had seen fighting in the Peninsular War when serving as an ADC to former KDG commanding officer General Sir Henry Fane. Bringhurst's epitaph mentions he fought with Fane in Portugal, Spain and France. Battersby, like Bringhurst, was an ADC to a general in the Peninsular War and afterwards in the South of France. Battersby worked for General Sir Kenneth Howard, who commanded a brigade and was involved in much of the fighting in the Peninsula and the South of France.

5

REGIMENTAL
STRUCTURE

The 1st, or King's Dragoon Guards 'was always a strong regiment'[1] in terms of numbers when compared to the other British cavalry regiments. It is not known why this was the case, but its having been the strongest British cavalry unit can be dated back to the changes in regimental establishments in 1793. Prior to this, in 1783, each dragoon regiment was fixed at six troops, which was increased to nine troops on the outbreak of the French Revolutionary Wars in 1793. However, when the cavalry regiments concerned were ordered to the Netherlands in 1794, they were still on the six-troop establishment, except the KDG which remained authorised with nine troops. From that date until Waterloo, the KDG maintained a larger than normal establishment, such that in 1815 it was almost double the size of the other British heavy cavalry regiments.[2] It was much larger than the Household regiments with which it was to charge at Waterloo. In 1812, the KDG had been recorded as having twelve troops in six squadrons, which comprised forty-seven officers and 1,037 men.[3] By comparison, the 1st and 2nd Life Guards regiments had four squadrons each.[4]

At the end of March 1815, the KDG's establishment was twelve troops with fifty-nine officers and 1,081 men, according to the *The Digest*.[5] However, the regiment did not send all its six squadrons to fight on the Continent in April 1815, as it left two behind at the regimental depot it had just established at Ipswich. *The Digest* listed the number of KDGs by rank who were dispatched from 12–17 April to join Wellington's army in the Low Countries as follows: '8 Troops of the regiment embark for Ostend, consisting of 1 Colonel, 8 Captains, 9 Lieutenants, 4 Cornets, 5 Staff, 1 Troop-Quartermaster, 47 Sgt's, 33 Cpl's, 8 Trumpeters, 8 Farriers, 488 Troopers, and 537 horses.'[6]

The lieutenant-colonel, who did not join the regiment, was George Teesdale, who presumably was left behind to command the depot. The two majors who did not travel with the regiment were Major the Honourable George Dawson, who was present at Waterloo but served as the quartermaster-general to the Prince of Orange, and Robert Acklom, who, like Teesdale, was probably left behind to help run the depot in Ipswich. In addition, four captains, fifteen lieutenants and eight cornets did not travel with the regiment to Ostend. The two members of the staff who were not present at Waterloo were the paymaster adjutant and the veterinary surgeon. Interestingly, all but one of the sergeants went to fight at Waterloo, whilst fifteen corporals stayed behind at the depot. Of the men, one farrier and one trumpeter remained with each of the four troops that were left in the depot, along with 312 mounted and 120 dismounted troopers.

★★★

In terms of regimental posts, the pinnacle of the KDG's structure was its regimental colonel. This was often a job for life and had a purely ceremonial and administrative role. These officers did not command their regiments in the field, but were present at parades and reviews and were responsible for clothing their units. They received a salary and were paid an allowance with which to equip their regiments. This appointment was usually given to a top general in the British Army. At the time of Waterloo, the KDG's colonel of the regiment was Sir David Dundas. Dundas became colonel in 1813, having been the commander-in-chief of the British Army.[7] He had a distinguished military career in the Seven Years War and in the French Revolutionary Wars. He had begun his military career as a gunner and had then been a colonel in the 7th Light Dragoons from 1795–1801 and then the 2nd Dragoons from 1801–13.

Dundas had been instrumental in reforming the training of the British cavalry, having written a text book which was made mandatory reading for all officers who served in that arm. This book was *Instructions and Regulations for the Formations and Movements of the Cavalry*, printed by the War Office in 1796. However, Dundas really made his name for another military manual. That book was *Principles of Military Movements for the Infantry*, which was published in 1788 and issued in 1792 as *Rules and Regulations for the Movements of His Majesty's Infantry*. It was significant as the first universally accepted set of instructions for drill and manoeuvres in the British Army that ensured it operated on a uniform basis. As a result of this manual, Dundas was nicknamed 'Old Pivot' from the pivots which were fundamental to his method of infantry manoeuvring.[8]

Lieutenant-Colonel William Fuller was the next most senior officer. He had been the KDG's commanding officer since joining the regiment in 1805. As commanding officer, Fuller held the ultimate executive power for the KDG on a day-to-day basis and when in the field. Fuller's second-in-command was Major

Henry Graham. He was only a couple of years junior to the commanding officer, having been commissioned into the KDG as a cornet in 1794. His speed of promotion had not, however, been as rapid as Fuller's, who had achieved his majority in eight years, whilst Graham was still a captain at Waterloo in terms of army seniority after twenty-one years' service. He had been in command of 2nd Troop until 17 May 1815, when he had handed over command to Battersby and was appointed 'Major of the Regiment'.[9] On Fuller's death at Waterloo, Graham, as second-in-command, briefly assumed command of the regiment until he too was killed.

Working alongside Fuller and Graham in regimental headquarters was the adjutant, Lieutenant Thomas Shelver. Shelver, like most KDG adjutants of that time, had been commissioned through the ranks. He had been made a cornet in 1812 and had been promoted to lieutenant in 1814. As adjutant, he was responsible for drill and the behaviour of the sergeants. He had to ensure brigade and regimental orders were adhered to and that all foot and mounted exercises were executed properly. All parades, guards and detachments fell under his remit. He held a parade called 'adjutant's drill', which was a regular practice of mounted and foot drill. In the evenings, the NCOs would file their reports with him. He was expected to keep rosters of officers and the TSMs. He was also present at all courts martial that involved the KDG. The adjutant was allocated a literate soldier to work as his clerk.

In most of these tasks, the adjutant was backed up by the RSM, who was effectively his second. The RSM was the senior soldier amongst the other ranks and acted as a bridge between the commanding officer and the adjutant in regimental headquarters and the TSMs who were responsible for their rank and file. The KDG's RSM, Thomas Barlow, was clearly competent, as his discharge papers attested his excellence and he had enjoyed swift promotion through the ranks, having joined aged 16 in 1801. He was a devout Methodist and his faith rubbed off on many KDG soldiers who turned to this denomination.

The last components of the KDG regimental staff were the paymaster, the regimental surgeons and the quartermaster. Regimental Paymaster John Webster was not present at Waterloo, but his assistant, the Regimental Paymaster Sergeant Richard Houghton, was there. He was attached to 1st Troop and presumably was part of the group of dismounted KDGs who did not take part in the fighting but worked with the farriers in the rear party. Webster's job was to keep the accounts of the regiment and ensure everyone in the regiment was paid correctly on the twenty-fifth day of each month. Troop captains signed in the Quarterly Pay-Lists for the funds they had been allocated with which to pay their soldiers. When abroad, the paymaster would have also worked with the KDG's agent, who was Alexander Adair of Chidley Court, Pall Mall, London, who effectively acted as the regiment's banker.[10] The paymaster was also responsible for ensuring lodging money was paid to those soldiers who had been given permission to live outside the barracks.

The regimental surgeon was John Going, and under him served assistant-surgeons William Macauley and Richard Pearson. The surgeons ran the regimental hospital when in barracks. When the regiment was sent to quarters in towns on home service, they were found a temporary location, namely a suitable building in which to house the surgeons and their staff. This was paid for by the inspector general of hospitals. When it came to campaign conditions or when the regiment was in the field, a tent was allocated to the medical staff. Going would have submitted a daily list of casualties to Fuller once he had received the reports of the orderly sergeant, which described the soldiers and their various illnesses. The surgeon also tended the commanding officer a weekly report which recorded all patients in the regimental hospital and their 'state'.[11]

The KDG was fortunate to have had a man of Going's calibre as its surgeon at Waterloo. Relatively few regimental medical officers had official qualifications and many had just been given training as hospital assistants. By the time of Waterloo, Going had vast experience and held a medical degree, having qualified with an MD from Edinburgh in 1789. He had started life as a regimental surgeon's mate until eventually being commissioned as a surgeon in the 11th Foot in 1793. He went on to become a surgeon in two cavalry regiments before being appointed a staff surgeon in 1800. The following year, Going was appointed as the regimental surgeon to the KDG. Macauley had five years' experience prior to Waterloo and had progressed from hospital mate to assistant-surgeon of the 63rd Foot in February 1810 before joining the KDG in the August of that year. The third of the KDG's three medical officers, Richard Pearson, also had four years' experience by 1815, having started as a hospital mate on the Irish Establishment. He had joined the KDG in 1813 as an assistant-surgeon.[12]

Regimental Veterinary Surgeon William Clarkson was not present at Waterloo. However, Assistant Veterinary Surgeon Spencer joined the regiment when they were in Paris in August 1815. The regimental veterinary surgeon was responsible for the health of the horses. He inspected all sick and lame horses every Sunday morning, when the horses were paraded in front of him. He was present at Evening Stables to inspect all the regiment's horses on a daily basis. The vet worked in close conjunction with the farrier-major. When the regiment was in barracks, he joined the veterinary surgeon at First Stables.[13]

One more officer who comprised the headquarters staff was Regimental Quartermaster John Brown, a Scotsman from Haddington. He had joined the KDG as a private in 1795 and had been commissioned through the ranks to quartermaster just before Waterloo in June 1815. His duties included having sole responsibility for the regimental stores, uniforms, horse appointments, arms and ammunition. When moving to new quarters, his job was to select and pay for appropriate lodgings. In the field, he went ahead of the regiment to mark out with pegs suitable areas for the men to bivouac by troops. Horses were another area of his responsibility, as he was expected to ensure the smooth running of the regimental stables and its provision of fodder. He detailed men to collect meat on market days and ensured that the barracks in general, and soldiers' messes in particular, were kept in an ordered and hygienic state.

The quartermaster also kept accounts of all the regiment's kit in special books. These concerned clothing, accoutrements, arms, ammunition, fuel, forage and provisions. He kept a letterbook with all the commanding officers' correspondence concerning the subjects in the aforementioned books.[14] He also had to ensure all the soldiers' necessaries and equipment were correctly marked. To help him with his book-keeping, as well as to assist the other members of regimental headquarters, there were a number of literate soldiers who worked as clerks. These men had to deliver a set of accounts for each troop on a monthly basis. The clerks had to deliver a muster roll which detailed where all the regiment's men were located, for example listing those on furlough or men who had died or deserted. They also had to prepare a monthly return of all allowances.[15] Working as Brown's assistant was Troop Quartermaster James Rigg. For administrative purposes, Rigg was attached to 2nd Troop and it appears that he also acted as that troop's sergeant-major in action at Waterloo, as this troop was the only one not to have a troop sergeant allocated to it.

Outside of the KDG's headquarters staff there were some other regimental appointments. The most senior of these was the riding master. He oversaw all riding tuition, ensured the appropriate techniques were taught and that the soldiers achieved the required standards of horsemanship. The commanding officers were kept constantly appraised as to their men's progress as they received returns which reported on and ranked the officers and soldiers as either first- or second-class riders. The riding master received five guineas per officer he successfully taught to ride, and was also paid two guineas for every horse he broke in. He worked with the rough riders, who were the riding instructors, with at least one assigned to every troop. They ranked as corporals and were paid an additional four pence a day for teaching the soldiers to ride.

The regimental farrier-major's job was to ensure all the regiment's horses were correctly shod. To do this he presided over regular hoof inspections, as he was answerable to the commanding officer on this most important of duties. His main job was the supervision of the farriers' work at the regimental forge. He also had to ensure the forge carts, that were used to carry the horseshoes to the different troops, were kept in good working order. The farriers, of which there was one per troop, always carried pincers, hammer and spare nails. According to Regimental Standing Orders, the farriers could always be found at the rear of their troop on field days or when on campaign. They were also used to carry out corporal punishment on the soldiers in their troop.

Other regimental appointments included School Master Sergeant John Thomas and Regimental Armourer Sergeant Edmund Halson. Both men were present at

Waterloo and attached to 1st Troop. Halson's job was to clean and repair all the weapons used by the regiment, which were swords, carbines and pistols. He was also responsible for the repair and upkeep of the metal appointments such as spurs. He had to pass on to the commanding officer a printed form that detailed all repairs that had been carried out. In addition to his sergeant's pay, the troop commanders paid him extra sums of money for the work he carried out for their respective troops.

Regimental Trumpet-Major William Dixon from Newbury would have been at Fuller's side at all times when in the field to ensure he could pass on the commanding officer's orders by trumpet. He was ranked as a sergeant and associated with them. All the other seven trumpeters, allocated to each troop commander, reported to him. He gave these men lessons for trumpet and bugle and ensured they could sound all the 'calls' as listed in the *Calls Book* and to play all the 'Field Calls' on foot and when mounted. [16] On foot parades, he acted as the sergeant to the trumpeters and drilled them. If there was a regimental alert to turn out on horseback, rather than reporting to troop assemblies, he would sound this command on a bugle. When the regiment turned out for parade he was to sound the 'General', which was a form of alert. [17]

The operational units of the KDG were its six sabre squadrons, which were distinguished by letters, starting with 'A' and running to 'F'. Each squadron was broken down into two troops, which numbered from 1st Troop to 12th Troop on a regimental basis. Whilst squadrons were purely tactical units, the troops were administrative establishments, with each commanded by a captain. [18] The average number of mounted men in each KDG troop that could have taken part in the first charge at Waterloo was around sixty-eight all ranks. Each troop was broken down further into three companies, presumably each commanded by one of the troop's officers as, along with the captain, there was a lieutenant and a cornet in each of these units. The smallest tactical sub-unit was the squad, the number of which depended on the size of the troop. [19] In most cases a sergeant would have been in charge of the squad, as was the procedure in the 3rd Dragoon Guards. [20] So the number of squads would probably have been governed by the number of sergeants available.

The regimental captains ran their troops as semi-autonomous units. They were administrators who managed their men's lives. They were instructed to be 'thoroughly acquainted with the men under their command, so as to be able at all times to inform the commanding officer with the effective strength of their respective troops, describing the number sick, employed and how employed'. [21] Amongst their many duties, they ensured the soldiers in their troop were properly accommodated, disciplined, trained and paid. They also ensured their men were correctly fed by visiting them at messing hour. They visited their troop's sleeping accommodation and stables daily to ensure they were clean and that Regimental Standing Orders were being adhered to. They were also expected to visit and examine the sick men in their troop. As well as ensuring their horses were in good condition, troop captains were to ensure that their men were accountable for all their arms, clothing and ammunition.

When in quarters, the troop captains were to visit the troop accommodation and stables daily and ensure the landlords in whose lodgings they were staying were correctly paid. On forage days they were to inspect the forage was sufficient in quantity and quality. In the field they commanded their troops as tactical units and delegated control of two of the three companies to one of the troop lieutenants or cornets. The senior troop captains would lead squadrons, which comprised their troop and one belonging to one of the junior captains. Apart from the commanding officer, the four senior KDG officers at Waterloo, and probably the squadron commanders on the day of the battle, were in order of seniority Major Graham and captains Turner, Naylor and Elton. The next senior captains were Bringhurst, then Sweny, Battersby and the most junior was the 23-year-old Thomas Quicke. The captains' experience varied, from Quicke, who had served for just seven years prior to 1815, to Turner, who had served for twenty years before Waterloo.

Regimental Standing Orders spelled out the junior officers' duties and what was expected of them. They had to attend Riding Master's Drill with their own chargers. New officers had to attend adjutant's drill to ensure they were 'perfectly competent in the several duties'. Subalterns were not allowed more than one batman and were not allowed to take any private soldier as his servant until approved by the commanding officer. All officers were expected to attend parades for Field Days, Reviews and Divine Service on Sundays. The Orders also spelled out that junior officers were to always be correctly attired and carry the appropriate arms. Officers were expected to ensure discipline was rigidly enforced. Regimental Standing Orders gave examples of when officers should ensure soldiers saluted them.[22]

In addition to helping their troop captain in training and drilling their men, the subaltern officers had to carry out the duties of the orderly officer. This was allocated to all cornets and lieutenants on the basis of a roster. The orderly officer had to remain in camp for the full twenty-four hours of his duty and was responsible for checking the smooth running of the regiment. He was distinguished from the other subalterns by the wearing of a pouch belt. His routine was set out in detail in the KDG Regimental Orders of 1819, which summed up the job as to be 'responsible for its [the regiment's] regularity in every particular, and to see that every article is in its place and properly hung up according to order, both in rooms and stables'.

The captains of troops also worked closely with their TSMs, who worked under the direction of the adjutant to oversee all the mounted or foot drills carried out by their troops. The TSM was responsible for the soldiers' attention to and the enforcement of the Regimental Standing Orders. He was also responsible for teaching all new officers the manual and troop exercises, for which he was paid half a guinea from each officer.[23] The TSM in turn relied on the sergeants, who ran the squads that comprised their troops. The sergeants' job was to focus on their men's behaviour and cleanliness of their person, their rooms in barracks and bivouacs when in the field. They had to ensure their squads were punctual and properly turned out. They kept a roll of the troop to which they belonged and to the squad of which they were the senior NCO. They were chosen as sergeants by being good, well-dressed horsemen who were excellent at drill, sword fighting and field exercises.[24] When acting as orderly sergeant they had to wear a small sword with their number one uniform, with gaiters and a sash, and carry a cane.[25]

In most KDG troops at Waterloo, there was about one more corporal than there were sergeants. Corporals were effectively the sergeants' deputies, who shared the responsibility for the discipline and guidance of their respective squads. They stayed with soldiers in their squads for most of the working day to ensure that jobs were properly carried out. Article No. 28. of Regimental Standing Orders stated, 'Corporals are to be chosen from such men as are active and zealous, and who from a perseverance in good behaviour have established a superiority.- In appointing serjeants no attention to be paid to seniority of corporals, but such as have manifested their inclination to the service, by a strict attention to their dutys to be preferred.' At Waterloo, the KDG's order of battle was that of the eight troops, with the regimental posts like the trumpet-major and saddler attached to 1st Troop and the headquarters elements attached to 2nd Troop. William Elton commanded 1st Troop. He was born in 1785, the second son of Sir Abraham Elton, 5th Baronet. He grew up at the beautiful Elton family seat of Clevedon Court in Somerset, which the present baronet still owns. According to a descendant family biographer, Sir Abraham chose the KDG for his son as a commission cost less than in the Foot Guards.[26] This was certainly the case ,as the price for the rank of ensign in the Foot Guards was £145, or 19 per cent more than a commission in the KDG at the time of Waterloo.[27] Elton joined the regiment as a cornet in 1804, was made a lieutenant the following year and gained his captaincy in 1809. Elton's troop sergeant was James Fairclough, a tall former weaver from Warrington, who was literate and whose conduct was described as 'excellent in every respect' on his discharge from the army.

George Battersby commanded 2nd Troop. The Battersbys were an old Yorkshire family and George's branch had emigrated to Ireland in the reign of King William III. They had settled in County Westmeath, where George was born in 1788. He was commissioned as a cornet in the 23rd Light Dragoons in 1808, becoming a lieutenant in that regiment in 1809. He fought in the Peninsular with his regiment from June 1809 to December 1810, when he was appointed as an ADC to Major-General Sir Kenneth Howard. Amongst other battles, he was present at the Battles of Talavera, Fuentes de Oñoro, Arroyo de Molinos and Almaraz. He was promoted to captain in 1813 and continued to work for Howard in the fighting in Spain and France until April 1814, when he transferred into the KDG and took over Graham's 2nd Troop. As there was no troop sergeant-major listed for 2nd Troop and Quartermaster-Sergeant James Rigg was assigned to this troop, it has been assumed that at Waterloo he acted as Battersby's troop sergeant-major.

The commander of 3rd Troop was a scion of an ancient Northumbrian family, the Wallaces of Asholme, Knaresdale and Featherstone. Robert Wallace was born in 1789 and grew up at Sedcop House in Kent. His uncle James had been the attorney general and his cousin Thomas was a politician, who was ennobled as Baron Wallace. He joined the army as a cornet in 1806, was made a lieutenant in 1808 and received his captaincy in 1814. His TSM was John Levitt from Peterstree in Suffolk.

John Sweny commanded 4th Troop. He was the eldest son of a Dublin chemist and was the only ex-ranker amongst the squadron captains. He enlisted as a volunteer in 1799, and by 1800 had been promoted to the rank of corporal in the 4th Dragoon Guards, in which he subsequently became a TSM. In 1805, he purchased a cornetcy in the KDG and directly was made adjutant. His lieutenancy came the following year and he had been made a captain in 1812. His TSM was James Page from Merton near Croydon. Page must have done well at Waterloo, as he leapfrogged at least one more senior TSM to be promoted RSM after Barlow had been made adjutant.

John Bringhurst was in charge of 5th Troop. He was the son of the rector of Woodstone in Huntingdonshire. Unusually for a KDG officer of that time, he was a graduate who had joined the regiment as a cornet in 1806, having matriculated from Cambridge in late 1804. He was promoted lieutenant in 1809 and was made captain after just two years in 1811. Prior to Waterloo, he had been ADC to Major-General Sir Henry Fane in the Peninsular War and in southern France in 1814. The 5th Troop TSM was Thomas Linton from Burton in Staffordshire, who had been a shoe maker before joining up.

James Naylor, the captain commanding 6th Troop, was born in London and had joined the army rather later in life, having been commissioned aged 31 into the Essex Militia as an ensign in 1797. He was promoted to lieutenant the following year and then transferred into the 62nd Foot for just two months in August 1799, before transferring into the KDG as a cornet in the October. He was made lieutenant in the regiment in 1803 and promoted to captain in 1806. He kept extensive diaries during the period of the Flanders campaign. After the deaths of the commanding officer and Major Graham, and the wounding of the senior captain, Turner, Naylor assumed command of the KDG. When Major Lygon, commanding the 2nd Life Guards, left the field with a wounded horse, Naylor took command of the remnants of the Household Brigade. The 6th Troop TSM was David Benwell from Kingsclere in Hampshire. Although he and his father had been farm labourers, his grandfather had been a yeoman farmer of standing in the local community.

He was probably in some way responsible for recruiting the many KDG men who came from the vicinity of Kingsclere.

Thomas Quicke, the captain of 7th Troop, at 23 years old, was the youngest and most junior troop KDG commander at Waterloo. The Quicke family were landed gentry, having held their family seat in Newton St Cyres, Devon, since the Reformation. Thomas was born there in 1793 and became a lieutenant in what was very much the family regiment at the just legal age of 16 in 1808. Thomas's eldest brother John had served in the regiment, married the daughter of a former KDG captain, Thomas Cumming, but had left to help run the family estate before Waterloo. Thomas's younger brother George had joined the KDG as a cornet in 1813. Thomas was made a captain in December 1814 and took commanded of 7th Troop. His TSM, John Tracey, was from Ireland and had started life in the 5th (Royal Irish Regiment) Dragoons; on that regiment's disbandment for insubordination and a fear it had been infiltrated by Irish rebels in 1799, he transferred into the KDG.

The most senior troop captain was Michael Turner, who commanded 8th Troop. He was born in 1776 and had grown up in the stately home of Stoke Hall near Ipswich in Suffolk. He was commissioned into the KDG as a cornet by purchase in 1797, was made a lieutenant in 1799 and promoted to captain in 1805. On Fuller's death he took command of the regiment until he was severely wounded. The 8th Troop TSM was Edward Wright, a former labourer from Chilwell in Nottinghamshire. By the time of Waterloo he was a particularly experienced soldier, having already served for nineteen years.

It is interesting to contrast the battle experience of these men with their French enemies at Waterloo. Only Bringhurst and Battersby had fought before, whilst many of their mounted opponents at Waterloo were seasoned veterans who had been in action more or less continually since the Battle of Austerlitz in 1805.

6

CLOTHING AND EQUIPMENT

The issuance of clothing and equipment was controlled by army regulations. However, the provision of them was from a number of sources. Most of the larger, expensive items of uniform and 'appointments' were paid for by the colonel of the regiment. He was given an allowance by the government to procure these items from contractors. This explains why the various British cavalry regiments used different equipment at that time. The regiment itself issued the soldier's 'accoutrements', horse and weapons. The cost of the smaller items of uniform and some 'necessaries'[1] were paid for by the soldier, being deducted from his pay. The uniforms provided by the colonel were: a sleeved cloak, renewed every twelve years; a pair of iron shod boots, renewed every six years; a pair of gloves and a helmet, renewed annually; and a coat, waistcoat and pair of breeches, renewed every two years.

The only exception to this uniform at Waterloo was that the soldiers wore grey overalls with a red stripe down the side and riding boots[2] with spurs, instead of white breeches and jackboots, and short gloves instead of gauntlets,[3] which were only worn on home station.[4] The KDG at Waterloo wore 'full regimentals', which was a dragoon guard uniform. Their blue facings with blue gauntlet cuffs identified them as 1st or King's Dragoon Guards. On their heads they wore the 1812-type two-pattern dragoon helmet, as used by all British heavy cavalry apart from the household troops. This helmet had a peaked leather skullcap reinforced with gilt and topped off with a 30in black horsehair mane. Above the peak it had an oval metal badge labelled with the regimental title of the reversed royal GR cipher surmounted by a crown, and on the front plate of the crest was a Medusa's mask. It had fluting moulded to its sides and a chin strap which was attached to ornaments located just above the ear in the shape of a rose. Some later paintings portrayed trumpeters with red manes, but there is no evidence for this from contemporary images of KDGs.[5]

The coat issued was the red 1812 heavy cavalry jacket, which had the regimental facing colour of blue on its collar, turn-backs and dragoon guard gauntlet cuffs, which distinguished them from dragoons who wore pointed cuffs.[6] The dragoon guard officer was also distinguishable from his dragoon peer in that the cloth of his jacket's facings (including collar and turnbacks) were made of velvet, whereas the latter's were made of cloth.[7] The coat was single-breasted and edged up to the collar, with gold lace for the officers and yellow worsted for the other ranks. The lace had a central stripe or train of blue, which was barred with worsted and was distinctive to the regiment in its pattern. This lace was also on the front of the coat and along its blue turnbacks which came over the hips. The coat's skirts were 9½in from the waist down to the bottom edge, and where they were at their lowest were 6in wide. The turnbacks that ran down from the waist were tailored so as to sit just above the saddle when the dragoon was on his horse. Where the turnbacks joined at the rear of the coat, the officers had gold rosettes, and on their shoulders they had twisted gold cord. The other ranks had blue shoulder straps trimmed in lace.

The officers and men wore a white leather sword belt which was worn around the waist and had leather slings that attached the scabbard and sabretache. The sword belt worn by the other ranks had a rectangular brass plate bearing a crowned star, upon which was superimposed a garter with the initials 'KDG' in its centre. The officers' version was a large, gilt, rectangular plate with a silver mount. Some contemporary portraits have shown officers wearing belts with the light cavalry pattern of snake clasp fasteners, as used by the Household Cavalry. However, the type of officers' sword belt buckle may have come down to a question of personal taste rather than necessarily a regimental distinction.[8] On campaign, all ranks wore a sabretache of black leather without decoration, attached to the sword belt by two white leather straps.[9] The sabretache was a leather document wallet used for carrying any books and paperwork the soldier needed. They also provided a useful flat surface on which to write notes when mounted.

The men wore a waistcoat under their jackets. Around their waists they wore a yellow web girdle, much like a cummerbund, which had two blue stripes. The officers had long cords and tassels suspended from their girdles. The gloves with which they were issued were white gauntlets.[10] As well as their dress, the men's hair also had to be uniform. Each troop had a man responsible for cutting hair.

There were various different orders of dress for the heavy cavalry. These were described in the Royal Horse Guards' (Blues) Standing Orders of 1814.[11] Whilst they may not have been exactly the same as those used by the KDG, they are a useful guide to what they probably wore. 'Review Order' was the uniform just described when the soldiers carried all their accoutrements. In this form of dress, troopers' cloaks were rolled with the buff side outwards and stowed behind the saddle. This 'Review Order' uniform was worn for drill, parades, going to church, on the march or in the field. The soldiers spent most of their days in barracks wearing working or stable dress. 'Review Order on Foot' was as described in 'Review Order' above but without the horse. 'Order for Divine Service' was the same as 'Review Order', only buff leather replaced the white breeches and gloves. Officers and other ranks were to carry sidearms.

'Marching Order' was the same as 'Review Order', only cloaks were carried before the saddle. The baggage cases were done up and stable collars were worn by the horses. Reins were to be fastened and horse furniture was not to be carried. Officers were to wear gloves, frocks and overalls, and the men were to wear second-best dress. Horsecloths were stowed between the blankets and waterdecks. Corn sacks were often carried and suspended from the saddles. If the haversack was not being used, it was carried in the baggage, and if used, it was hung on the right shoulder but suspended on the left side of the body along with the canteen. Unless being used under the saddle, the blankets were wrapped in the waterdeck to keep them dry. Water buckets were carried on a rear ring attached to the saddle, and carried inside them were billhooks and nosebags. Breast lines were carried on the baggage cases and the picquet posts were attached to the carbines. Larger camp equipment was either transported on waggons or by bat horses, which many officers used.

'Light Marching Order' was as above, except the privates did not take their carbines and baggage was minimised and matched to the job in hand. 'Field Day Order' dictated that all accoutrements except collars and horse furniture were to be taken. Officers were to wear frocks, overalls and gloves.[12] The other ranks were to wear their second dress and to carry their cloaks at the front of their saddles. 'Light Field Order' was the same as 'Field Day Order', except that carbines were not carried. With 'Under Arms on Foot', officers were to wear morning dress with a sword. The soldiers were to be fully accoutred and to be wearing ordinary day dress. For 'On Foot with Sidearms' and in 'Under Arms', officers were to wear a waist belt and small sword. Soldiers were to wear their swords. 'On Foot without Arms' was as just described but without swords, and all were to carry a regimental cane in the right hand. Officers were to wear sashes and did not need to carry a cane if they were armed with a sword.

With 'On Foot Escort Duty', corporals were to be armed with swords and privates to wear pistols and cartouche belts. All were to be dressed in second-best coats. If an officer was taking part in this escort, he was to be mounted and wearing light marching order. Under the heading 'Dress of Sergeants and Sergeant Majors', the KDG Standing Orders stated, 'On duties on foot and under arms they are dressed with sashes, with knots hanging on the right side, pouch belt, carbine and sword belt, with gloves hanging on the swivel.' Another regulation dictated, 'When corporals and privates are ordered to escort deserters ect, they will parade with arms as on all foot parades, flints and ammunition complete and in trousers.' Officers were to be in morning dress, wearing sidearms and carrying whips.

Quartermasters, and presumably later TSMs, were always to be on horseback at general parades, but not on watering parades. The latter were taken by the orderly officer. The trooper's dress for these occasions was to hold a switch and to wear gloves, a stable jacket, trousers and shoes. The horses were to have their cloths folded and fastened by surcingles and they were to wear bridoons. 'Working and Stable Dress' was the form of dress most commonly worn when in barracks. For the men this comprised trousers and waistcoats. 'Guards' was ordinary day dress, unless the soldiers were leaving the barracks, in which case they wore watering capes and caps. 'Morning Dress' for officers was to wear watering caps, gloves, frocks and to carry sidearms when in public. The privates were to wear jackets, trousers and caps. 'Ordinary Day Dress' was worn when it was time for the officers to have lunch after Midday Stables. Soldiers could adopt this dress code earlier. The officers wore dress coats, gloves, breeches, boots with spurs and wore sidearms. Soldiers and NCOs wore second dress with leather breeches and shoes.'

'General Directions' was when soldiers had put on a particular form of dress for an event like a church parade and then had no specific tasks thereafter. The dress was modified to suit the task in hand. Officers' 'Morning Dress' was dress coats and black velvet socks. 'Court Dress' was only for the officers and probably only applied to the Household Cavalry officers, as well as the Blues, rather than to those in the KDG. 'Order for Officers Attending Balls and Assemblies in Cantonments' was 'Ordinary Day Dress', but always wearing 'proper' spurs with their boots.

As well as most of the larger items of the soldier's uniform, the colonel had to provide the 'appointments'. These were the saddlery and horse furniture. Apart from the full regimental uniform, the soldier was responsible for paying for all his other items of clothing which were, as discussed, called 'necessaries' and were renewed when the need arose. They also included items such as washing and cleaning kit and grooming equipment. The dragoon was also issued with 'accoutrements', a collective term for the items of equipment that related to the soldier's weaponry. These items were expected to last twenty years.

The weaponry of the KDG at Waterloo was a sword and pistol for all, and the private soldier also carried a carbine. The KDG's main weapon was the 1796-pattern heavy cavalry broadsword, which was based on the Austrian pallasch of 1769 for heavy cavalry. This sword was given an iron scabbard in 1775 and it was this version that the British adopted. It was different from previous British cavalry swords, as it was designed to be mass produced in an attempt to cut costs during the French Revolutionary Wars. It was first used in action by the British heavy cavalry in the Peninsular War. The KDG used two versions of this sabre, one for the officers and another for the other ranks. The sword knots also differed; both were of white leather, but the officers' knot had a gold bullion tassel. Both the officers' and soldiers' versions of this sabre were sheathed in an iron scabbard with wooden liners and had a steel chape to strengthen it. The scabbard had two rings, from which it was attached to the waist belt.

The 1796 other ranks' disc hilt-pattern sword weighed 2lb 5oz and its blade was, for the most part, straight with one cutting edge, 35in long and 1½in broad. The blade was fullered, so that it had grooves on either side to reduce its weight. Until just over a month before Waterloo, this sabre was chopper-ended in that the last 7in of the blade were slightly angled backwards down to its hatchet point. The hilt comprised a grip of bound ribbed wood covered in leather and a circular steel guard. The shape of this guard gave its name to the classification of this sword as disc-hilted, and it was single knuckle-bowed. The disc itself was perforated with six holes, which were visible and helped to lighten the weapon. The sword's single knuckle-bow, to protect the hand, was an extension of the disc guard, which was bent back to attach to the bottom of the hilt.

The officers' 1796-pattern honeysuckle-base sword was broadly similar to that just described for use by the other ranks. Its main difference was its semi-basket guard was not a single knuckle-bow but a cup-shaped one-piece casting which would have covered the fist. Its base was carved in the shape of a honeysuckle flower, which led up to a pierced scroll decoration that covered the knuckles. The knuckle-bow was perforated, both to decorate and lighten the weapon, and when it narrowed to join the top of the handle the perforations in it were carved to resemble a ladder; this design led the sword to be described as 'ladder-hilted'. Its grip also differed from the soldiers' sword, as it was overlaid with fish skin which was bound with wire. The blade too was different, as it was frequently blued and etched with the gilt decorations of foliage and the 'GR' royal cipher and coat of arms.[13]

The sword's original hatchet point was designed to be used for slashing rather than thrusting. There had been some debate in the British Army prior to Waterloo as to the more effective method of using a sword when mounted. John Le Marchant, an ex-commanding officer of the 2nd Dragoon Guards, had made great advances in the training of the cavalry with swords. In 1796, he had published the *Rules and Regulations for the Sword Exercise of Cavalry*. Whilst this book certainly improved the swordsmanship of the British cavalry, its shortcoming was that it focused on light rather than heavy cavalry; yet its instructions were ordered to be adopted throughout the cavalry. In it, Le Marchant advocated the use of the cut over the thrust, and thus the heavy cavalry sword had a hatchet point and soldiers were trained to cut.

The French, on the otherhand, were of the thrust school. The French general, Marshal Saxe, suggested that the blades of his men's cavalry swords should be blunted to encourage them to thrust only.[14] However, Uxbridge's foresight was to save many a British cavalryman's life at Waterloo with his last-minute decision to give his men the ability to thrust as well as cut. This was revealed in the 6 May 1815 entry in the *The Digest*, 'The regiment inspected by Lt. General The Earl of

Uxbridge, who gave directions for the broadswords to be ground to at the point to
a different form than heretofore. The point to [be] made at the centre of the blade.'
Only the last 12in of the blade was sharpened on both sides, but this was enough
to enable the KDG to kill their opponents with the use of the point. This method
of dispatching the armoured French cuirassiers was portrayed in a contemporary
illustration which is shown in the plates.

Although Uxbridge's decision to adopt the spearpoint helped to level the playing field, the KDG's French opponents still had the advantage of having had a
slightly longer sword. Lieutenant Waymouth of the 2nd Life Guards, who charged
with Naylor's KDG squadron at Waterloo, complained of 'the great disadvantage
arising from our swords, which were full six inches shorter than those of the
Cuirassiers'.[16] In reality, the An XIII-pattern (the An XI was similar and was also
used) Klingenthal swords of the KDG's French cuirassier opponents at Waterloo
were only about 3½in longer than the British swords. However, the British heavy
cavalry sabre was too heavy for long periods of cutting and thrusting, and the fact
it was weighted to the hilt, meant that the tip made less impact when cutting. Also,
its scabbard tended to rust and the sword often rattled in it, and the blade was
often blunted by repeated drawing.[17] One heavy cavalry officer described it as 'a
lumbering, clumsy, ill-contrived machine. It is too heavy, too short, too broad.'[18]

However, in the sword's defence it made more of a mess of its opponents than
the An XIII, as described by George Farmer in the Peninsula. He stated that whilst
the sleek French weapon made only a small clean wound, the British sword produced horrific injuries, adding, 'the wounded among the French were thus more
revolting than the wounded among ourselves'. Hence there was a morale dimen-
sion to the British weapon that rendered, 'men [the French] more timid'. Although
Uxbridge's instruction to convert the KDG's swords from hatchet to spearpoints
enabled the KDG to thrust at Waterloo, some felt the 1796-pattern sword was too
light and flexible for effective thrusting.[19] The cuirassiers' sword and their armour
could have given them some advantage over the KDG and the rest of the British
heavy cavalry at Waterloo. However, Uxbridge expressed his doubts about the
Frenchmen's armour, saying, 'I think the Cuirass protects, but it also encumbers,
and in a mêlée I am sure the Cuirass causes the loss of many a life.'[20]

The KDG weas also issued with firearms. Only the corporals and privates carried
the 1796-pattern heavy cavalry carbine. These short-range weapons were intended
to enable the dragoon to fire either when on his horse or skirmishing dismounted.
The soldiers were also issued with a 1ft 3in bayonet for this carbine, which was
hardly ever used. The weapon was 3ft 5½in long and had a 26in barrel. It weighed
around 8lb and had a .75in calibre. Its stock had an attached side-bar on the opposite side of the lock that allowed the carbine to be hung from a spring clip on the
soldier's shoulder belt. It was carried butt uppermost in a bucket attached to the
right side of the horse by the saddle. It was rarely fired when mounted, as it was

difficult to be accurate, and reloading was tricky and took a long time. The sword was the safer option, unless dismounted.

Both the officers and other ranks also carried a pistol that was housed in a holster on the side of their saddle. The soldiers were issued with the Nock 1796-pattern heavy dragoon pistol. This had a 9in barrel, was 1ft 3in long with the same .75 calibre as the carbine, and weighed around 2lb 8oz. The pistols had very rounded butts and no brass plate but just a plain trigger guard. The pistols were very rarely used as it was virtually impossible to hit one's target when mounted, unless the target was at point-blank range. The officers tended to buy their own pistols, which were generally a little more accurate due to their superior craftsmanship, but were still pretty useless.

The KDG's most important piece of equipment was his horse. As there was a shortage of black chargers at the end of the eighteenth century, only a few regiments were mounted on them. The KDG was one of these regiments, along with the 1st and 3rd Dragoons. Whilst the privates just rode blacks until 1811, the trumpeters rode greys and the officers bays, browns or chestnuts.[21] The trumpeters were still mounted on greys in 1805, as the King was recorded as having approved the colonel of the regiment, Sir William Pitt, to instruct the commanding officer to 'purchase as many grey horses as are necessary to mount the Trumpeters of your regiment at present mounted on horses of differant colour'.[22] With the exception of the Household Cavalry, the KDG and the rest of the heavy cavalry rode horses with nag tails, whilst the French did not dock their horses.[23] Notwithstanding having been surrounded by Household Cavalry at Waterloo, this differentiation in horse tails would have helped the KDG to distinguish friend from foe on the smoke-blanketed plains of the battlefield.

The size of army horse was also regulated and had to measure between 15 and 15.3 hands. It had to be aged around 4 to 5 years old when purchased. The ideal horses for heavy cavalry were deemed to be: close, compact, broad with strong thighs and good sound feet with open heels.[24] In 1798, the average size of the KDG horse was 'fifteen hands one inch and a half'.[25] The KDG and other British heavy cavalry tended to use hunters which were either Thoroughbred crosses or larger Thoroughbreds. Whilst these may not have been ideal for military use, there was an ample supply of these types of horses in Britain and Ireland at that time.[26] British horses tended to be younger and larger than the ones ridden by the French cavalry. Also, French horses had an age limit of 7 years, whereas the British mounts soldiered on 'with no maximal years of service'.[27]

Each soldier was allocated one horse, and there were five or so extra horses allocated to each troop; they also had a troop 'bat' horse.[28] Officers either had their horses bought for them by the colonel of the regiment or bought them themselves. They were allowed more than one and used 'bat' horses to carry their kit. Subalterns were clearly allowed food for three horses, as Lieutenant Hibbert explained in a letter written from Flanders in 1815:

I got my horses over very safe, that is without having been kicked or lamed in the least; few other officers can say the same. I found that one horse was not sufficient to carry my baggage and therefore was obliged to get a fourth for which I paid £15. I shall be obliged to find food for him myself, as we are only allowed for three.

The number of horses for which fodder was provided increased with rank, so presumably KDG squadron commanders were allowed food for four horses and the commanding officer, five.

The British Army had clear-cut regulations for the care of horses instituted in *Instructions on the Care and Feeding of Horses*, first published in 1795. The troop farriers were required to oil the upper bony part of the horse's tail or dock every Saturday. On the first and fourteenth days of each month, the horses' tails were to be trimmed square and their troop letter to be branded afresh. Soldiers were required to carry a curry comb, rubbing cloth and picker in their horse's nosebags. KDG Regimental Standing Orders listed all the soldiers' duties with their horses on a daily basis, which will be described in the following chapter.

According to Army General Orders in 1810, horses were to be fed daily the following: 10lb of hay or straw, 12lb of oats, and if oats were not available, 12lb of barley or Indian corn. Again, Regimental Standing Orders dictated feeding times and methods:

> [T]he forage for the twenty four hours is to be delivered out by the Regimental Quarter Master at Head Quarters, and under the superintendence of a Subaltern Officer at out quarters, at morning stable time. The horses are to be fed three times a day in equal proportion at each stable time.

On campaign it was much more of a hand-to-mouth existence, as soldiers had to live off the land and seek forage for their horses, which could mean they were reduced to collecting green corn and gorse. Watering times were also prescribed in Regimental Standing Orders, which instructed that at Morning Stables, 'the horses are to get half a pail of water each'. And 'at half past ten the bugle sounded for horse parade, [and] after the parade is inspected by the commanding officer, the horses are rode out to water'.

The arrangement of horse furniture and the way it was packed was according to the set standard of the British heavy cavalry system. The saddle was the 'Heavy Cavalry Universal Saddle' introduced in 1796, which was an improved version of the Eliot-pattern light dragoon saddle.[29] This saddle was made of brown leather built over a wooden tree with a goatskin seat. The breast plates were connected to the slots into which the front arch of the saddle was housed. The saddle had loops connected to it, from which were hung various items of equipment. Officers' saddles were similar to those of the men, but were of better quality and in some cases more ornate. They differed in having sideboards with fans that stuck out of the rear of their saddles and on which their valise rested. The soldiers' saddle did not have this feature, so their pillion equipment was carried directly on their horses' backs.

At the back of the saddle, stowed behind the cantle, was a tubular cloth valise. Around this was wrapped the waterdeck, which was a red waterproof canvas sheet. This measured 52in square and was large enough to cover the saddle and bridle when placed on the ground. When rolled around the valise, the canvas sheet displayed the regiment's initials in blue on both the ends, with the letters 'K' and 'D' next to each other, with a 'G' below them.[30] The soldiers' mess tins were strapped on top of the valise. A rolled cloak was tethered with three straps over the front arch of the saddle that covered the pistol holsters. The cloak was covered in a flounce, which was a leather guard to prevent the reins from chaffing, as was a folded blanket that was placed under the saddle to stop the horse's back from being rubbed.

A girth, surcingle, breastplate and divided crupper kept the saddle in place, and the stirrups were square-sided. The heavy cavalry bridle comprised a curb and snaffle, or bridoon, double-bit which had curved side-bars which often featured a brass boss with the regimental insignia. To tie up their horses, the soldiers were issued with a white leather head-collar or halter.

On campaign and when in marching order, the KDG soldier would carry a lot of kit on his horse. The regulation amount was a quarter of the horse's weight, or around 250lb. The only equipment the dragoon kept on his right side was his carbine, which was attached by a swivel hook to a white 3in-wide carbine belt that hung over the soldier's left shoulder. This belt was attached with a brass buckle and had a slide to adjust its length. Attached to this belt with a pair of leather straps was a curved cartridge pouch for thirty rounds of carbine ammunition, which was positioned in the small of the man's back. The carbine's butt was secured in a leather bucket that was attached by a picket ring to the offside of the saddle, with its barrel attached to the pommel by a strap. When not in action, a picket-stake would be strapped to the carbine.

Most of the men's kit was, however, attached to the left-hand or nearside of his horse. Tied to the offside rear of the saddle was a leather case that contained spare horseshoes and a nosebag, next to which was sometimes hung a hay-net and a canvas bucket which contained such items as hatchets and tent pegs. On the soldier's left-hand side he would wear a sword belt, attached to which was a sword in its scabbard and from which a plain black leather sabretache was attached with white leather straps. In 'Marching Order', the dragoon would have slung over his right shoulder, and hanging on his left side around the level of his waist, a white canvas haversack which contained his daily ration of bread and any extra food he could procure. On his left side there would also be slung a blue wooden water canteen on a canvas strap. When extra fodder had to be carried, corn sacks were draped over the saddle.

When on campaign, even the packing of the soldier's saddle bags was to conform to a uniform pattern. In the near end bag were to be packed one pair of trousers, one pair of leggings, three pairs of stockings and one bag for small items. In the centre bag the dragoon was to pack his shag breeches, a mirror, a pair of shoes and a cleaning kit to include pipe clay and a pipe clay dish, a blackball and five brushes. The off end bag was to contain six turnovers, three shirts, a pair of scissors and a wash kit which consisted of a shaving box, razor and case, as well as a comb. In the flap the horse care-related items were packed, consisting of clothes worn when tending the horses, namely the stable jacket, shoes and forage cap, as well as the tools of the trade: curry comb and brush, snaffle bridle, mane comb and sponge oil. On the top of saddlebags was stowed the horsecloth.[31]

7

DAILY LIFE

Daily routine in peacetime for the KDG depended on where the regiment was located: in barracks, in quarters or in the field. Most time, however, was spent in barracks, and this chapter describes what a normal regimental day would have looked like in 1814, when the KDG was stationed, in its last garrison posting prior to Waterloo, at Clonmel, the county town of Tipperary in Ireland. The detail that follows is taken from the daily routine as outlined in the KDG's Regimental Standing Orders.[1] The beginning of the working day was heralded by the orderly trumpeter, who would sound a warning call to the regiment at 5.30 a.m. to indicate that they had fifteen minutes to get into 'stable dress'. This was the soldiers' attire for Morning Stables and consisted of a shirt, trousers and waistcoat. In order to attend to Morning Stables, the soldiers would take with them their horse's nose bags containing their stable appointments. At 6 a.m., on the sounding of the call for Morning Stables, the troop was marched down to the stables, halted and fallen out to their duties.

One of the soldiers' first tasks would have been to half fill pails with water from the pumps located near to the stables and water their horses. They would then have rubbed them over and cleaned their horses' boxes. This they did by shaking the dry litter and then folding it into neat bundles, which they hung on hooks at the rear of their horses. They then raked their horses' dung into piles before removing it to a heap outside. Two of the men on duty would sweep the stable floor until all that could be seen was clean cobbles. Some of the soldiers would be detailed off to collect forage. In the KDG, the routine on the treatment of the horses' litter depended on the weather. On fine days, it was taken out of the stables and spread on the cobblestones to dry, where it was left until Evening Stables. When it was raining or snowing, the litter was swept into a neat pile in the middle of the stables instead.

At around 7.30 a.m. there would be another call on the trumpet when the orderly TSM would order the 'dismiss' to be sounded, which would invite the soldiers to retire to their squad rooms to wash, get back into stable dress and make their beds properly. Once done, they would be allowed by their squad corporals to prepare and eat their breakfasts. This meal normally consisted of broth with meat in it and some bread with which to mop it up. Each squad room had the names of the soldiers it contained written up outside its door. There were two rooms per squad, as in the cavalry there was one room for every eight men; whereas in the infantry it was one room for twelve men.[2]

Each man had a bed with a bolster, a mattress and a couple of sheets and blankets. Clean sheets were provided twice a week, on Thursdays and Sundays. They were also provided with a table and some candlesticks. The men were expected to cook their own meals in a basic kitchen which contained early nineteenth-century cooking utensils such as wooden ladles, a porringer and iron pots. There would also be a wooden urinal, covered in a cloth, that was positioned in the corner of the room. Soldiers were well fed relative to their civilian peers. On a daily basis, the official rations per soldier were as follows: 1lb of beef, or if not available ½lb of pork; 1½lb of bread or flour; ¼ pint of pease; 1oz of butter or cheese; 1oz of rice; and 5 pints of beer.[3] When on campaign, the amounts of food rationed were less, being just 1½lb of beef or 10oz of pork and 1½lb of bread or flour.[4]

At 8.45 a.m., whilst the privates were having breakfast, the orderly officer would mount the guard. On the arrival of the orderly officer, the regimental guard was turned out by the orderly sergeant. He would have worn his best uniform or 'full regimentals' with a sash, with which he would have worn a small sword, and he would have carried a cane. Regimental Standing Orders were particular that when the guard was ready, the orderly sergeant was expected to have looked the duty officer straight in the face and then to have announced that the guard of 1st, The King's Dragoon Guards was ready for his inspection. Once the orderly officer had inspected the guard, he would indicate to whom he had awarded the title of being the commanding officer's orderly. This selection was based on which soldier was the best turned out member of the guard, and for this privilege he was excused the tedium of sentry duty. However, he still had to be available for any errands demanded of him by the orderly sergeant.

There were various discrete calls on either the trumpet or bugle which served as specific warnings for different types of parades. For mounted parades, 'Boots and Saddles' would normally have been sounded at 9 a.m. or an hour and a half previous to the named hour of the mounted parade. Then half an hour before this mounted parade there would have been another reminder, this time on the bugle. When it finally came to start the mounted general parades, it would have been announced on the bugle. For foot parades it was slightly different. Troop parades were announced on the trumpet twenty minutes before the named hour, and general parade on foot sounded on the trumpet at the named hour. At 9.30 a.m., there was yet another call, but this time on a bugle, to alert the KDG to Midday Stables. The duty troop sergeant would then call the troop roll in front of his TSM.

After stables, at 10.30 a.m., the troops took part in the horse parade, which was summoned on the bugle by the trumpet major. The horse parade was an opportunity for the whole regiment and its chargers to be inspected by the commanding officer. After the horse parade had finished, the orderly officer's next job was to lead the regiment to ride out to water their horses outside the barracks in the nearby meadows, just outside the town of Clonmel. At this time any new recruits would stay behind for a visit to the riding school. Here the rough riders of their respective troops would teach the newly arrived soldiers how to ride.

After watering their horses, the KDG privates washed their mounts. Once completed, the TSM would inform the orderly sergeant who, in turn, relayed this information to the orderly officer that the troop was ready for his inspection. The orderly officer would then check the horses, and in particular their tails to see they were clean and combed. The men would then 'feed away'. When in barracks, dragoon guard horses were given on a daily basis 13lb of hay, 9lb of barley or straw and 11lb of oats. Later, when they were on active duty in the Low Countries, the oats were replaced by straw or bran.[5] In the KDG, the forage for the whole day was delivered by the quartermaster to headquarters. The junior officer responsible would then ensure it was dished out in the right amounts to the different troops at each stable time, as the horses were fed in equal proportions three times a day.

The completion of feeding was announced at around 1.30 p.m. by the duty trumpeter, who sounded the 'dismissal'. The soldiers would then return to their rooms to cook some broth for their lunches. However, the troops were not allowed to touch their food until the orderly officer had inspected it and was satisfied that it was up to standard in its quality and quantity. If the food was not satisfactory, it was to be filed in his report to Adjutant Thomas Shelver. The next trumpet call came at 6 p.m. to announce the officers' dinner. Evening Stables was sounded after that at 6.45 p.m. Troop roll calls were then made and, according to Regimental Orders, 'any man absent at any of the troop roll calls will of course be confined and reported'. Once the troop roll calls had been completed and no soldiers found to be absent, the dragoons were marched to Evening Stables.

At this duty, the horses were brushed, given their third and final feed and bedded up for the night. The announcement of the completion of duties would have been passed down the chain of command from the squad corporal via the squad sergeant to the TSM, who would finally report to the orderly sergeant that their respective troops had completed their last stables tasks. Once all the TSMs had carried out the same reports for their troops, the orderly sergeant would report to the orderly officer that the KDG was ready for inspection. The orderly officer would then check the horses' feed and stable conditions, and once satisfied he would have instructed the orderly trumpeter to sound the 'dismissal'. Watch Setting was at 9 p.m., when the orderly officer made a final check of the canteen to ensure there was no further drinking by the men. He then went on to visit the regimental NCOs guards to ensure all were present and correct in their attire and had completed their tasks. At this point in the day, the orderly officer's tasks would have been completed, unless there was an emergency or an event that warranted his attention; for the men, it was lights out.

The last major aspect of the KDG's peacetime working life in the years immediately before the Battle of Waterloo concerned the training and the tactics that they were taught. The fruits of their learning and practice were then put to both good and bad use in the way they fought on 18 June 1815.

8

TRAINING AND TACTICS

Although Horse Guards set out the guidelines for training, the way new recruits were instructed was a matter for the individual regiments. Around the time of Waterloo, the KDG seemed to have developed a friendly team-based approach to teaching its new soldiers. On arrival, the new recruit was attached to a 'conviviale' or buddy who was to be their chaperone for their first few months at the regiment. According to Regimental Standing Orders, this 'conviviale' was to be 'a respectable good soldier', and it went on to state that, 'Non-Commissioned Officers to instruct such recruits as are in their Squads, in particular of their duty, and to take pains to inculcate on their mind that good conduct and spirit which may lead them to attain the first ranks of their profession.' The first priority for training new recruits was to teach them to ride. This was the responsibility of the riding master, who supervised the troop rough riders in their instruction of new recruits. The commanding officer was kept constantly appraised as to the recruits' progress, and they were eventually ranked by the riding master as either first- or second-class riders.

The key areas of instruction in the cavalry were in riding, foot and mounted drill, the use of weapons, formation riding and mounted tactics. There were uniform guidelines for the cavalry in sword drill and mounted manoeuvres, as set out in two instruction manuals first published in 1796. The first of these, *Rules and Regulations for the Sword Exercise of the Cavalry*, was written by John Gaspard Le Marchant. Mounted manoeuvres were dictated by General Sir David Dundas's *Instructions and Regulations for the Formation and Movements of the Cavalry*. The foreword to this manual instructed that these rules and regulations 'shall be observed and practised by the several regiments of cavalry in his majesty's service'. However, the most important discipline of horsemanship and the rest of the British cavalry's training in the early nineteenth century was largely left to the commanding officers to carry out at their depots and within their regiments. In many cases, the British and French used different methods of training, riding and fighting that was to be reflected in how they fought each other at Waterloo.

The style of horsemanship was an area where there was a marked difference between the French and the British. The former had centralised training based on their riding schools, where emphasis was placed on the control of the horse through the ménage system of training. The ménage-seat was described in Adams's 1805 book *An Analysis of Horsemanship* as, 'that medium position in which the rider sits when the horse works straight, i.e. not going only straight forward, but without any bend in the position of the horse'.[1] France had brought out riding manuals in 1788 and 1805 which were considered to be the best of their time, and the French cavalry's training was based on the progression of the rider. Their six-month period of instruction for the novice rider was double the time the British recruit was given, and enabled them to ride as opposed to just being able to sit on a horse.[2] They introduced central regulations for the care of their horses in 1794. These were the most advanced of their kind at the time and made the French cavalrymen self-sufficient in the general and veterinary care of their horses.[3]

In contrast, the British did not standardise their riding instruction and horse care. There were isolated attempts, such as the establishment of the Cavalry Depot at Maidstone and Lord Paget's equitation centre at Woodbridge in Suffolk, but the majority of riding instruction was a regimental responsibility, carried out in their own riding schools. Paget was helped by Le Marchant at Woodbridge. Here, cadres of officers and men were trained and then returned to relay these instruction methods to their own regiments. Unlike the French emphasis on the control of the ménage, the British adopted a more sporting attitude to riding based on hunting and racing, where speed was more the objective. This was called 'military riding' and was the British Army's method of riding from 1765 to 1865.[4] As a result, the horses used reflected the respective nation's styles of riding, the French using less powerful but more controllable mounts, whilst the British horse was bred for speed and endurance.

The British 'sporting' style was criticised by a writer using the pseudonym 'Eques' in the 1811 edition of *The Royal Military Chronicle*, who stated that British horses were harder to control with a 'preponderance to the shoulder'. This critic went on to insist that horses should be more carefully broken in and that the lack of British horsemanship owed a big part to the army's lack of riding schools. He had a point as, by the late eighteenth century, only two regiments, the Royal Horse Guards and the 2nd Dragoon Guards, had their own riding schools. 'Eques' went on to moan, 'It has surprised me to observe how much of this [horsemanship] essential part of an officer's education is neglected.' Lieutenant-Colonel Tyndale of the Life Guards produced *A Treatise on Military Equitation* in 1797, in which he commented that 'it is seen in countries where the ménage-system is unknown, that their cavalry are almost always beaten by inferior numbers of well-trained or indeed indifferently trained cavalry'.[5]

Notwithstanding much commentary on the superiority of French over British military horsemanship, the KDG and its peers in the British cavalry were well-trained and competent horsemen. The men were schooled by the rough riders, under the auspices of the regimental riding master, in their troops and were instructed to a high level of competence. Like the rest of the British heavy cavalry, the KDG rode with extended legs in long stirrups. The advantage of the British style of aggressive riding was reflected in their success in the charge. The British cavalry regulations published in 1813 urged the rider in the charge to lean back, use the spur and not interfere with the horse's mouth, giving it full head. This was clearly going to lead to horses charging out of control and caused the troops to become dispersed. This weakness was something which their more disciplined French adversaries avoided.[6] It was, therefore, not much of a surprise when one of the characteristics of the British heavy cavalry's performance at Waterloo was its lack of control. This drawback was to cost the KDG and, with the exception of the Blues, the rest of the British heavy cavalry dearly that day.

The use of the sword was another area where British and French cavalry differed. As discussed, the former favoured the cut and the latter the thrust. The British approach was enforced by Le Marchant's doctrine that the cut was better. He felt that a thrusting cavalryman was vulnerable to a fatal parry riposte by his adversary, and for that reason he endorsed the cut. His manual outlined mounted swordsmanship based on six different sword cuts, which ranged from the offensive strike to the defensive parry.

Le Marchant's book set out exercises for cavalry privates to start dismounted standing 4ft from a circle that simulated an opponent's face. In this drill, the soldier would employ the six cuts, with the emphasis on using their wrists rather than their arms in a scything motion and not to bend their elbows, which would be vulnerable to cuts from their enemies. This was then practised on horseback, with the additional mounted sword exercise called 'running the ring'. Here, the soldier had to put the point of his sabre through a metal ring and then extricate his blade, which would be dragged away from him with the use of a pulley. This trained the soldier to not only stab his enemy but to also be able to withdraw his sword and move on to face his next opponent. It was also a useful practice in horse control when fighting. Mounted sword instruction was carried on in conjunction with the riding masters. A last aspect and useful drill of Le Marchant's manual was the focus given to men using their initiative when fighting.

The main drawback of Le Marchant's manual for the KDG and the other heavy cavalry regiments was that it focused on the light cavalry's curved slashing weapon, to the exclusion of their weapon, the heavy cavalry straight sabre. However, it was still a useful handbook and the skills and discipline it instilled no doubt helped the British cavalrymen in their one-on-one duels with the French cavalry at Waterloo.

In terms of command and control in mounted manoeuvres, Wellington was adamant on the need for cavalry discipline, as he made clear in one of his dispatches:

> The formation and discipline of a body of cavalry are very difficult and tedious and require great experience and patience in the persons who attempt it. After all it is doubtful whether they will succeed, whether the body of cavalry thus formed will be worth the expense of maintaining it; for at the same time that nothing can be more useful in the day of the battle, and nothing more useless, than a body of regular cavalry half and insufficiently disciplined.[7]

This was a comment made by the Duke many years before Waterloo, when he was fighting in India at the end of the eighteenth century. It is revealing in that it showed he appreciated that the control of cavalry was difficult but also that he thought it was unlikely that it could be achieved.

General Sir David Dundas's *Instructions and Regulations for the Formation and Movements of the Cavalry* was the standard operating procedure for the command and control of regiments of cavalry through 108 different mounted manoeuvres. Dundas, along with the Duke of York and the Adjutant General Sir William Fawcett, ran the British Army in the late eighteenth century. They were so impressed with Prussian military practice that they copied some of that army's equipment and tactics. Dundas, who was later to become the KDG's colonel of the regiment, intended to produce a guide to mounted manoeuvres in response to the poor state of British cavalry drill.[8] The book addressed the different movements made by a regiment in changing formation and position. The book discussed movements in echelon, open and close column, line, counter march, etc. The manual was mandatory reading for the British Army, as in the foreword of Dundas's manual was a royal instruction that 'every Officer of Cavalry shall be provided with a Copy of the Regulations'.

There were two main formations in which cavalry regiments were to move. 'Closed column' was mainly used for moving into position. It was easy to control and enabled regiments to move efficiently and quickly from their assembly areas to their forming up points prior to deployment. In this manoeuvre, the regiment moved with a narrow frontage of a troop, with thirty soldiers arrayed in two lines in 'loose files', that was knee to knee. There would be an officer on both flanks of the first line, with a corporal placed behind on the flanks of the second line. This was a tight formation as the ranks had only half a horse-length spacing between them. The officers would form on the left flank of their respective squadrons, and the commanding officer and his trumpeter would be positioned on the front left of the leading troop. According to Naylor in his diary, the KDG adopted this formation on the morning of 18 June when it moved from its bivouac area to the Household Brigade's concentration area west of the Brussels–Charleroi road in between the farms of Mont St Jean and La Haye Sainte. He wrote, 'Before daybreak we were on the alert but remained inactive till 11 o'clock when we formed in column of Squadrons.'

The second formation outlined for cavalry to use when manoeuvring was that of deployment in 'line'. This was the normal formation that was adopted prior to making the charge. The regiment's squadrons were deployed abreast and in two lines, with each horseman riding knee to knee and with little space between the two ranks. This formation had four broad variations: the single line, the double line, the echeloned line and the chequered line. The single line was that adopted by the KDG in its first charge against the 1st and 4th Cuirassiers to the west of La Haye Sainte.[9] In this formation, all the squadrons were packed in a line with spacing of 27 yards between each, to form two dense waves. On the basis that the KDG was a four-squadron regiment, its frontage at Waterloo would have been around 382 yards.

In this manoeuvre, the commanding officer was to be positioned at the very front of the centre of the regiment, with his squadron commanders behind him. The central squadron was the 'squadron of direction' which would lead the others in the regiment in their first charge. The other squadron commanders then had to take their positions off it. According to Naylor, Fuller placed himself in front of him as he was the central squadron leader.[10] The other officers were positioned at the flanks and the centre of the front line of their troops, covered by their sergeants and corporals. Their job was to keep the front rank's dressing straight. About two horse lengths behind the two lines of the regiment was a supernumerary rank containing officers, TSMs, sergeants and trumpeters. Also in this third line, at the extreme right, according to the text book, would have been RSM Thomas Barlow. The eight troop farriers remained further behind still with the rear party, which was not to take part in the action.

Deployment in line was always going to be a difficult formation for Fuller to have governed at Waterloo. The long length of his regiment's line probably made it impossible for him to have viewed the whole of his regiment's frontage, even from a central position, and thus very hard to control. By only having the commanding captain in front of each squadron, there were insufficient officers to prevent their troops from racing away in the charge, which is precisely what happened at Waterloo. Another problem with this manoeuvre was its insufficient consideration of broken ground and obstacles. At Waterloo, before they could commence their charge, the men of the KDG had to thread their way between the three infantry squares of the KGL and one of the Hanoverians. Even when they had formed up, they then had to negotiate the obstacle of the sunken *Chemin d'Ohain* and afterwards the large obstacle of La Haye Sainte's farm complex.

As well as ordaining methods of cavalry movement, Dundas's book also covered tactics. In contrast to Le Marchant's light cavalry-focused sword manual, these *Instructions and Regulations* were mainly a heavy cavalry handbook. Little attention was paid in it to the skirmishing and piquet work of light cavalry, as its tactical focus was fixed on the heavy cavalry charge. The charge was specified to start at a walk, with the sword resting on the soldiers' right arms. The crescendo of movement increased with the move to a fast trot and then, within 250 yards of the enemy, an increase of pace to the gallop. At 80 yards out from their targets, the charge was to be made 'with the greatest velocity' and soldiers were to carry their swords carried horizontally across their heads, with the sharpened edge pointed towards the enemy. However, Lieutenant Waymouth of the 2nd Life Guards bemoaned this method of sword carriage at Waterloo when he stated it was 'the custom of our Service to carry the swords in a very bad position whilst charging, the French carrying theirs in a manner far less fatiguing, and also much better for either attack or defence.'[11]

The charge was normally carried out in two ranks and in line. Speed was of the essence in this manoeuvre, on the basis that, 'the spur as much as the sword tends to overset an opposite enemy'. However, Dundas stressed that, along with the speed of the charge, cohesion was important, and that once made, 'the great object is to rally and renew its efforts in a body'. He also explained the actions a regiment should take if the charge was unsuccessful. That was to 'retire as well as it can, to make way for those that support it, and [it] must rally as soon as possible under the protection of others'. Interestingly, the manual counsels against charges over broken ground, as the KDG had to execute in its first charge at Waterloo, 'If the ground is open, the shock must be given with vigour; if it is so embarrassed as to prevent the acting in body; less can be expected in such a situation adapted to another arm, and improper to bring cavalry into with advantage.'[12] Whilst Dundas's theory was reasonable, it was hard to apply in the conditions that faced the heavy brigades at Waterloo. The circumstances made it hard to combine the vigour necessary for an effective charge with the control required to ensure cohesion over the broken ground over which they had to charge, which was covered in obstacles.

The French manual's directions on manoeuvre and the charge were similar to those of the British, but with less emphasis on speed and more on control. Charges were carried out in lines of two ranks, with most of the officers in front of the first rank to ensure control. The NCOs controlled the second line and were posted on the flanks to help cohesion and shape when charging. Unlike the British, there were few soldiers in the third or supernumerary rank, with just some trumpeters, three officers and a couple of sergeant-majors. Soldiers were instructed to move to the charge in silence, so as to hear the words of command. It was not until 50m from their target that the *charge à la sauvage* would be given. The soldiers were then to stand up in their stirrups and shout '*avancez*', with the front rank instructed to point their sabres at the enemy. However, with control in mind, the French cavalry usually carried out their charges at the trot or walk.

It seemed that the KDG dragoon was as well trained as his French adversary at Waterloo. He would have been a proficient horseman and good with his sword.

Where his training could in some way have let him down was in the lower emphasis placed on command and control in British cavalry relative to that in the French.
If the officers had kept their squadrons together, reorganised after their first charge
and then returned to their own lines, rather than charging into those of the French,
many of the horrendous losses might have been averted. In mitigation, however,
the battlefield conditions before the first charge made control nigh on impossible.
In conclusion, it says much for the KDG's training that a regiment unbaptised by
fire could have done as well as it did at Waterloo against battle-hardened French
cavalry with as much as ten years' experience of fighting.

FROM THE PLAINS OF CLONMEL TO FLANDERS FIELD

In the four or so years leading up to Waterloo, the KDG had been stationed in Ireland. It had started its duties in Dundalk in 1810, and had proceeded from there to Dublin the following year. At the end of 1812, the regiment moved to Clonmel, which was to be its barracks until it returned to England. The KDG left Ireland from Cork Harbour in two waves. Seven troops left in November 1814, followed by the remaining three troops in January 1815. The regiment disembarked at Bristol and dispersed as follows: four troops to Coventry and two troops each to Warwick, Leicester and Nottingham. There was little recorded to assess the state of the regiment on the eve of the Flanders campaign in 1815.

On 20 March 1815, Napoleon, having returned from exile on Elba, entered Paris, so King Louis XVIII and his family left France to Bonaparte. Notwithstanding Napoleon's overtures of peace to the monarchs of the larger European states, the four leading nations – Austria, Britain, Prussia and Russia – signed a declaration at the Congress of Vienna that decreed Napoleon an outlaw. This made the War of the Seventh Coalition inevitable. A further agreement was made on 25 March with the Treaty of Alliance, in which these leading European powers each pledged 150,000 men to defeat Napoleon. In response to this, Bonaparte mobilised the French armies and hastily began to rearm and re-equip his forces. However, only two of the four Allied armies were ready to invade France by the beginning of May. One army, under the command of Wellington, consisted of an Allied force that comprised armies from Belgium, Britain, Hanover, Holland and several German principalities. The other was a Prussian army under Marshal Blücher.

The KDG was then ordered to the Low Countries to join the British contingent of Wellington's Allied army. The regiment proceeded from the Midlands to the London area. Hibbert mentioned that their route was via Highgate and Hampstead to Durfleet.[1] *The Digest* of 12 April 1815 recorded that eight troops of the regiment were embarked for Ostend. The regimental transports left Tilbury, Purfleet and Gravesend on 16 April, and spent a night anchored off Southend and another day in the Margate Roads. The crossing was not a pleasant one, as Hibbert described. 'We had a very rough passage from Gravesend, and were obliged to come to anchor frequently for fear of being driven on the shoals in the river.'[2]

The KDG arrived at Ostend on 19 April and started to disembark on 20 April.[3] However, as Hibbert went on to describe, conditions were not great:

[W]e disembarked at twelve and did not finish until eight o'clock in the evening, when we set out for Bruges and arrived there about twelve. It was a cold rainy evening and when we arrived not a soul was up, and no billets for the horses or men, therefore they were obliged to remain out for two hours before any billets could be procured.[4]

Not all the regiment arrived in Ostend on 20 April, as RSM Barlow, in a letter home, stated that he 'came within sight of Ostend on the morning of the 24th on that day we disembarked; at ten o'clock the same evening'.[5] Colonel Fuller arrived later still with headquarters division on 27 April.[6]

★★★

Whilst Wellington and Blücher wanted to go on the offensive and invade France, they were not prepared to do so until they had the assistance of the Austrians and the Russians, so that all four armies could make a simultaneous attack on Paris. However, at the end of April 1815, the other alliance armies were still mobilising and thus were still not yet ready to assist in any invasion of France. So the British and Prussian commanders decided to go on the defensive until the Austrians and Russians could join them on France's borders. Wellington's army and the Prussian forces were drawn up on France's north-eastern frontiers, to contain any attempt by Napoleon to take the Low Countries and to await the appearance of their allies prior to an invasion of France. The two armies' front line stretched for around 130 miles, from Ypres in the west to Maastricht in the east.

Wellington's forces were concentrated on Brussels and to its west and southwest. This was to comply with his lines of communication to the sea. The Prussians were located to the south and east of the Belgian capital, with their headquarters at Liège. This allowed them to run their lines of communication east towards Prussia and to be in a position to defend any moves by the French in the direction

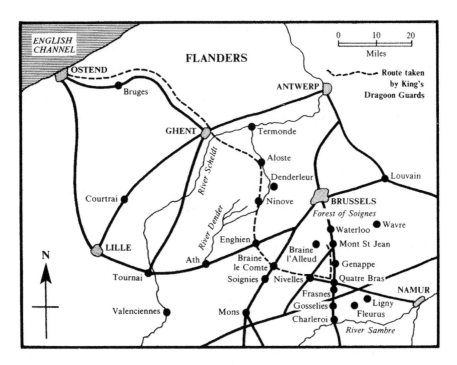

Route to battle: the KDG's route from Ostend to Waterloo. (Elizabeth Mann and Michael Russell Publishing Ltd)

of their country. If the French invaded the Low Countries, Wellington's priorities were to protect his lines of communication to Ostend, from which port his British troops were resupplied, as well as to defend Brussels. As the first threat would be to Brussels, Wellington sited his army to cover four of Napoleon's most likely routes to that city, as well as to Ghent. These routes were: from Valenciennes via Mons to Brussels, which he thought the most likely; from Tournai via Ath to Brussels; from Lille via Menin to Ghent; and from Tournai to Ghent. The fifth possible axis of a French attack was from Charleroi to Brussels, which was covered by Blücher's I Corps under Lieutenant-General Count von Ziethen.

Wellington's army was divided into four main groupings and positioned in such a way they could all concentrate within twenty-four hours. His dispositions were as follows: his reserve corps in and around Brussels; I Corps, under the Prince of Orange, on his left flank, with headquarters at Braine le Comte; II Corps, under Lieutenant-General Lord Hill, on his right flank, with headquarters at Ath on the River Dender; and to the east and in the rear of II Corps, the Cavalry Corps, under Lieutenant-General, the Earl of Uxbridge, with his headquarters at Grammont. It was to the latter location that the KDG marched from Ostend. Here the regiment was commanded by the Duke of York, via his military secretary in a letter, to join the Household Brigade.[7]

The route taken by the KDG from Ostend to its cantonments in the Cavalry Corps area around Grammont was first to Ghistelles to Bruges and on from there to Ghent via Ecloo. The KDG arrived in several parties at different times, so a halt was called at Ghent until the whole regiment could be assembled for the march to the south. According to Hibbert, his troop had enjoyed a pleasant march from Ostend with the Inniskillings and Greys, through some pretty countryside, and, in contrast to the Prussians, got on well with the locals, as he described in one of his letters:

> The country we have hitherto passed through is most beautiful; from Ostend to Ghent the road is paved and as level as a bowling green the whole way, but the country on each side is a perfect garden, the cottages and gardens far surpass England and the inhabitants are uncommonly civil especially to English men who are much liked in Flanders. They detest the Prussians; they gave us to understand that it was impossible to satisfy them in any particular, and the common men would generally plunder them of everything they had before they departed from their billets. They said we behaved like gentlemen, and therefore tried to anticipate our wishes in everything they could.[8]

However, Hibbert also demonstrated in his letter of 28 May that the British too could be forceful in extracting food from the locals:

> The people in the farmhouse in which I am quartered are most uncommonly stingy, and they would not cook me my dinner unless I gave them a franc; they soon altered their tone when they found that if they did not do it by fair means they must do it by [unreadable]. In fact they refused to give us anything to eat at first and were very saucy, but we broke open their larder and when our bellies were full, we condescended to talk to them. I mean to pay them for what was consumed, nevertheless.[9]

Captain Naylor also had a pleasant journey down to the Cavalry Corps concentration area with the 163 men and 159 horses under his command; this would have corresponded to a two-troop squadron. Some of the other ranks must have brought their wives, as Barlow wrote, 'Sgt Majors Levitt and Benwell['s] wives are come out with us, we have in all 23 women, the regulations is one woman to 25 men, each woman earns half allowance free of expense.'[10] He marched his soldiers via the canal road to Bruges, where he dined and spent the night at the Coronne Impériale. Then on 22 April, lack of horse fodder meant that Naylor's troop had to go foraging that evening. The following day, Naylor had some time off. He went to look at Ghent's churches with some officers from the Scots Greys, had dinner and saw a play. On 24 April, Naylor stated in his diary he had to look for additional horses, probably for the five unmounted men under his command.

Barlow was four days' ride behind Naylor and did not arrive at Ghent until 27 April, having marched via Ghistilles and Ecloo. Like Naylor, Barlow was having a pleasant progress south, as he penned home:

> The country where I now am is one of the most beautiful I ever saw and the inhabitants are very good to us. I should like for you to be here very much, was it not for the great inconvenience you would be party to on the march, for as you could not speak the same language as the people, you could not very readily procure lodgings. I am endeavouring to learn French[.] I have made a little progress in the attainment of it so much so as to be able to ask for food.

Naylor stayed at Ghent for just over a week, from 23 April to 1 May. This city was home to the French government-in-exile and King Louis XVIII and his family. Barlow saw him and wrote, 'The King of France is here and I have had the pleasure of seeing him twice since I came[;] he has with him a great many French soldiers and a great many have deserted from Boneparte [*sic*] lately and joined the King.' The officers not only saw but were introduced to the exiled French monarch, as Naylor recorded in his diary. It appeared the last elements of the KDG arrived at Ghent from Ecloo on 27 April, under the commanding officer Fuller, where they 'joined the 1st Division of the regiment, and quartered in the Environs. His Majesty [King Louis XVIII] was pleased to express much satisfaction at the appearance of the Heavy Cavalry.'[11]

On 1 May, after a few days which allowed the troops to reform as a regiment, the KDG commenced its move to its cantonments in the Cavalry Corps area in the Dender Valley, with its headquarters located in Sint-Lievens Esse. The other troops were located in the area of Aspelare in the villages of Egem, Liederkerke, Aloste, Denderleur, Sint Antelinks and Nederhasselt.[12][13] On 27 April, the KDG officers were presented to King Louis XVIII and a couple of days later, Naylor was again off in search of horses. It appeared the KDG was pretty short of horses, as from the regimental return on embarkation there was a shortfall in mounts of at least 75 horses; and this did not include the requirement for second and third mounts for the officers and bat horses to carry the regiment's baggage.

Until hostilities began in mid-June, life centred around the normal troop business of watering, troop and regimental parades, field days and reviews. The reviews escalated both in size and in the military importance of their reviewing dignitary. Lord Uxbridge inspected the KDG on 6 May, during which parade he told the regiment to file their swords down from a hatchet to a spear point. There was then a review of both heavy brigades, with the exception of the Royals who had not yet arrived, by the Prince of Orange and other distinguished guests at Heldergems on 24 May. Hibbert recorded, 'The Duke de Berri in particular was highly delighted, and said that his brother could not but be re-established in his possessions, when he had so excellent a body of forces to assist him.'[14]

The crowning review was that of most of the British cavalry and the horse artillery by both Wellington and Blücher on Schendelbacke Common near Gramont on 29 May. Also in attendance were the Prince of Orange and the Duke of Berri. According to Barlow, it was a hot and long day, the regiment having remained in the saddle from 5 a.m. until 7 a.m. Hibbert described this parade:

> You may conceive what a sight it was when a line was composed of sixteen regiments of cavalry, and all in the most beautiful condition imaginable. This line was exactly three miles in extent – a comfortable sight for the French rascal[s] had they been there. Martial [sic] Blucher was highly delighted, and all the foreigners who were present. Lord Wellington made his appearance at one o'clock and did not dismiss us until six, so we had had quite enough of it by the time we got home, which was about nine. We were altogether about fifteen hours on horseback, and nothing to eat or drink; added to this it was the hottest day I ever felt and many men fainted in the ranks.[15]

There was one further inspection before Waterloo, and that was by Lord Edward Somerset on Welle Common on 9 June, at which he instructed the soldiers' kits to be reduced by nearly a third in weight by cutting down on the 'necessaries' being carried. Somerset then took two squadrons of KDGs with the two Life Guard regiments and the Blues on a field day on 15 June.

The other incidents of note during this waiting period in May in the Dender Valley were recorded in *The Digest* as the couple of moves the regiment made that month. First there was a move on 13 May of quarters for all except headquarters to the villages of St Marie Anderhove and St George Anderhove. Then, on 24 May, the KDG took new cantonments, with headquarters having been moved to Denderleuve on the River Dender. The other squadrons were moved to the villages of Welle, Indergem and Kerexken in the area of Alost and Ninove. The other significant event recorded in *The Digest* were the late arrivals of the remaining officers. Captain Battersby joined with his servant on 17 May. He then replaced Major Graham as 2nd Troop leader, with Graham having been appointed the regimental major until his seniors, lieutenant-colonels Teesdale or Acklom, arrived. Lieutenant Brooke joined the regiment on 18 May and Captain Bringhurst on 27 May.

When not working, there appears to have been plenty of time for the officers, men and horses to have rested and relaxed. This was especially important for the horses, which would have been worn out by the long march from Ostend. The forage in the lush Dender Valley was reported to have been plentiful and of good quality:

The horses were living in clover, for their racks and mangers were full of it, and their stalls of clean straw up to their bellies, though this bounty was in some measure repaid by the manure, which was so valuable that the production of one horse in twenty-four hours was worth at least three or four pounds of hay and perhaps four times the quantity of clover.[16]

The moving of cantonments was probably to ensure there was plenty of fresh forage for the regiment. This period of rest and copious eating paid dividends in terms of the reportedly superior condition of the British heavy cavalry's horses to those of the French cavalry at Waterloo.

If Naylor and Hibbert were typical examples of troop captains and subalterns in the KDG, then we have a good indication of the officers' pastimes over this period in their record of events. Naylor spent his days off shopping and visiting friends. Amongst his purchases was silk for a waistcoat, a saddle from a brother officer and some silver forks and spoons at Alost. Naylor called on a range of people, mainly for dinner. He met officers from outside the KDG, having called on Lord Uxbridge on 18 May and dined with Captain Kelly and Lieutenant Irby of the Life Guards and Major Bridges of the 12th Light Dragoons on 3 June. Otherwise he tended to dine with the commanding officer and the other senior captains commanding troops. Hibbert had a somewhat quieter time, having complained in one letter that 'the only amusement I have now is riding'. He regretted forgetting his flute and wished that the corn in the fields was cut so he could go partridge shooting.

Whilst Naylor was buying silk for waistcoats, Barlow, then a TSM, was purchasing linen for drawers and pantaloons. He was suffering from the fact that his shirts were falling apart and he could not replace them at that time. When he was not writing, Barlow seems to have spent much time cooking, having reported he and RSM John Brown had knocked up some Yorkshire puddings and they intended to tackle a gooseberry pudding as that fruit was plentiful in the vicinity of their quarters. Barlow indicated that he and his friend Brown were well fed at that time:

[W]e have for breakfast coarse rye bread, coffee – for dinner stewed meat and potatoes – for supper the same as dinner, sometimes they make us hasty puddings, our chief drink is buttermilk[;] I have grown very fond of it. The good nature of the people exceeds all I ever saw or could expect far before the English[;] we cannot talk their language but they provide everything for us without being asked.[17]

Brown, like Barlow, was missing his wife terribly:

Mr Brown is not yet appointed, he is much better than when I wrote to you, having received a letter from his wife; she is very unhappy and her children not very well; he says he would rather go home than have the commission he expects. I can assure you that an order for my return home would please me better than if I was appointed Generalissimo[. H]owever, as I am a soldier my duty is obedience.[18]

The circumstances of the KDG private soldier during this period of waiting in cantonment has not been well documented. The best indication from a primary source was contained in a letter written by Private Charles Stanley to his cousin, dated 15 May 1815:

> We have one gud thing Cheap that is Tobaco and Everrything a–Cordnley Tobaco is 4d Per 1b Gin is 1s 8d Per Galland that is 2½ Per Quart and Everrything In Perposion hour alounse Per Day is One Pound of Beef a Pound and half of Bred half a Pint o Gin But the worst of all we dont get it Regeler and If we dont get it the Day it is due we Luse it wish It is ofton the Case i asure you My Dear Lad I hop Wot Ever may Comacros your mind to trobel You wish i hope nothing will I hope you never will think Of Being a Soldier I Asure you it is a Verry Ruf Consarn … I have not ad the Pleasure of Ling in a Bed since In the Cuntrey thank God the Weather is fine Wish is in hour faver we Get no Pay at all onley hour Bed and mete and Gin we have 10d Per Day soped from us wish we shal Reseive wen six months is Expired.[19]

However, this daily ration of meat and bread was very much in line with what British troops got issued in the field, if not better.[20] And it appears to have been in the same proportions as the amount Wellington decreed should have been rationed to the Brunswick troops in a letter of 13 May 1815, which was, 'two pounds of bread, half a pound of meat, and vegetables'.[21] Stanley's complaint over the delay in having been paid was echoed by Barlow, who wrote in a letter dated the day after Stanley's that, 'I have not received any pay from 25 April last, my rations amount to 6d per day, so that I have due to me 2/6 per day from that time.'[22]

It was not just the other ranks who were affected by the lack of pay. Hibbert too complained of the lack of funds, but at least he had private means as a back-up:

> We have had no pay issued as yet, nor do I think we shall get any for some months to come. Mention this to my Father when you next see him, and tell him that if I was to draw upon his bank at Ghent or Brussels they would deduct thirty per cent upon the drafts. But it must come to this in the end; that is if we get no pay, and I have not more that will last me six weeks.

However, the officers' and soldiers' wages were to be paid a few weeks later, as Naylor recorded drawing his troop's pay up to 24 May from the paymaster on 5 and 11 June.[23] Also, Hibbert asked his mother in a letter dated 11 June to, 'Tell

Father that we received all the pay due to us the other day, and therefore I shall be enabled to go on without drawing on England.'[24] Overall, this period of preparation during May and the first fortnight of June 1815 was useful to the KDG and the other regiments of the heavy brigades. The officers, men and horses had been well rested, fed and trained; something that was to stand them in good stead on 18 June at Waterloo.

HOSTILITIES OPEN: 16 JUNE TO THE MORNING OF 18 JUNE

On 31 May, the KDG was formally incorporated with the two Life Guards regiments and the Blues into the First (Household) Cavalry Brigade, under the command of Lord Edward Somerset. The beginning of June saw a field day on the fourth and another inspection by Lord Edward Somerset on the sixth. The only regimental event of note, according to *The Digest* and Naylor's diary, was the punishment of Private Marvin and his co-conspirators at 6 a.m. on 14 June. They paid the penalty for drunken horseplay with a loaded carbine, as described by Hibbert in one of his letters:

> I got off an unpleasant duty owing to it, which is seeing four men flogged tomorrow for getting drunk on duty. One of them as a frolick loaded his carabine with three ball cartridges, one on top of the other, and very deliberately shot at the other three who were before in order, as he said, to let them hear the noise the balls made in passing. It was lucky that none of them were killed.[1]

The regiment's daily humdrum schedule was about to end. Before dawn on 16 June, the KDG was ordered to Nivone, Uxbridge's cavalry corps headquarters, 'with all expedition'. At 3.30 a.m. on the previous day, Bonaparte's *Armée du Nord* had crossed the French border into Belgium just south of Charleroi. This was part of a thrust north on the road that ran north through Quatre Bras and Genappe to Brussels. Napoleon's forces first engaged soldiers from the von Zieten's I Prussian Corps. By that evening, the leading French elements had reached Frasnes, where they stopped for the night. As Wellington had believed the French would use Mons

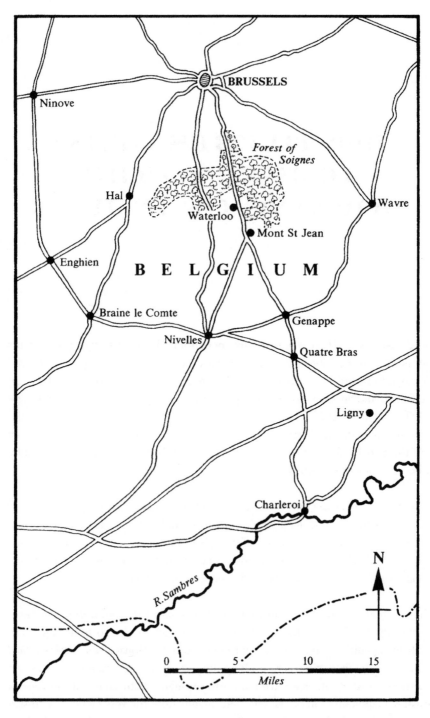

Area of operations June 1815: the region south of Brussels. (Elizabeth Mann and Michael Russell Publishing Ltd)

as their axis to Brussels, his forces only received their orders the day after the French invasion of Belgian territory.

The fact that Napoleon's advance was a surprise was borne out by the fact that two squadrons of KDG were exercising with the rest of the Household Brigade on the day of the French invasion.[2] In a letter written on 14 June, Barlow was 'still in a state of inactivity'[3] and TSM Page described the order to march in one of his letters as a sudden one.[4] Also, all the cavalry's top brass, including the Earl of Uxbridge, Lord Edward Somerset, the KDG's commanding officer, Fuller, and subalterns Brooke and Huntley, were all attending the Duchess of Richmond's Ball in Brussels on the night of Napoleon's crossing into Belgium. In a letter to his wife, RSM Barlow recorded the regiment's early start the next day:

> On the 16th June at 3 o'clock in the morning our late and lamented Shelver [as he was to be killed at Waterloo] called me up and informed me that an order had been received to march immediately; about five o'clock the regiment moved for Niuvelle [Nivelles], distance of about 45 miles.[5]

The regiment first had to re-form and march to the cavalry corps headquarters at Ninove. Naylor summarised the key events on the KDG's long march to Nivelles in his diary, starting from their arrival at Ninove:

> We arrived about 8 o'clock and remained an hour when the Brigade under Lord Edward Somerset consisting of 1st and 2nd Life Guards, Blues and 1st Dragoon Guards marched for Enghien which place we left on our right and proceeded to Braine Le Comte where we halted an hour to wait, and marched at 5 o'clock for Nivelle[. B]efore our arrival at Nivelle we heard a cannonade and at times could distinctly see a smoke at some distance. When we came to Nivelle many wounded were arriving and we were informed that an action had commenced at 4 o'clock. General Picton's Division consisting of the 1st, 28th—32–42–79–92–95 etc.[6] had suffered much as well as the Belgians; they had been repeatedly charged by the French cuirassiers.[7]

The regiment's march to Nivelles had been a slow one, with the roads choked with Allied cavalry and transports. The KDG's first destination described by Naylor above was Enghien, 'on the main road between Brussels and Paris, the point of assembly for several corps that had been stationed in and about that part of the country'.[8] Captain Cavalié Mercer of the Royal Horse Artillery recorded that just as he left Enghien, 'a column of household troops made its appearance, advancing from Ninove, and taking the same direction'.[9] So from Enghien onwards to Nivelles, Mercer took pretty much the same route as the KDG and the rest of the Household Brigade. However, he had set out earlier than the regiment and was some way in front of it. He had later received instructions that he was to join the Household Brigade. In his book, he gave a much more prosaic description of the regiment's route than Naylor's scant diary entry, and his account paints a clear picture of the sights and sounds of the KDG's route march on 16 June.

According to Mercer, 16 June was a scorching hot day. Enghien, as described by Naylor, was a park in which many gentlemen and ladies gathered in their finery to watch the Allied troops pass by. He found the countryside more 'bare and fore-boding' than what he had already experienced in the Low Countries. The KDG progressed south-east from Enghien and into the area of what is now Rebecq, and had crossed the River Senne over its old stone bridge. At this point, the regiment had headed south to Braine-le-Comte, some 5 miles away. According to Mercer, south of the Senne the countryside became prettier and was more wooded. The KDG arrived at Braine-le-Comte at 4 p.m., where they rested for an hour. This location was clearly an Allied resting area as, when there, Mercer had recorded he had seen 'several regiments drawn up in close columns, dismounted and feeding'. He went on to state that the town had pretty gardens and Mercer's party attracted groups of spectators, many of whom were priests.[10]

At 5 p.m., after their breather at Braine-le-Comte, during which the horses were fed and watered, the KDG had then pushed east to the hamlet of Long Tour. Here it, and the rest of the cavalry as reported by Mercer, had left the road 'for the adjoining fields' as the baggage train of some of the Allies, among them Hanoverians, had caused a traffic jam. At this point, the route climbed sharply and obliquely into a wooded ridge of hills, somewhere to the north of Houssière. Mercer recalled, 'the dull tramp of the horses, the rattling of sabres, and the voices of command, all magnified by the echo of the forest, which one might have fancied himself speaking under a vault.'[11]

It was around this point in their journey, described by Mercer as the Bois de la Houssière, that the order was given to the KDG and other cavalry regiments to lighten their horses' loads by untying their hay nets, as mentioned by Captain Taylor of the 10th Hussars, who had the same itinerary as the KDG:

> In passing through a deep wood beyond the town [Braine-le-Comte], we began to hear firing; on our issuing from the wood it became quite distinct, and soon we were enabled to see the line of smoke of the Action at Quatre Bras from the high banks of the road. An order arrived from Lord Uxbridge to throw away our hay and to trot at nine miles per hour, towards Nivelles, which we did accordingly.[12]

From the Bois de la Houssière on the plateau, it was just over 7 miles' march to Nivelles. On leaving this wood, the KDG must have been made aware for the first time that a battle was raging out to its south-east at Quatre Bras. Mercer was eloquent in his description of what he experienced at this point of his journey:

A most extensive view lay before us and now for the first time, as emerging from the woods, we became sensible of the dull, sullen sound that filled the air, somewhat resembling that of a distant water-mill, or still more distant thunder. On clearing the woods it became more distinct, and its character was no longer questionable – heavy firing of cannon and musketry, which could be distinguished from each other plainly.[13]

Mercer painted a picture of the town of Nivelles as a mass of towers and buildings, and highlighted a ruined castle, 'sweetly touched by the light of the setting sun, whilst the greater part lay in deep-toned purple obscurity'. He also pointed out that much of the din came from the townsfolk who were watching the Battle of Quatre Bras from the heights outside the town. Mercer contrasted the quiet serenity of the countryside through which they had just passed with the pandemonium and movement of Nivelles, which was punctuated with 'clattering peals of musketry' and the 'explosion after explosion' of the cannon. He believed 'the whole populace of Nivelle was on the streets' and described many as observing the spectacle from their houses or standing about 'like frightened sheep'.[14]

Barlow summarised the KDG's approach and arrival in Nivelles in far fewer words than Mercer in his letter home:

[W]hen within about 5 miles of that place we distinctly heard the Enemy's Cannonading, the Light Cavalry who were in our front threw away their forage and advanced to face the Enemy but did not get up time enough to prevent the Enemy Cavalry from pressing our Infantry very hard, but our brave fellows kept their ground till the Cavalry arrived when the Cowardly French ran away – on our approach to the field of battle we met a great many wounded Officers and men coming in.[15]

This event was also recorded by Naylor, who stated that the regiment, on its arrival at Nivelles, witnessed the wounded from Picton's division pouring into the town.

Having passed through Nivelles in an easterly direction towards the fighting at Quatre Bras, Fuller finally called the regiment to a halt some 2 miles east of the battlefield, as Naylor described in his diary:

It was almost dark (about 8 o'clock) when we arrived in the field and formed close column on the side of the road. By this time the firing had nearly ceased and after remaining about an hour we marched to our bivouac in front of Genappe, the horses remained saddled[,] the enemy being in a large wood two miles in our front.[16]

It must have taken about an hour to reach their bivouac location near Houtain-le-Val, as Barlow recorded in a letter that at 'about ten o'clock we Bivouacked in a field of corn'.[17] This field was located to the rear of the farm house at Quatre Bras. The soldiers were tasked to fetch water for the horses from this farm, and to feed them on some corn that they had found nearby.[18] It had been a long day, as TSM Page recounted in a letter home, 'We marched this day 40 English miles and slept in open corn-fields, our horses being saddled, ready to mount at a minute's notice, the French being in a wood close to us.'[19] The KDG then spent some time relaxing before sleeping by its horses. However, no food was forthcoming as rations had evidently not been brought along, as Barlow wrote, 'and although we had no food or clothes to cover us we slept soundly, til two o'clock, when we prepared to advance upon the enemy.'[20] This lack of food was corroborated by Page, when he complained in a letter home about his predicament on the eve of the battle on 18 June, 'What seemed worst of all during these three days, we could draw no rations, consequently we were without anything to eat or drink.'

The KDG was not the only cavalry regiment not to have managed to get its soldiers' rations ahead of the Battle of Waterloo. Fellow heavy cavalryman Sergeant William Clark of the Scots Greys wrote that in the evening of 16 June, 'With two of my comrades, walked back to the village in the hope of being able to purchase some liquor or bread, both of which we stood in need of as we had brought no rations from Denderhoutem.'[21] It appeared that the cavalry's baggage trains had not been able to get through to their front-line positions, as John Edgecombe Daniel, an officer in the Commissariat Department assigned to the 7th Hussars, explained, 'it was a cold and cloudy night, during which neither baggage nor supplies appeared, so the troops had to suffer terrible privations.'[22]

However, the Royals appear to have been better organised, as one of its captains, Alexander Clark Kennedy, wrote that the 1st Dragoons, 'were aroused in the morning of June 16th by the trumpets sounding to turn out about four o'clock. The troops were got together as quickly as possible and three days['] biscuits & c, having been issued to the men.'[23] The Royals, like the KDG, had been bivouacked in the fields to the west of Quatre Bras, and had also linked its horses in column, saddled and bridled ready for action.

The battles of Quatre Bras and Ligny were fought on 16 June. Whilst the KDG and British forces were bivouacked next to the battlefield of Quatre Bras, the Battle of Ligny had been fought just over 7 miles to the south-east. The former was a contest between Wellington's Allied army and the French under Marshal Ney. Although it ended in a stalemate, with almost equal casualties on both sides, the Allies had just managed to move sufficient reinforcements into the area of this strategic crossroads in time to have checked the French advance northwards towards Brussels. However, with the exception of some skirmishing after the battle by the 11th Light Dragoons in Sir John Vandeleur's 4th Brigade, the British cavalry arrived too late to fight at Quatre Bras. As a result, Kellerman's cuirassiers did much damage to the British 5th Brigade under Halkett. The 69th was caught in line not square and lost its king's colour. The cuirassiers were only prevented from taking the crossroads by accurate musketry and cannon fire. By the time that night fell, only the arrival of the British 1st (Guards) Division had managed to delay the French long enough to arrest their progress north and west.

The Battle of Ligny also took place in the afternoon of 16 June. Napoleon commanded the French forces which were successful in breaking the Prussians' strong defensive position on a ridge behind the Ligny stream. The Imperial Guard smashed the Prussian line and Marshal Blücher, who had his horse shot underneath him, had only just escaped. The French General d'Erlon was then supposed to have trapped and destroyed the broken Prussians, but had his orders countermanded by Ney, who wanted him at Quatre Bras. The net result was d'Erlon's corps spent the afternoon between the two battlefields and the Prussians escaped to the north to Wavre. This was within reach of Wellington's fall-back defensive position on the Mont St Jean plateau. This escape of the Prussian Army was crucial, as it stopped Napoleon from carrying out his intended strategy of dividing the two Allied armies sufficiently to be able to destroy one army at a time. However, Napoleon's defeat of the Prussians at Ligny did make the Allied position at Quatre Bras untenable, and Wellington had to move his men north on 17 June towards the plateau of Mont St Jean, to the south of Waterloo.

★★★

Having had an uneventful night, the KDGs were woken at 2 a.m. on 17 June in preparation to advance on the enemy. An hour before dawn, a British cavalry patrol had come into contact with a French picket at a farm near Piraumont, as Page recounted, 'On the morning of the 17th at daybreak firing again commenced, so far it is what we call skirmishing.'[24] Naylor stated that the regiment was, 'At day light ready to mount.' Mercer was located in the proximity of the KDG and described what they would have seen at this point to their front, looking east, 'the corn trampled down, particularly in the plain, plentifully besprinkled with the bodies of the slain. Just in front of the farm of Quatre Bras there was a fearful scene of slaughter – Highlanders and cuirassiers lying thickly strewn about.' Naylor continued his diary entry for the day, writing that they were, 'At 8 o'clock ordered to water our horses a small distance in our rear.'[25]

Later that morning, Wellington, on learning that Blücher and his men had escaped from Ligny north to Wavre, told Blücher's chief of staff, General Count von Gneisenau's envoy, that he intended to take up a defensive position south of Waterloo. But he made it clear that he would only do this if the Prussians were prepared to support him with at least one army corps. He stressed that if a force of this size could not be pledged by the Prussians, then he would have to withdraw his army to the north of Brussels and that city would be lost to Napoleon. At 10 a.m.,

Wellington issued orders to his generals, the gist being that the Allied troops were to retire from their respective locations to the Mont St Jean ridge to the south of Waterloo.[26] The line infantry regiments and Foot Guards at Quatre Bras moved north along the main Brussels–Charleroi road, covered by a light infantry screen. The last of the infantry left the area of Quatre Bras around 11.30 a.m.[27]

According to Naylor, the cavalry were ordered at noon, 'to take position in a large plain adjoining the position of the enemy. Sometime previous to this our Baggage and Infantry had commenced a retreat, at 5 we began to retreat and cover the movement of our infantry.' Presumably this 'large plain' was the flat land to the north of the Quatre Bras crossroads described by Mercer as, 'To the left [north] the ground descended gradually for two miles where it appeared bounded by a long wood extending to Brussels. In front it descended to a plain a mile in breadth.'[28] The cavalry taking a position on the 'large plain' was part of the British plan to mask the retreat of the Anglo-Allied infantry on the west of the Namur road, with all the cavalry drawn up in two lines touching the road. The KDG and the rest of the heavy cavalry formed the second line.[29] Naylor had either lost track of time or there was a transcription error in his diary, as the cavalry retreat began far earlier than at 5 p.m. as he stated. Other eyewitnesses recorded the cavalry withdrawal had commenced at 2 p.m. and at 2.30 p.m.[30]

Ney had been holding his forces back south of Quatre Bras on the morning of 17 June as he did not want to drive Wellington north to the proximity of his ally Blücher. However, at noon, on discovering the Anglo-Allied infantry were retreating towards Brussels, Napoleon issued an order to Ney to engage and destroy them with best speed. When the leading elements of the French cavalry were around 2 miles to the south of Quatre Bras, at Little Marbais, they were spotted by Wellington and Uxbridge through their telescopes.[31] It was at this point, between 1.30 p.m. and 2 p.m., that Uxbridge, with Wellington's permission, gave the order for the cavalry to retire, as described by Barlow in one of his letters, 'An order was given to retreat when the Infantry and Artillery retired covered by our Heavy Brigades of Cavalry; then came behind us the Hussars and Light Cavalry.'[32]

Uxbridge organised his cavalry in three columns; a main one with one flank column on either side. He placed the Household Brigade, with the KDG in it, and the Union Brigade in the centre column, and ordered them to follow the retreat of the infantry on the main Brussels–Charleroi road. The heavy brigades then moved north to the high ground behind the village of Genappe and took up position on either side of the main road. They were held there by Uxbridge to cover the retreat of the Anglo-Allied light cavalry, who were retiring north with the French vanguard hot on their heels. Uxbridge initially placed the Household Brigade on the right and the Union Brigade on the left of the main road. However, he changed his mind and ordered Somerset's men to form column of half squadrons on the left of the main road to Brussels. The KDG, with the rest of its brigade, stayed in this position for around twenty minutes before Uxbridge ordered the 7th Hussars to charge the leading French elements, a body of lancers.[33]

After much toing and froing between the British light cavalry and the French lancers, Uxbridge withdrew the 7th Hussars and in their stead launched the 1st Life Guards. The 7th Hussars had made no impression, given the strong position of the French lancers in being protected on both their flanks by the houses of the village. It could be argued that they probably should not have been sent in to do this job in the first place. The Household troops' charge came later, when there was more chance of defeating their enemy's cavalry. It was a great success, as they smashed the French lancers and drove the remnants back into Genappe. Barlow described this action:

[O]n our retreat one of the most dreadful storms of rain, thunder, and lightening came on that I have ever witnessed which continued without abatement for about an hour, the rain literally came down in torrents and we were completely drenched; immediately after the French Cavalry charged our Light Cavalry and had it not been for a most Gallant Charge made by the 1st Life Guards they would have suffered severely[. T]he Blues and our regiment then formed in open columns of divisions on the road to charge, but did not[. T]he Brigade then formed in line ready to receive the enemy who came up with Artillery and fired at us as we were formed but did not do us any injury[.] The Blues lost a few men during the retreat.'

Page also recorded in a letter how the initial June sunshine had given way to an extremely powerful electric storm which had made life very uncomfortable for the KDG and the other soldiers that day:

As the French advanced there was one of the heaviest storms of rain ever known, accompanied by thunder and lightning. The fall of rain was so heavy that in the fields that were covered in corn, our horses sunk in every step up to near the hock. It is out of my power herein to express our situation – our boots were filled with water, and as our arms hung down by our sides the water ran off a stream at the ends of our fingers.[34]

Naylor also commented on the rain in his diary and explained that the KDG was lined up to fight at Genappe, but because of the success of the 1st Life Guards ended up not charging the enemy:

We continued to retire and form on either side of the road, as we passed through Genappe we experienced the most severe fall of rain I ever beheld. A short distance from Genappe the 1st Life Guards charged a body of Lancers who were pressing our rear. They charged in column of divisions on the road and we formed for the same purpose, but the enemy retiring we did not charge.

The only KDGs who appear to have gotten involved in the fighting on 17 June was the left-hand squadron[35] under Captain Sweny, which had been ordered to skirmish with the enemy dragoons who were pursuing the British cavalry.[36] However, Sweny evidently got his bearings wrong and had to be saved by Barlow, as the latter explained:

> Capt Sweny was ordered out with a division to skirmish with the enemy but owing to the misconception of his orders took his division into a place where they were likely to be taken prisoner. I was despatched to fetch them away and although much exposed to the Enemy's balls brought every man away safe.[37]

Sweny's TSM, Page, described his part in this event:

> [I] took a horse on 17th June with a Frenchman's complete kit of arms, saddle bags, ect on him. The horse had one of his ears nearly cut off. I gave him to a farrier to take care of for me while I was skirmishing with French Dragoons, but he lost him altogether.

After the British cavalry's encounter with the French in Genappe, the rest of their 6-mile retreat to the Mont St Jean ridge was uneventful. *The Digest* described the last events of the retreat to Mont St Jean:

> The Heavy Brigade retreated to the village of Mont St. Jean. The Household Brigade formed columns by regiment on their prospective bivouacs, on the grand route from Genappe to Brussels on the right, and a cross road from Waterloo to Nivelles, in the rear of the Brigade, one mile in advance of Waterloo.[38]

Naylor wrote, 'We continued our retreat until we took position in front of Waterloo for the night, where we bivouacked during an incessant rain and without any refreshment or forage.' The KDG went in and set up its regimental bivouac in the Household Brigade concentration area, which was some 300 yards north-west of the Elm Tree Crossroads. With the arrival of the KDG in its bivouac area just south of the Mont St Jean farm, we have now returned to where we left them poised to charge at the end of chapter two. All the soldiers knew was that they had to charge the enemy cavalry to their front. But who were these French horsemen and what were their backgrounds? The KDG, along with the other regiments in the Household Brigade, were blind-sided to their enemy, being on the reverse slope of the plateau. Yet, unlike its sister regiments in the brigade, the KDGs had never fought the French as a regiment before. So they would have been largely ignorant of their adversaries, even if they could see them. Thus only the handful of officers and men with combat experience would have appreciated the ominous significance of those 'crests of the cuirassiers', which Elton described as his last sight before urging his horse on in the first KDG charge at Waterloo.

WATERLOO I: MOUNTED OPPONENTS

It was clear that the regiment initially faced cuirassiers in its first charge. Nearly all those KDGs who recorded the events of Waterloo from differing troops mention this fact. William Elton of 1st Troop mentioned having fought 'cuirassiers of the Imperial Guard'.[1] Hasker in 3rd Troop reported, 'About two o'clock we were obliged to mount and ascend the acclivity, sword in hand. There we found French cuirassiers cutting down our infantry.'[2] Naylor of 6th Troop recorded that, 'An attack was made through a line of enemy supported by a line of cuirassiers and a reserve of lancers.'[3] John Derry in 8th Troop talked of fighting a brigade of cuirassiers.[4] And Hibbert, who was not present at the battle, described the regiment had 'cut to pieces a large body of cuirassiers'.[5]

The cuirassiers were the most numerous of the elite French cavalry units. In the Napoleonic era, they only ranked after the Imperial Guard and the two regiments of carabineers which paraded on the right of the line. They comprised some of the tallest men in the French cavalry, with a minimum height of 5ft 9in, and only rode large horses of over 15 hands. They were experienced soldiers, who were required to have served for a minimum of twelve years before they were considered for cuirassier selection. Nicknamed 'Napoleon's *Gros Frères*', they were his armoured enforcers, of whom he boasted 'are of greater value than any other type of cavalry'. And as such he paid them five centimes a day more than their peers in the other types of cavalry regiment. They were the Emperor's baby, which he created out of the old French *régiments de cavalerie*, and numbered one to twelve.

In 1802, Napoleon instructed the 1st Cuirassiers to be the first of these regiments to be equipped with the Mk I cuirass. Under the cuirass, these soldiers wore a single-breasted, very short-skirted habit. They wore overalls of linen or hide and on their heads wore the distinctive cuirassier helmet with a horsehair mane. They were issued with the IX or XIII model pistols and were provided with the mark XI model musketoon. However, many cuirassier regiments disdained the use of these weapons and relied only on their An XIII or An XI-pattern sabre with a 38in twin-guttered blade, which was housed in an iron scabbard.

The two regiments of cuirassiers which initially faced the Household Brigade around La Haye Sainte were from général de division Comte Edouard Milhaud's IV Reserve Cavalry Corps. With the exception of two companies of horse artillery, Milhaud's corps was a cuirassier-only unit and comprised two divisions, the 13th, under Pierre Watier, and the 14th, under Jacques Delort. Each division contained two brigades. Watier's first brigade was commanded by Jacques-Charles Dubois and his second by Étienne Travers. The KDG's initial opponents were from Dubois's brigade, which comprised the 1st Cuirassiers, under Colonel Ordener, and the 4th Cuirassiers, under Colonel Habert. The KDGs in the left-hand squadrons that charged in the most easterly direction, along with the Union Brigade, were also to face the men from the 2nd Brigade, under Travers. This brigade consisted of Colonel Richardot's 7th Cuirassiers and Colonel Thurot's 12th Cuirassiers.

Delort's 1st Brigade, under the command of Pierre Farine, consisted of the 5th and 10th Cuirassiers, the former commanded by Colonel Baron Gobert and the latter by Colonel Baron Lahuberdière. The 2nd Brigade was commanded by Jacques Vial and consisted of the 6th and 9th Cuirassiers, under colonels Martin and Bigarne respectively. Some of the KDGs in the right-hand squadrons that charged west of La Haye Sainte were to fight Delort's men later in the afternoon in the fields below La Belle Alliance.

The KDG's initial opponents in the first charge and its principal adversaries during the battle were the 1st and 4th Cuirassiers. The commanding officer of the former, Michel Ordener, was a hero of the Empire and still only 28 years old. His 1st Regiment was *la crème de la crème* of the cuirassiers,[6] seasoned veterans and victors of many Napoleonic battles in the ten years leading up to Waterloo. They had won battle honours at Austerlitz (1805), Eylau (1807) and Moscow (1812). Amongst the many actions they had seen, notably they had fought at Jena (1806), Wagram (1809) and Leipzig (1813). On 18 June 1815, they numbered 452 officers and men.

Riding on the left wing of the 1st Cuirassiers to the west of La Haye Sainte were the 4th Cuirassiers,[7] its sister regiment in Dubois's 1st Cavalry Brigade. They were smaller than the 1st Cuirassiers, numbering 359 officers and men in three squadrons, under the command of Colonel Baron Habert. These cuirassiers wore the same uniforms as Ordener's men, but the two regiments' facings were different. The 4th Cuirassiers wore *aurore* or orange, whilst the facings of the 1st Cuirassiers were red. Like Ordener's men, they too were battle-hardened, having participated in the fighting in Italy (1805), Germany (1806–7), Austria including Wagram (1809), Russia (1812) and Germany including Leipzig (1813). More recently, they had just defeated a unit of Prussian cavalry at Ligny.

Some historians have alleged there were French cavalry units other than Dubois's brigade involved in this first assault on La Haye Sainte. Houssaye mentioned Travers's Brigade and Siborne said they were cuirassiers from Kellerman's III Cavalry Corps. Barbero, based on comments by eyewitness Octave Levavasseur, one of Marshal Ney's ADCs, suggested the French cavalry which first invested La Haye Sainte was an ad hoc force, which was led by one of Ney's ADCs, the Belgian Colonel Crabbé. Levavasseur explained that Ney had called an orders group of his cavalry colonels and instructed each to second a squadron to this composite unit, which was to 'follow by the left [west of La Haye Sainte] and sweep up all that you find between the enemy artillery and his infantry when passing through the ground occupied by the enemy behind La Haye Sainte'.[8]

However, it seemed unlikely to have been Travers's Brigade, as it was almost certainly involved in the counter-attack against the British heavy cavalry's first charge and so could not have been in two places at once. Kellerman's cuirassiers also seemed to have been an improbable choice of unit for this job, given how far they were initially located from this action, and their corps was not tasked to support d'Erlon's assault, as Milhaud's had been. As for Crabbé's force, it must have been considerably smaller than the thirty-odd squadron force alluded to, on the basis that there was a squadron from each regiment allocated to it. This was because there simply was not enough real estate around La Haye Sainte on which to field them.

Most historians seem to have gone with Dubois's men as having been involved in the first mounted assaults on La Haye Sainte, as testified by a rare primary source, eyewitness Michel Ordener. Yet Levavasseur was also an eyewitness, so his account should not be ignored. What seems most likely was that both Crabbé's unit and Dubois's men were involved. Crofton suggested there were eleven cuirassier squadrons involved in the initial moves against La Haye Sainte, and given that the 1st and 4th Cuirassiers comprised seven squadrons, the remaining four squadrons could well have been Crabbé's contribution to this assault.[9] Levavasseur only credited Crabbé's force with having achieved an uncontested charge to take the enemy's guns and in the chasing off of the Allied infantry pickets in their way, without a shot being fired. As he made no mention of Crabbé's men having engaged the Lüneburg Light Battalion, his evidence would not conflict with Ordener's claim that his 1st Cuirassiers had done that job. Also, Levavasseur did not mention fighting with Allied mounted troops. He stated that on looking behind themselves, Crabbé's force saw that they were being pursued by enemy cavalry. This was the KDG and the rest of the Household Brigade in hot pursuit of the 1st and 4th Cuirassiers.

After this initial clash, the KDG had to face other cuirassier regiments which were sent from Milhaud's IV Cavalry Corps in the French counter-charge. There have been conflicting eyewitness reports as to which cuirassier regiments were sent against the Household Brigade in the west and which counter-charged against the Union Brigade further to the east. Those British dragoons in action on the eastern edge of this ridge would have been fighting amongst the sixteen French guns that had been moved forward to that position.[10] Milhaud praised Delort's division for the recapture of these guns, where predominantly the Union Brigade, and in particular the Greys, were fighting.[11] Yet Delort himself implied that his men were involved over to the west, against the Household Brigade, in a letter in which he congratulated his subordinate, who commanded the 1st Brigade in his division. In this letter he stated that Farine:

> [D]istinguished himself in the charge made the same day against the cavalry brigade of the British royal Guard, commanded by Lord Somerset and where the same cavalry was put in disarray by two brigades of the Division, ie by the 5th, 10th, 6th and 9th Cuirassiers.[12]

In another publication, Delort credited Farine for having led the 6th and 9th Cuirassiers in their destruction of both the Household and Union brigades. However, Delort was confused, as it was Vial's 2nd Brigade which contained the 6th and 9th Cuirassiers and Farine's 1st Brigade comprised the 5th and 10th Cuirassiers.[13] As a result of this mistake by Delort, many historians have also got Farine's and Vial's regiments muddled up.[14] Delort's eyewitness statement as to the brigade commander who was responsible for the repulse of the Household Brigade was repeated by the French nineteenth-century historian Houssaye, who also stated that it was Farine's cuirassiers who had counter-attacked the British 'horseguards'.[15] So Delort's division was praised for actions in the Union Brigade's area by Milhaud, and yet Delort had praised his men for having stopped the Household Brigade. It therefore seemed that the cuirassiers of Delort's 14th Cavalry Division were involved in the fighting with both the British heavy brigades.

Eyewitness Michel Ordener also referred to only the 7th and 12th Cuirassiers as having taken out the Union Brigade. He was quoted by his biographer as having stated that these regiments, 'threw themselves onto Ponsonby's dragoons and whilst laughing swept them away and destroyed them'.[16] This is backed up by many of the regimental histories of the cuirassier regiments in Milhaud's corps.[17] Maybe Ordener was being partisan in solely recognising the efforts of the sister brigade in his division in this conflict. However, another Waterloo veteran, Hippolyte de Mauduit, also recorded the sole participation of the 7th and 12th Cuirassiers of Travers's Brigade in this action against the Union Brigade. This was shown in a map of the battlefield in his book on Waterloo in which he portrayed, by the use of dots, the route to this conflict taken by only Travers's men.[18] Although Mauduit was unlikely to have seen this event, as he was located way to the south of La Belle Alliance with his Imperial Guard regiment, he did base his history on eyewitness accounts.

On the basis of this evidence, it appeared that Travers's Brigade had certainly fought on the eastern end of the French forward gun line on the intermediate ridge north of La Belle Alliance ridge. Their presence there also made sense, as they would have been the first of the cuirassier regiments available to be have been used in the French counter-stroke. As the other front-line brigade, that of Dubois, was in the process of being chased back to the French lines after its tussle with the Household Brigade, Travers's men were the only remaining unit in the front line of Milhaud's division. However, it must be noted, there were conflicting accounts of the initial placement and movement of Milhaud's cuirassiers.[19] Yet it seemed unlikely that just Travers's men took on the Union Brigade. This was suggested in another, and earlier map than that of Mauduit, made a year after the battle by a Belgium-based surveyor, Willem Benjamin Craan. He, like Mauduit, based his map on eyewitness accounts and indicated both of Milhaud's divisions as having taken part in this fighting against the Union Brigade.[20]

There was also the possibility that the remnants of Dubois's brigade had managed to rally in time to reinforce Travers's men in repulsing the British heavy cavalry. Ordener was recorded in his biography to have stated that, subsequent to his initial foray on to the Mont St Jean plateau, Milhaud had given him command of a brigade which comprised his regiment and the 7th Cuirassiers.[21] Later in this book, a Sergeant Roy, formerly of the 7th Cuirassiers, was quoted as having written that, 'At Waterloo I have seen and I can certify that it was Colonel Ordener who, using a clever manoeuvre, made a circle of steel around the English cavalry which was nearly completely destroyed.'[22] This action could have referred to the event Barlow described when 'a body of the French Cavalry and Lancers surrounded us'.[23]

However, it is unlikely Ordener and his men had a hand in the destruction of the right-hand squadron of the KDG, that Elton described as having been drawn on and surrounded by a 'very superior numbers of cuirassiers & lancers'.[24] One Waterloo expert believed that Ordener did not assume command of the 7th Cuirassiers until after 4 p.m., which, if it was the case, would have ruled out this scenario.[25] Also, it seemed highly unlikely Ordener and his men could have had the time to participate in such an intricate counter-attack, having just been chased back to the area of La Belle Alliance by the British heavy brigades. Although there were no large-scale cavalry actions after the heavies' first charge, there were some of around brigade-size strength during the French grand cavalry charges between 4–6 p.m. So it seemed more probable that Ordener carried out his 'circle of steel' later in the afternoon than during the French counter-attack to the first charge by the British heavy cavalry.

The conflicting eyewitness accounts have meant that it has not been possible to be categorical as to which cuirassiers fought which regiments of British heavy cavalry in the French counter-attack after the heavies' first charge. The truth seems that the British heavy cavalry and the cuirassiers all became jumbled up around Lobau's infantry squares on the intermediate ridge south-east of La Haye Sainte and north-east of La Belle Alliance. However, it is unequivocal that the Household and Union brigades in total faced all the cuirassiers of Delort's division and those of Travers's brigade. This would have comprised a total of seventeen squadrons of over 2,000 French sabres. On the basis of eyewitness reports, it would have appeared that the bulk of these cuirassier regiments in Milhaud's corps were located at the western end of the intermediate ridge, in the area of the Household Brigade. Whilst the KDG observers described masses of cuirassiers, there were very few mentions of sightings of French heavy cavalry amongst eyewitness accounts from the Union Brigade. In the latter brigade, most reports of French cavalry were just of lancers on their withdrawal north to the British line.

As has been seen, the KDG did not just face cuirassiers, but lancers as well. The lance wounds suffered by many of the regiment's officers and men were testament enough to their other mounted opponents. Naylor was not the only KDG to mention lancers. Derry mentioned that Major Graham had been 'pierced by a French lancer'.[26] Elton mentioned that many in the regiment had been, 'surrounded by vastly superior numbers of lancers and cuirassiers' and that his friend had, 'killed four of the enemy's lancers, who seem to have attacked him [from] behind'.[27] Hibbert mentioned that when the regiment rode back from the enemy positions, 'they were met by an immense body of lancers'.[28] The large amounts of lancers would seem to rule out one recent historian's theory that they could have been from just one squadron of lancers that was seconded to Crabbé's force.

But who were these lancers? By the time of Waterloo, the French Army contained seven regiments of lancers, all of which were present at the battle. These were Le Régiment de Chevau-Legers de la Garde Imperiale (the Blue and Red Lancers) and the line lancer regiments numbered from one to six. When historians have referred to the use of French lancers at this stage of the battle, when Napoleon sent in his counter-stroke to the charge of the British heavy brigades, they have mostly referred to Colonel Bro's 4th Lancers in Baron Charles-Claude Jacquinot's 1st Cavalry Division. Many have mentioned the other regiment in the same brigade commanded by Gobrecht, namely Colonel Martigue's 3rd Lancers, as also having been involved in this cavalry action. Bro's regiment only comprised two squadrons, so it is likely that the three squadrons of the 3rd Lancers were also used in this French counter-stroke. This 2nd Lancer Brigade was positioned at the extreme east of the battlefield on the French right flank and was used with devastating effect on the Greys, whom they attacked on their return to the Allied lines after their assault on the French gun batteries to the north-east of La Belle Alliance.

However, recent historians have questioned this view, having argued that it would have been very difficult for the 4th Lancers to have engaged the Greys on the eastern wing of the Union Brigade and then to have had the time to move across the battlefield to cause havoc with the KDG and others in the Household Brigade on their return from the French lines. One of these historians who took this view also believed these lancers were probably from the Red Lancers of the Guard Cavalry.[29] A few French contemporary histories mentioned the Red Lancers' involvement at this juncture. It seemed the earliest mention of their involvement in this action was by Le Maréchal de Camp Berton in his 1818 book on Waterloo. He has some authority as, although he was not present at Waterloo, he had been nearby at Wavre, where he was a brigade commander in the 10th Cavalry Division.[30] Subsequent to this assertion that the Red Lancers were involved in attacking the heavy brigades, there have been several other historians who have used similar language to Berton's to describe this event; this would suggest that he was their sole source of this information on this issue.[31]

However, there were two British eyewitnesses who described having seen the Red Lancers in the area where the British heavy brigades were fighting at Waterloo. Lieutenant Archibald Hamilton of the Greys recorded, 'In the hopes of stopping them we followed and passed between the columns of the French infantry, when their red lancers closed behind us. One of the red lancers put his lance towards my horse's head.'[32] The presence of these lancers operating in the area of the KDG's operations is also borne out by Lieutenant Waymouth of the 2nd Life Guards, who wrote, 'As I was taken prisoner in this charge [the Household Brigade's first charge], I am unable to add anything more of my own knowledge, except the position in which I saw some Cuirassiers and the Red Lancers.'[33] Waymouth marked a line on a map that indicated where the Red Lancers were posted behind a cuirassier formation just to the north-east of the crossroads at La Belle Alliance. Although Waymouth wrote that he could not remember precisely where these two units were, his indication corresponded almost exactly to where they were shown to be located on Craan's map.[34] This showed the route these lancers took to the front line from around the area of Plancenoit, as well as the location of Delort's cuirassier brigade.

So those KDG who reached the French ridge around the area marked by Waymouth could well have experienced the Red Lancers. We know many of the KDG charged with the 2nd Life Guards, as Waymouth went on to write in his next letter that on more than one occasion, 'finding myself near Major Naylor, of the King's, may have also passed to the left [east of La Haye Sainte]'.[35] Most French historians mentioned that it was Ponsonby's brigade that the Red Lancers engaged. However, by the time the KDG and 2nd Life Guards hit the French gun batteries and positions, they were already mixed up with the Royals and Inniskillings, with whom they had merged in their charge south.

However, other contemporary historians are dubious of the Red Lancers' involvement with the Household Brigade at this stage of the battle. Andrew Field, who has written on Waterloo from the French perspective, believed that it was unlikely, 'a Guard regiment would have been taken from the third line for such a task. They would have to have passed through both Kellerman's 3rd Cav Corps and Reille's infantry.' He quite reasonably wondered why if they were involved in such a conflict it was not mentioned by Antoine Fortuné de Brack.[36] De Brack's account of his experiences at Waterloo were described in a letter to General Pelet written in 1835. It appeared to be the best and most in-depth eyewitness account of the actions of the Red Lancers of the Guard to have been found to date. In this letter, he referred to his regiment's first actions on 18 June 1815 as during the massed French cavalry attacks. His comments on the counter-attack against Ponsonby's men made no mention of the Red Lancers, but were limited to these words, 'Under the sabres of our cuirassiers and the thrusts of our 4th Lancers of the Line, commanded by Colonel Bro they strewed the ground with their dead.'[37]

Yet it was difficult to reconcile the lack of claims by Red Lancers as to their success against the British heavy cavalry at this stage of the battle with Allied eye-witness reports of having sighted them. A possible explanation was that, whilst they did not proactively engage in fighting the British heavy cavalry at this juncture, they did provide a barrier of lances to block the British attempts to pierce the French positions at the west end of the forward gun line. This theory was under-pinned by Red Lancer de Brack's recollections:

> At Waterloo, our four regiments of the guard were on the same line. The English charged that line. We crossed our spears with the other lancers [so as to form a defensive phalanx against the British cavalry]. In the process of carrying out this manoeuvre the enemy showed up suddenly in front of us, and as they had to avoid [the phalanx of lances], they were consequently pushed on to our regiments with short arms [cuirassiers].[38]

Other than the 3rd and 4th Lancers in the 1st Cavalry Division, there were four regiments of French lancers at Waterloo. On the extreme west of the French line were the 5th and 6th Lancers of Piré's 2nd Cavalry Division, who were located to the west of the Nivelles road, just to the south-west of Hougoumont. It is highly improbable that they would have been moved from their task of protecting the French west flank and unlikely they could have travelled that far east to have engaged the KDG and then returned to that position, from where they attacked the square of the 51st Regiment around 4 p.m.[39] There are certainly no reports of them fighting British heavy cavalry at this juncture.

The two remaining regiments of French lancers on the field that day were the 1st and 2nd of Subervie's 5th Cavalry Division. Levavasseur in his autobiography mentioned his party of cavalry, under Crabbé, as having been rescued by, 'General Colbert, the commander of the cavalry, whom having recognised us brought the squadrons which were not involved in the struggle [with the British cavalry]'.[40] This Colbert could have been either Louis-Pierre-Alphonse in charge of Subervie's 1st Brigade of Lancers or confusingly it could have been his brother Pierre-David, who commanded the Red Lancers. Napoleon had ordered Lobau, to whom Subervie was most probably attached, to move east in case the Prussians fell on his right flank; and that is what Lobau did by around 4–4.15 p.m. Thus Subervie's lancers could have participated in the French cavalry counter-attack at around 2.45 p.m. Naylor mentioned seeing French lancers in the enclosed fields around Plancenoit, and that would correspond roughly to the area where Subervie's men were located.

However, there were few accounts which recorded the participation of Subervie's lancers in the French cavalry's counter-attack. The history of the 12th Cuirassiers mentioned, 'The Emperor galloped up to and ordered General Milhaud to charge this cavalry, already stopped by Subervic's [sic] and Jacquinot's divisions.' French historian Edgar Quintet also stated that Subervie mentioned to him that he had been in the vicinity of the French counter-attack, and so could have taken part with his men. Yet Quintet did not go so far as to quote the French lancer commander as having said that he had actually participated in this action.[41] A third mention of Subervie was made by Mauduit, who wrote, 'But already the Subervic [sic] and Jacquinot's divisions made a skillful and audacious manoeuvre and cut off their line of retreat and scattered the English dragoons all over the battlefield.'[42]

Given Elton stated that the right-hand squadron of KDG had been surrounded by 'very superior numbers of cuirassiers & lancers', and that Bringhurst of that squadron had been killed by lancers,[43] it seemed, on balance, that Subervie's men were very probably involved with the KDG. This is because it appeared unlikely that Jacquinot's men could have covered just under the 2 miles in that congested and cluttered battlefield of Waterloo from their initial positions south of Papelotte to the west of the Brussels–Charleroi road in time or at all to engage the KDG. Also, Subervie's lancers' initial positions, just to the east of the chausée at La Belle Alliance, corresponded pretty much exactly to where the KDGs and other British heavy cavalry from the west flank broke the French line in pursuit of Dubois's men in the first charge. Yet this is all conjecture, as none of these reports of Subervie's involvement with the heavy brigades were from primary sources and no eyewitness accounts have yet been discovered to have proved their involvement with the British heavy cavalry at this juncture of the battle.

It may never be known which French lancers, if any, also attacked the KDG along with the French 3rd and 4th Lancers. Yet, on the balance of available evidence, it would appear the Red Lancers were in the area of the French counter-attack on the Household and Union brigades, as reflected in Waymouth's observations and according to their movements shown on Craan's map. Their static presence in that location, possibly presenting a phalanx of lances as a defensive bloc, would also tally with Naylor's comments in his diary of having made a charge, 'through a line of the enemy supported by a line of Cuirassiers and a reserve of Lancers'. On the other hand, given their reported location, it was more likely to have been Subervie's men whom Naylor saw when he had charged too far to the south-east into the area of the 'enclosure, a large field in which there were Lancers'. This area was described in a footnote as being 'in the direction of Planchenoit'.[44] So neither is there enough evidence to be emphatic as to whether there were French lancers from units other than the 3rd and 4th regiments involved in the counter-attack on the British heavy brigades; nor can one argue that the Red Lancers and Subervie's men were not involved in this action in any way.

From the eyewitness evidence, one can only be sure that the French 3rd and 4th Lancers were involved with the British heavy cavalry. This assertion was under-pinned by comments made by the Red Lancer de Brack in a letter to a French journal in 1818, in which he defended the record of the French lancers.[45] In the section on Waterloo, he praised Bro and his 4th Lancers for meting out retribution to the English Horse Guards for taking an Eagle, killing fifty English cavalry who were trying to escape, and for leaving 300 English corpses on the battlefield.

So what did the 3rd and 4th Lancers look like? As French lancers were merely re-roled dragoons, their uniforms were very similar. All that appeared to have distinguished the two types of French cavalry, apart from the front ranks carrying lances, was the slight differences in their helmets.[46] The lancer helmet was essen-tially a reworked dragoon helmet. In addition to the basic helmet, it had a rear peak as a neck guard and its crest was different in that it contained a neo-Grecian horsehair crest somewhat similar to that worn by the British Household Cavalry regiments at Waterloo. Whereas the French dragoons, along with the British dra-goon and dragoon guards regiments like the KDG, wore a floating horse-hair mane from their helmets.

Otherwise, the French lancers' uniforms were pretty much identical to those of the dragoons. The 3rd and 4th Lancers, whom the KDG faced at Waterloo, wore a green habit-veste that had pointed cuffs as opposed to the straight and buttoned cuff-flaps of the dragoons. These tunics had white linings and had, like the cuiras-sier regiments, different-coloured lapels, cuffs, collars and turnbacks by which the regiments could be identified. In the cases of the 3rd and 4th Lancers, their regimental colours were respectively pink and crimson. On the front of their tunics they had thirty-two yellow metal buttons and the facings did not have piping. On the flaps of their tunics they had an arrowhead badge, which was common to the first four regiments of lancers of the line. Below their tunic, the lancers wore a white waistcoat and for trousers they wore middle-green breeches; as opposed to the dragoons, whose breeches were off-white. These breeches were reinforced with black leather and had a double line of lace in their regimental colour which ran down the side of the leg.[47]

The 3rd Lancers, prior to having been made lancers in 1811, was the 8th Regiment of Dragoons. This regiment was raised in 1674. Between 1805 and 1808, it had fought at: Austerlitz, Jena, Eylau and Friedland. From 1808 to 1812, it had fought in the Peninsular War. In the years before Waterloo, it had been fighting in Russia and in the German states. At Waterloo, it comprised three squadrons of 406 men, under the command of Colonel Charles-Francois Martigue, a seasoned officer with twenty-nine years' service under his belt at the time.

The 4th Lancers was, prior to its 1811 conversion to lancers, the 9th Regiment of Dragoons and was established in 1673. Initially called 'Lorriane', the regiment was named the 9th Dragoons in 1791. Its military track record was much the same as its sister regiment, the 3rd Lancers, having fought at Jena, Eylau, Friedland, in Spain, at the great Battle of Borodino in 1812, and at Leipzig and Hanau. Adkin stated that the 4th Lancers was a two-squadron regiment of 296 men,[48] which is at odds with de Brack's letter in which he stated, 'Bro charged at the head of his three squadrons.'

The last unit of mounted opponents that the British heavies faced during and after their first charge was another regiment from Général de Division Baron Charles-Claude Jaquinot's 1st Cavalry Division, to which the 3rd and 4th Lancers belonged. It was the 365 officers and men of the 3rd Chasseurs à Cheval, under Marquis de la Woestine, which was brigaded with the 7th Hussars. The latter was posted off to the flank during this part of the battle and did not engage the British heavies at that time. The 3rd Regiment of Chasseurs à Cheval had been founded as a regiment of dragoons in 1675 and had become the 3rd Regiment of Chasseurs in 1791. Amongst other battles, it had fought in Italy in 1805, at Vilsbiburg, Essling and Wagram in 1809, and in 1812–13 at Krasnoe, Borodino, Dresden and Leipzig. The chasseurs were a light horse formation and one of the most versatile forms of French cavalry. They were similar to and often brigaded with hussars, and could also work in the dismounted role. Their key job was in reconnaissance and small-scale skirmishing work. They wore a black shako and a green uniform consisting of a coat, side-buttoned overalls and short boots. They were armed with either an An XI-pattern light cavalry sabre, a carbine and bayonet. However, during the French counter-stroke they appear to have operated to the east of the Union Brigade area, and probably not many came into contact with the KDG over to the west. There were certainly no KDG eyewitness descriptions of having engaged Chasseurs à Cheval during or after the first charge.

Yet the KDG was not to face the lancers until later in the battle, as its first opponents were the elite 1st and 4th Cuirassiers. Fate had put the opposing nations' first numbered heavy cavalry regiments on a collision course. Coincidentally, the French 1st Regiment of Cuirassiers was directly on the axis of charge of the English 1st Regiment of Dragoon Guards or KDG. The contrast in battle experience of the two regiments was stark. Whilst the 1st Cuirassiers had been on active service almost continually for the previous decade, the KDG were rookies as none of its men had seen any action with the regiment during their years of soldiering. The last battle in which the KDG had fought as a regiment was at Beaumont in 1794, beyond the memories of most of the KDG who served at Waterloo. Yet these two regiments would not be strangers when they were to meet, as they had crossed swords on three previous occasions at the battles of Oudenarde (1708), Malplaquet (1709) and Fontenoy (1745). Would the 1st Cuirassiers, with two losses and one win and with all its recent battle-hardened years of experience, level the scores with its greenhorn British opponents from the KDG?

Watercolour painting of an officer of the 2nd or Queen's Regiment of Horse 1687. (1st The Queen's Dragoon Guards Heritage Trust [QDGHT]. Most of the items portrayed which belong to this trust are on display at Firing Line, Cardiff Castle Museum of the Welsh Soldier)

The Queen's Horse capturing the French kettle-drums at Ramillies in 1706. Photograph by Raven Cozens-Hardy of an oil on canvas painting by Robert Alexander Hillingford. (Officers' Mess 1st The Queen's Dragoon Gaurds [OMQDG])

The King's Dragoon Guards and Queen's Bays at the Battle of Warburg in 1760. Photograph by Raven Cozens-Hardy of part of an oil on canvas painting. (OMQDG)

Lt-Col William Fuller, the KDG's commanding officer, whose last recorded words were, 'On to Paris!' Photograph by Elizabeth Vickers of a copy of a painting. (QDGHT)

King's Dragoon Guards recruiting poster displayed in the Angel Inn, Honiton, Devon. Photograph by Elizabeth Vickers. (QDGHT)

Capt. Henry Graham, the Major of the Regiment – 'the Major, neither watchful nor prayerful was pierced by a French lancer, fell down dead'. Photograph by Elizabeth Vickers of a watercolour painting. (QDGHT)

Capt. John Bringhurst, of whom Elton wrote, 'the sacrifice of all the Frenchmen that ever existed would not console me for Bringhurst alone'. Photograph by Raven Cozens-Hardy of an oil painting on canvas. (OMQDG)

Lt James Leatham wearing his Waterloo medal the wrong way around. Photograph by Elizabeth Vickers of an oil painting on canvas. (QDGHT)

Lt Robert Hawley, from a long line of soldiers and whose father William had commanded the regiment, and who lived to the ripe old age of 93. Oil painting on card. (Canon Anthony Hawley)

Cornet the Hon. Henry Bernard, the youngest officer to die at Waterloo, who, according to Hibbert, 'not being able to keep up with the French, they killed him on the road'. Oil painting on canvas. (Lady Frances Carter)

James Reed of Wootton St Lawrence, Hants. A private at Waterloo, he is portrayed here later in life as a sergeant. Photograph of a copy of a painting, owned by Reed's descendants. (QDGHT)

Pte, later Cpl, John Derry in old age. The Leicester man who at Waterloo, 'went, cutting and slashing on all the way, till horses were spent'. (Peter Derry)

Mounted KDG officer in stable dress. Photograph by Elizabeth Vickers of a pencil sketch by Capt. James Naylor KDG. (QDGHT)

Mounted KDG officer in home service uniform marked by his gauntlets and white breeches. Photograph by Elizabeth Vickers of a watercolour painting by R. Wymer. (QDGHT)

Dismounted KDG private in home service uniform, 1812. Photograph by Elizabeth Vickers of a print of a watercolour painting by R. Wymer. (Author's collection)

Mounted KDG private in home service uniform, 1812. Photograph by Raven Cozens-Hardy of an aquatint by I.C. Stadler after Charles Hamilton Smith, 1812, from *Costumes of the Army of the British Empire*. (OMQDG)

Mounted KDG private in the grey breeches and boots of campaign uniform, 1813. Photograph by Raven Cozens-Hardy of a watercolour painting. (OMQDG)

KDG 1812-pattern heavy cavalry helmet. Photograph by Elizabeth Vickers. (QDGHT)

A 1796-pattern British heavy cavalry other ranks' sword with a hatchet point. Photograph by Elizabeth Vickers. (QDGHT)

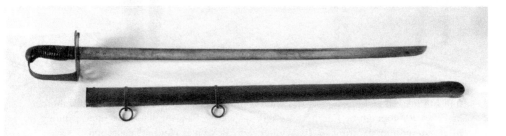

Sword arm protect   Attack & Def^ at Sp^ —

'Sword arm protect, attack and defence at speed.' Photograph by Elizabeth Vickers of a pencil sketch of sword drill by Capt. James Naylor, KDG. (QDGHT)

French 4th Cuirassier. As well as the numbers on his valise and his horse's shabraque, this soldier's regiment was distinguishable by his aurore or orange facings. Photograph of print by Rozot de Mandes. (Philip Haythornthwaite)

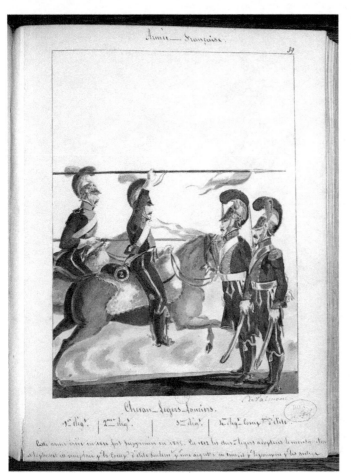

The French *Chevau-legers lan-ciers: 1ere, 2eme, 3eme et 4eme regiments.* Photograph of a print from Valmont's *Costumes militaires français 1791 à 1815.* (© Collection Yves Martin)

The charge of the Household Brigade – Waterloo 18 June 1815. The KDG are just discernible in the haze to the left of the Life Guards. (Collections du Musée Wellington, Waterloo)

Burial of the dead in the aftermath of the Battle of Waterloo, print by James Rouse in William Mudford's *An Historical Account of the Campaign in the Netherlands*. This portrayed the ground over which the KDG charged to the east of La Haye Sainte. (The Syndics of Cambridge University Library, Lib.3.81.2.)

Lord Somerset's heavy brigade … charging and overthrowing French cuirassiers, showing the KDG in combat to the east of La Haye Sainte. Photograph by Elizabeth Vickers of a watercolour painting by Charles Warren. (QDGHT)

The Foot Guards headed by the Duke of Wellington and the 1st King's Dragoon Guards advancing to the right of La Haye Sainte, showing a KDG getting around his adversary's armour by a skilful thrust of the point to the neck. Photograph by Elizabeth Vickers of a watercolour painting. (QDGHT)

The King's Dragoon Guards and French dragoons at Waterloo 1815. Photograph by Elizabeth Vickers of a print of a drawing by Jan Anthonie Langendijk. (Royal Collection Trust © Her Majesty Queen Elizabeth II, 2016)

A mounted KDG considers giving quarter to a dismounted French cavalryman; the KDG can be identified as an officer by his honeysuckle base sword. Photograph of an oil on canvas painting by R. Caton-Woodville. (Elizabeth Mann)

Uxbridge waves his sabre to the trumpeter to sound the recall on the east of the *chausée* south of La Haye Sainte, in an engraving by Robert Havell after a painting by J.M. Wright. On the left are most probably KDGs from their location, their type of helmet and their label as 'guards'. (Philip Haythornthwaite)

The remnants of the KDG being addressed by the Duke of Wellington after their first charge at Waterloo. Photograph by Raven Cozens-Hardy of part of an oil on canvas painting. (OMQDG)

SACRED TO THE MEMORY OF LIEUᵗ FRANCIS BROOKE
OF THE 1ˢᵗ DRAGOON GUARDS
ELDEST SON OF SIR HENRY BROOKE BARᵗ
WHO FELL IN THE 22ᵗʰ YEAR OF HIS AGE
WHEN GALLANTLY CHARGING THE FRENCH
IN THE EVER MEMORABLE BATTLE OF WATERLOO 18ᵗʰ JUNE 1815
THIS MONUMENT IS ERECTED BY HIS PARENTS
AS A MEMORIAL OF THEIR AFFECTION FOR HIM
AND IN REMEMBRANCE OF HIS MANY VIRTUES.

The memorial to Lt Francis Brooke, KDG, in Aghalurcher Parish Church, Colebrooke Park, County Fermanagh. (Viscount Brookeborough)

The hoof of a charger that carried a KDG sergeant at Waterloo. Photograph by Elizabeth Vickers. (QDGHT)

Lt William Stirling, KDG, and his Waterloo medal. Photograph by Elizabeth Vickers of a miniature portrait of oil on wood, and of a medal. (QDGHT)

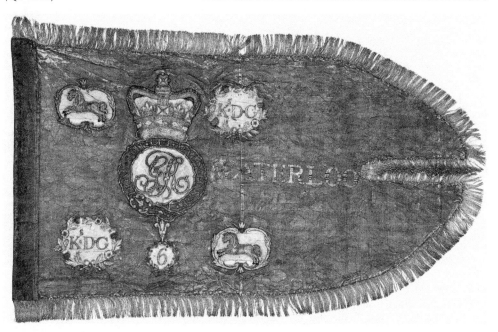

A guidon of 6th Troop KDG showing the royal cypher of King George III and 'Waterloo', the first battle honour to be displayed. This was not carried in battle and was in use some time between Waterloo and 1820. (QDGHT)

KDG patrol stopping off at an inn. Photograph by Raven Cozens-Hardy of a watercolour painting by Orlando Norrie. (OMQDG)

The capture of Cetshwayo – the Zulu king being led into captivity by the KDG and 60th Rifles. The three KDGs are capts Gordon and Gibbings and Lt Alexander. Photograph by Elizabeth Vickers of a print in a supplement to *The Graphic*, 18 October 1879. (Author's collection)

A KDG Marmon-Herrington armoured car in the streets of Benghazi, Libya, over Christmas 1941 during the Second World War. (QDGHT)

QDG Ferret scout car on patrol in the service of United Nations forces in Cyprus, 1986. (Author's collection)

QDGs in their Jackal armoured vehicle in Afghanistan during Operation Kapcha Baz on 9 March 2009. Photograph by Colonel Alan Richmond OBE. (Crown copyright)

The KDG Waterloo tradition lives on with the QDG! The dinner held by the QDG in Cardiff in September 2015 to commemorate the bicentenary of the Battle of Waterloo. (© Tempest Photography)

WATERLOO II: THE FIRST CHARGE OF THE UNION BRIGADE

The first charge made by the KDG and by most of the British heavy cavalry was fairly chaotic. At the start line there was cohesion; troops were arrayed by troop, squadron and regiment. Within minutes of their receipt of the signals to charge, the squadrons lost their defined lines and the soldiers rode where they could. This was because, having been on a reverse slope, they were blind-sided as to the enemy and obstacles the other side of the ridge. If there had been any orders as such, they appear to have been vague, as Waymouth of the 2nd Life Guards stated the, 'right of the brigade was thrown forward in order to sweep the high road along which the enemy's column were advancing against La Haye Sainte'.[1]

The KDG and the rest of the heavy cavalry's direction of travel was therefore not pre-determined, but dictated by which of the enemy they wished to engage and whatever obstacles around which they had to manoeuvre. This meant that in many cases regimental demarcation collapsed and soldiers from different regiments would end up fighting alongside each other. Waymouth, on the immediate left or east of the KDG, corroborated this when he recounted that he had, 'commanded the left half squadron of our Regiment and of the Brigade'. He said that during the first charge he had, 'more than once, during that advance, finding myself next to Major Naylor of the King's Dragoon Guards, and to whom I spoke'.[2] Waymouth went on to presume that Naylor commanded the KDG's left-hand squadron, but in fact Waymouth commented in a later letter that Naylor had attested that he had in fact commanded the centre squadron, which appeared to be a surprise to him.[3]

The first charge of the British heavy
brigades at the Battle of Waterloo.
(Callum Graham)

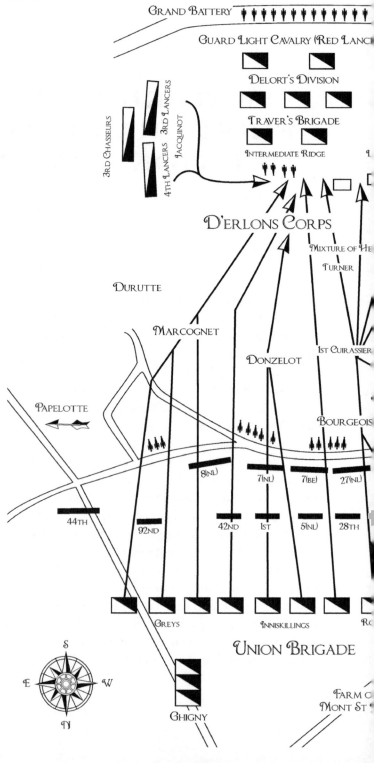

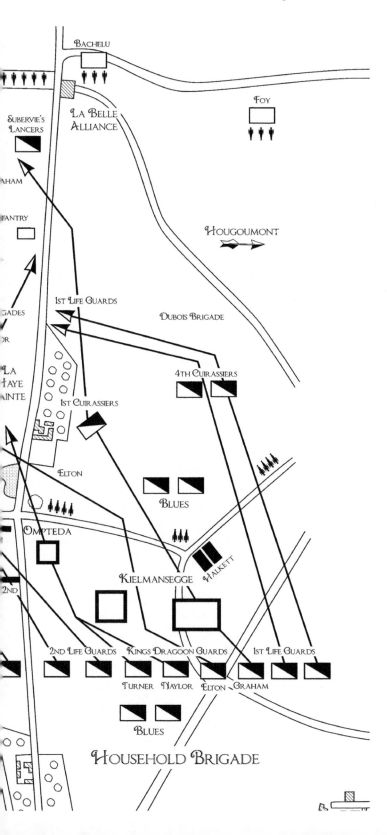

As there were four KDG squadrons, this would have meant there were another two of its squadrons which ended up further to the east of the 2nd Life Guards's left-hand squadron. These men had ended up outside not only their regimental formation but in the other heavy brigade's area, which was borne out by Captain Alexander Clark Kennedy, who commanded the centre squadron of the Royals:

> Troops of various descriptions got mingled together. One instance I can speak to, viz., a small party of the King's Dragoon Guards that had joined the charge on the other side of the Brussels road retired on the proper left of my squadron, and regained the position along with it.[4]

In fact the Household and Union brigades became totally blended, with the centre squadrons of the KDG charging alongside the Greys, the left-hand regiment of the Union Brigade.[5] Elton, who commanded one of the centre squadrons of the KDG, mentioned that Somerset charged with him, as did an officer in the Greys, as Lieutenant Hamilton wrote:

> The first time we charged, the first brigade of cavalry on our right charged at the same moment, and having received the fire of their square of infantry before we did ours, they wheeled about, and charged as we advanced; so great was the confusion that the general commanding them rode up against me, I being on the left of our brigade, and he in the centre of his.[6]

The KDG's first charge cannot, therefore, be seen as a discrete event as it was so mixed up with those charges made by the other regiments in the two heavy brigades. So when French accounts of the initial cavalry actions at Waterloo refer to fighting against Ponsonby's brigade, it could well have been some of the KDG that they had been fighting. For that reason, the KDG's first charge is better understood by first looking at the actions of all the other British heavy cavalry regiments in their first and most important charge, and then to weave the KDG's story into that broader narrative. On the other side of the hill, just prior to the first charge of the heavy brigades, the French columns of d'Erlon's four leading divisions were moving on to their objective. This was to breach the Allied line just to the north and north-east of La Haye Sainte. Napoleon's opening move had been a feint in attacking the right of Wellington's line. He had sent his II Corps commander Reille to attack the Allied strongpoint of Hougoumont, the fortified farm held by some Nassauers, Hanoverians and two battalions of British Foot Guards. However, rather than sucking in the Allied reserves as Napoleon intended, this assault on Hougoumont became a costly distraction for the French, causing them to commit Reille's corps for much of the afternoon in costly frontal assaults on the Allied troops' secure positions behind the farm's loopholed walls.

In the centre of the French position around the crossroads of La Belle Alliance to the east of the Brussels-Charleroi road was Lobau's VI Corps. To the west of that road and in the front line was Bachelu's 5th Division of Reille's II Corps; this comprised Campi's and Husson's infantry brigades. Behind them to the south was located Simmer's 19th Infantry Division, and behind them Jeanin's 20th Infantry Division. In the very rear were the regiments of the Young Guard, then the Middle Guard and finally the last line of defence, the Old Guard. To the east of the main road, almost opposite Husson's brigade, was Lobau's 3rd Cavalry Division, under Domon, which comprised Dommanget's and Vinot's brigades. To their south was Subervie's 5th Cavalry Division, which comprised Colbert and Merlin de Douai's brigades. It was not until 4.15 p.m. that Lobau's corps began to move east from their positions on the intermediate ridge, to take up positions to the rear of Milhaud's cavalry, facing east to counter the oncoming Prussian threat from that direction.

To their south were the brigades of Duhesme, Morand and Friant. On Napoleon's right wing was d'Erlon's I Corps. This corps was fresh as it had not been involved in the fighting on the previous couple of days. It was now eager to prove its worth on 18 June. From west to east, first in line was Quiot's 1st Division, of which Charlet's brigade had its left shoulders on the Brussels–Charleroi road. Next to them was Bourgeois's brigade, which took up position just north of the track that ran north-east from La Belle Alliance to La Haye. To Quiot's east was Marcognet's 3rd Division, comprising Nougues's and Grenier's brigades of infantry. On the extreme right of d'Erlon's corps was Durutte's 4th Division, with the infantry brigades of Pegot on the left and in the extreme east that of Brue.

D'Erlon positioned twelve of his infantry battalions in the front line, with eight of them arrayed in columns of closed ranks. The frontage of each division was 200 men, and twenty-four deep. This was not the usual French method of deployment but it is believed that Napoleon ordered it to facilitate better control of the many new recruits with which he had swelled his armies' ranks during the Hundred Days. Behind the three divisions in the front line was Donzelot's 2nd Infantry Division, which comprised the brigades of barons Schmitz and Aulard.

In the third line were the cavalry. The Guard's Light Cavalry Division under Lefèbvre-Desnouëttes was in the west, and to its right, further east, was Milhaud's IV Cavalry Corps of the Reserve. The Guard's Light Cavalry comprised Colbert's Red Lancers on the left and to the west, and to its right in the east, were located Lallemand's Chasseurs à Cheval. To that formation's immediate east was Delort's 14th Cuirassier Division of Milhaud's corps, and to its right was Watier's 13th Cuirassier Division, which was the eastern-most formation of Milhaud's corps. As discussed in the notes to the previous chapter, it appeared that Milhaud's cuirassier divisions subsequently changed formation into lines of division, with Watier's division in the front line and Delort's behind it in the second. From

Watier's division would come the KDG's first opponents from the 1st and 4th Cuirassiers in Dubois's brigade. Finally, on the extreme right flank in the far east of the French line, was Jacquinot's 1st Cavalry Division. This division comprised the 3rd and 4th Lancers, as well as the 3rd Chasseurs and 7th Hussars. Their job was to protect d'Erlon's eastern flank. They were later used with ruthless efficiency in their east-to-west sweep of the battlefield in the French counter-stroke after the first charges of the heavy brigades.

The opening French moves were marked by Crabbé's mixed cavalry unit's reconnaissance operations and Dubois's brigade's attack on the Hanoverians to the west of La Haye Sainte. These cuirassiers went on to menace the squares of the KGL and Hanoverians. The first of the French units that the Union Brigade was to hit were those of Bourgeois's and Donzelot's infantry, just after they had crossed the Ohain road and had moved through the hedges that lined this track. This had taken place at around 2.25 p.m.

All the Union Brigade regiments had three squadrons. Their attack was in echeloned line, as this was one of the better formations with which to attack infantry. The aim was to keep the brigade in formation to contact the French infantry with a series of hits by the three regiments. The Scots Greys had been echeloned behind the Inniskillings to their east, as Uxbridge had intended the Greys to stay in reserve. However, in their enthusiasm they too had joined the attack from the start, having charged on the Union Brigade's left flank. Lieutenant-Colonel Hamilton commanded the 443 sabres of the Scots Greys. In the centre were the 446 Inniskillings, under Lieutenant-Colonel Muter, who confusingly later changed his name to Straton. On their right was the western-most regiment in the Union Brigade, the Royals, whose right flank was the brigade boundary with the left-hand squadron of the left-hand regiment in the Household Brigade, the 2nd Life Guards. Their regimental strength was 426 all ranks.[7]

Muter explained that when brigade commander Sir William Ponsonby waved his hat, he had, 'advanced the Brigade in line … pointed to the French columns, and told me when he saw the fit moment he would make the signal for advancing'. He went on to describe how the Union Brigade passed through the Allied infantry, that they, 'part wheeled back to make room for the Cavalry – part passed through the intervals of Squadrons, and some, I fancy got through rather irregularly'.

Contrary to Lady Butler's depiction of the Scots Greys charging downhill at the gallop, the Union Brigade actually charged uphill and hit the French infantry on the northern edge of the ridge of the Mont St Jean plateau, which was the column that was reorganising itself on the sunken road. They could not get up much speed as they had to weave their way through the Allied infantry, as Muter had explained. The Scots Greys charged at a trot as they passed through the intervals of the 92nd Foot to hit Grenier's brigade, and in particular the 45th Ligne infantry regiment. They hit this unit as it was re-forming into line, having just crossed the sunken road. After a volley of fire that dropped a few of the Greys, the French were overwhelmed. At that point, Sergeant Ewart took that French infantry regiment's Eagle. However, the fourth echelon of Durutte's 4th Division was able to form square in time to withstand the Greys's attack.

In Marcognet's 3rd Division, one of the 45th Ligne's officers, Lieutenant Martin, described this assault:

> In this bloody confusion, the officers attempted, as was their responsibility, to re-establish a little order and to reform the platoons, for a troop in disorder can do nothing, let alone advance. At the moment that I succeeded in pushing one of them back in the ranks, I saw him fall at my feet from a sabre blow; I turned around quickly … it was English cavalry that had penetrated into the middle of us and cut us to pieces.[8]

After overwhelming Grenier's brigade, the Greys crossed the sunken Ohain road and charged on a roughly south-west course down the slope to confront Nogue's brigade, which had the time to form square. The French were able to pour volley fire from their muskets into the Greys, bringing many down. The Greys were to take numerous prisoners which they then sent to the rear. Notwithstanding the 'recall' having been sounded and in spite of 'all the efforts of the Officers to prevent it',[9] the Greys carried on the charge in a sweep to the south-west across the valley to the three French gun batteries on the intermediate ridge north of La Belle Alliance ridge. Once there, they sabred the French gunners and stabbed their artillery horses.

To the Greys's right, and in the centre of the Union Brigade, were the Inniskillings, who passed through Pack's brigade, which comprised the 42nd Foot and the 1st of Foot, and hit Marcognet's division, which, being slightly behind Quiot's and south of the sunken road, had a little more time to react. The Greys should have remained in reserve but moved into the front line, and this made the Inniskillings become the centre regiment. Ponsonby, the Union Brigade commander, charged at the head of the Inniskillings, who, once they had got their horses over this obstacle, immediately engaged the men of Charlet's brigade, who were in the process of attacking the farm of La Haye Sainte. Here they struck the 54th and 55th Ligne regiments, which could do little to repel the yelling Irish horsemen. The commanding officer remarked afterwards that he had seen his adjutant felled by a musket shot, so some resistance must have been offered by these units, although many of the French could not use their firearms.

Martin went on to describe the French infantry's inability to use their weapons and their vulnerability to this British cavalry as they were not formed in square:

> When infantry is in disorder and the cavalry has broken into its ranks, resistance is useless and it can massacre them almost without danger. This is what happened.

In vain did our soldiers try to get to their feet and raise their muskets; they were unable to strike this cavalry mounted on powerful horses with their bayonets, and the few shots that were fired in this confused crowd were as likely to hit our men as the English.

Having turned over this unit, the Inniskillings proceeded to take around 2,000 prisoners and had to employ a squadron to escort them to the rear. The regiment claimed that one of its soldiers, Private Penfold, had taken an Eagle, but it was dropped and lost to a member of the Royals. Once they had passed the infantry, they continued charging into the valley and their commanding officer commented that thereafter, 'there was no line preserved'.

On the extreme right on the west wing of the Union Brigade were the Royals. This regiment advanced by threes from the flanks of half squadrons and then, on Uxbridge's order, it wheeled into line with the Greys and the Inniskillings. The right-hand squadron passed through the 28th Regiment. Lieutenant Gunning, a troop commander in the Royals, explained how the Royals formed up with the rest of the brigade:

> The Union Brigade was in line, but by bringing up our left shoulders in the attack, we came in contact with the French nearly in column of squadron in echelon, so that the right squadron of the Royals came in contact with the left corner of the square of the enemy, and suffered most severely in officers and men.[10]

The French infantry had managed to fire their muskets at the Royals, and Clark Kennedy mentioned he saw around twenty of his dragoons fall after this volley. As the Royals came from further east, they did not wheel to their right to fall upon Bourgeois's 2nd Brigade but instead Bourgeois's men fell back to their right, thereby moving towards the shaken column of Donzelot's division. During this manoeuvre, the Royals were a little in advance of the other two regiments of dragoons and were the first to hit Donzelot's men, and in particular crashed into the 105th Ligne regiment, whose Eagle they took. There was controversy whether it was taken by Captain Clark Kennedy or Corporal Styles. However, it was the first Eagle to be taken that day and Styles triumphantly escorted it to the rear of the Allied lines.

At the same time as the Royals charged the 105th Ligne, the 28th Foot's left wing fired a volley into this French column and helped in mopping up the prisoners.[11] Gunning continued his account of the Royals's charge after the capture of the Eagle:

> The centre and left squadrons of the Royals did great execution against the middle of the enemy's squares. As a matter of course the Enniskillen's [sic] did not receive so much fire from the square as first fell on the Royals; but the Greys came in contact with the right corner of the square, and also received a severe

volley of musketry from the light infantry of the enemy on the extreme right of their attack; this body of troops retired in excellent order, and the broken regiment formed on them. After our charge the enemy were running in every direction for their own lines.

After the three Union Brigade regiments had made their initial contacts with the French, the Allied infantry descended from their positions on the Mont St Jean plateau and finished off those of the French infantry who wanted to fight, taking the rest prisoner. Once captured, the French soldiers were taken to the rear. A total of around 3,000 Frenchmen were taken prisoner.[12] The Union Brigade had rocked Donzelot's and Marcognet's divisions and had prevented them from breaking the Allied line. However, at this point the brigade lost cohesion, and both the Royals and the Inniskillings charged in roughly the same direction as the Greys towards the area of the three batteries of French guns which had been moved north from the Grand Battery to the intermediate ridge north-east of La Belle Alliance.

Many dragoons in the brigade ignored their officers' orders to stop and reorganise in order to return to their lines, as Ponsonby's aide-de-camp, Major de Lacy Evans, explained:

> You are rightly informed that Sir William Ponsonby did his best to prevent the further advance up the opposite ridge and towards the left of the French cannon, and so did all the Officers of any discretion about him; but finding that we were not successful in stopping the troops, we were forced to continue on with them in order to continue our exclamations to halt.[13]

This failure to stop was to cost the brigade and its commander dear, as Gunning wrote, 'At this moment the French infantry on our left advanced rapidly, and fired a volley of musketry among the scattered cavalry. By this volley General Ponsonby was killed, within twenty yards of me.'[14] The French, however, claimed Ponsonby had been killed by one of their lancers called Orban. This version was corroborated in a letter sent to Ponsonby's brother Richard, the Bishop of Derry.

Eyewitnesses from the Union Brigade, whose accounts were recorded in Siborne's *Waterloo Letters*, claimed that they did not face any enemy cavalry on the way south to the French gun lines. Some alluded to their brigade as having become muddled up early in the charge, as Clark Kennedy wrote that the Greys got, 'mixed with the Royals long before we got half-way down the slope'.[15] Not much has been recorded of what happened once the Union Brigade arrived at the French gun batteries. Wyndham recounted that Cornet Crawford of the Greys, 'tells me after this, they [the Greys] went up the high ground and took the guns, somewhere about twenty, and sabred the gunners and drivers, but could not bring away the guns'.[16]

13

WATERLOO III: THE
FIRST CHARGE OF THE
HOUSEHOLD BRIGADE

The Household Brigade was deployed into two lines by its brigade commander by wheeling by threes. The regiments were arrayed with the 2nd Life Guards in the east, with its left-hand squadron's left-hand men on the Charleroi road. These men were within sight of the Royals on the east of that road, who were in the right-hand or westernmost squadron of the Union Brigade. To the 2nd Life Guards's right was the KDG, which was the centre regiment of the brigade. To the KDG's right was the 1st Life Guards, who were the westernmost regiment in the Household Brigade. In the rear of the three front-line regiments were the Blues, who were supposed to have stayed behind the front line in reserve but moved into the front rank early in this first charge. Uxbridge positioned himself in the same place as 'the Officer leading the left squadron of the 2nd Life Guards (perhaps a little more to the right)';[1] Somerset placed himself in the centre of his brigade, in front of the centre squadrons of the KDG, as, according to Elton, they charged together.[2]

The left-hand KDG squadron was probably commanded by Captain Turner. The two commanders of the KDG's centre squadrons were Captain Naylor on the left, or east, bordering Turner's squadron, and Captain Elton on the right, or west, whose squadron bordered the right-hand or easternmost squadron under Graham. According to Naylor, the KDG's commanding officer, William Fuller, positioned himself next to him in the left-hand of the centre squadrons.[3] Records of the soldiers' pay show in which troops the privates and NCOs were posted. As far as the officers were concerned, apart from the squadron commanders, we cannot be sure which officer was where, with the exception of those in Graham's right-hand squadron, as Elton recorded in his letter, 'Major Graham, Bringhurst, Battersby, Brooke and Bernard were the officers of the right squadron'.

The number of KDGs present at the Battle of Waterloo was 606 all ranks. After deductions for sickness there were 592 all ranks. This comprised twenty-seven officers and 565 other ranks.[4] If the double-counting of the regiment's farriers in *The Digest* and in the *Official Return* were to be excluded, as has been argued was the case in note 4, then this number of 592 tallied exactly with the net number after adjustments of KDG all ranks in both the aforementioned documents. The net numbers of other ranks for the other Household Brigade regiments reported in this dispatch were as follows: 1st Life Guards, 210; 2nd Life Guards, 197; and Royal Horse Guards, 213.[5]

Unless further information should come to light that will show what the numbers in the KDG's rear party were, it will not be possible to calculate how many men actually charged. However, it has been possible to assess the maximum amount of men who could have charged, which was 554 all ranks after the farriers had been taken off as they would not have charged.[6] From this number must be deducted the rear party. A reasonable guess would be that this comprised the quartermaster and two mounted men per troop, who would have worked with the dismounted KDGs in the rear party. Once these seventeen men were deducted, the likely number of KDGs that took part in the first charge at Waterloo would have been around 537 sabres. Interestingly, Clark Kennedy reckoned that regimental numbers involved in the fighting were around 12 per cent less than that stated in Wellington's Dispatch.[7] When applying this discount to the gross number of 613 KDGs listed as the regiment's official strength of all ranks on 18 June in the Dispatch, including the sick and those on command,[8] the number of 539 corresponds more or less to the number of KDG sabres that participated in the first charge as estimated above.

Elton described the sequence of events that set the KDG off on their first charge: 'The infantry suddenly broke out of their line into solid squares & we saw the crests of the cuirassiers. The line without waiting for any particular orders, drew swords & set off at full speed. Every squadron took the interval of our infantry which was next to them.' This was echoed by Page, who wrote, '[T]he French infantry and cavalry came boldly into the bottom of a very large field while we were formed at the other end, they charged our infantry and as soon as they showed themselves to our front the word charge was given for our Brigade by Col Fuller.' Given the sudden order to charge, there did not seem to have been any explicit instructions given to the brigade.

The KDG charged on both sides of La Haye Sainte. The right squadron of two troops under Graham charged down the west of La Haye Sainte and then probably crossed the chausée south of that farm's orchard. To the left, or immediate east, of Graham was Elton's squadron. Ironically, this was the one squadron about whose route we know least but on which the most has been written in Elton's letter.

The actions he witnessed during the first charge resembled a journey to the north and the east of La Haye Sainte. Elton mentioned, 'Lord E. Somerset who charged with us.'[9] And yet Somerset's brother, Lord Fitzroy, recalled Lord Edward's movements were such that, 'He himself went to the right of La Haye Sainte'.[10]

Elton's description of the events he witnessed, however, described a route to the south-east, across the *Chemin d'Ohain* to an area directly north of the farm's garden, that was north-west of the sandpit or ravine, formerly occupied by the 95th Rifles. Elton stated that on initial contact with the cuirassiers his men had bettered their opponents and, 'Those [French] who could escape lost no time; the others were blocked up in a corner, a large fence on one side & a broad ravine on the other, these were all killed by our people.'[11] The KDG captain continued, 'Here [by the ravine] Lord Uxbridge had a round with one of their officers & though two of our men charged him and gave him plenty of cuts & thrusts on both sides, the man escaped into the lane where he was killed by the others.' Uxbridge never went to the west of La Haye Sainte, and presumably the lane Elton described was the *Chemin d'Ohain*, north of La Haye Sainte. Elton then mentioned that Somerset, with whom they charged, 'crossed the ravine & was followed by all of us'.

Lord Fitzroy concluded that he had seen, 'Lord Edward Somerset returning from that charge on the other side of the *chaussée*, i.e., in front of Picton'.[12] So they had ended up east of the farm, as the proposed route suggested they would have. Also, Elton mentioned that, subsequent to moving off for the first charge, he had not seen the right-hand KDG squadron. If Elton had charged down the west of La Haye Sainte, they would probably have seen Graham and his men haring off to the south. Whilst there is no clear-cut evidence, it just seems unlikely that Elton charged to the west of La Haye Sainte, as the ground to that side was wide open and clear of obstacles and yet Elton stated that he was travelling on, 'ground which could not be traversed at that pace'.[13] Maybe when Lord Edward stated he charged to the right of the farm, he was just referring to where he had started his first charge. However, the route that has been suggested here that Somerset and Elton and his right-hand centre squadron took was merely conjecture; what actually happened remains a mystery.

The left-centre KDG squadron commander was Naylor, who told Waymouth that he had charged to the left or the east of La Haye Sainte.[14] So the left-hand squadron under Turner, by process of elimination, would have gone to the left of La Haye Sainte as well. Derry, who was in Turner's troop, described his experiences in the initial stages of the charge:

Our Household Brigade of Heavy Dragoons charged the French Brigades of Curasseers Men Cloathed in Steel Armour. While passing thro' the lines of Infantry, they opening out in company then gave shout, 'Now we have lathered them do you shave them.' Lathered with bullets thus we met sword in hand & such a crash of armour knocked off helmets … they fled … and we followed on.[15]

If Elton had indeed charged to the east of La Haye Sainte, then three-quarters of the KDG would have gone to the left or east, only Graham's squadron having charged to the right or west of the farm. This conclusion differs radically from the orthodox view that one, or at the most one-and-a-half KDG squadrons went to the east or left of La Haye Sainte.[16] Just to complicate matters, this assertion of an almost total KDG charge to the east of the farm does not appear to have been borne out by Siborne, who wrote that when the 2nd Life Guards had pushed the cuirassiers on the east of the farm to the rear of La Haye Sainte, that, 'they were joined by the King's Dragoon Guards, who had crossed the road in front of the farm'.[17] This statement would imply that the bulk of the KDG had charged to the west of La Haye Sainte and crossed the *chausée* to the south of that farm. The truth was that the nature of the ground encountered during the first ten minutes of the charge must have broken the cohesion of the different KDG troops, and the speed of events made recollections unclear. However, the eyewitness accounts of Naylor and Elton implied three-quarters of the KDG passed to the east of La Haye Sainte in the first charge.

The Household Brigade charge was not only split by the large obstacle of La Haye Sainte's farm buildings and enclosures; it was also slowed down by the necessity to cross the sunken road of the *Chemin d'Ohain* that ran west to east to its front and by the dense vegetation either side that had to be negotiated. Once across this road to the south, the British horsemen then had to cope with treacherous ground on the slope down which the French cuirassiers were fleeing. The rain from the night before had created a lot of mud and made travelling at speed very difficult, as the horses' hooves either sunk into the ground or slipped on the greasy surface. This tricky descent was made worse by the gradient of the slope into the valley floor. The muddy state of the ground was to have tragic consequences for the KDG and other British heavies later in the afternoon when they tried to return from the first charge.

The crests that Elton and his soldiers saw on the ridge of the Mont St Jean plateau were those of the 1st and 4th Cuirassiers, who had just been engaging the KGL and Hanoverian infantry squares. The right-hand squadron of what was probably the 1st Cuirassiers had just moved into the sunken section of the Ohain road. The first of the cuirassiers to be engaged were north of this road, as Uxbridge described the first phase of the charge:

> Towards the bottom of the slope I found our infantry mostly in line, but getting into squares to receive the Enemy's Cavalry, and making intervals for us as our Squadrons presented themselves. Thus we passed through the Infantry as fast and as well as we could (but necessarily not with exact regularity), when again forming, we instantly charged and fell upon masses of Cavalry and of Infantry.[18]

Thomas Hasker in Wallace's 3rd Troop, which was in either one of the centre or left-hand squadrons, described the initial events in which he was involved:

> About two o'clock we were ordered to mount and ascend the acclivity, sword in hand. There we found French cuirassiers cutting down our infantry. We charged them; on which they turned about and rode off, we following them, and as many as were overtaken were cut down.[19]

The initial actions of the right squadron of the KDG have not been recorded, but were probably similar to those of the 1st Life Guards because of having charged next to them. These were recorded by Waymouth, who wrote, 'the right and centre regiments formed line by wheeling by Threes to the left, and immediately advanced to the attack'. He went on to quote his friend Captain Kelly of the 1st Life Guards, who stated that his regiment and the right half of the KDGs 'met the Cuirassiers in perfect line'. Contrary to the orthodox view of a hurtling downhill charge, the KDG and 1st Life Guards met the 1st and 4th Cuirassiers at a trot, given the soggy state of the ground. However, they had the advantage of surprise and many of them hit the French cavalry obliquely, thereby increasing their destructive potential.

A series of vicious hand-to-hand duels ensued. In one such contest, RSM Barlow was reported to have defeated a French cuirassier officer and relieved him of his sword, which he subsequently presented to his commanding officer, Fuller. One of the more remarkable aspects of this episode that the participants recalled was the din of the English cavalrymen's swords as they struck the cuirassiers' helmets and cuirasses. To Private Coulter of the 1st Life Guards, the noise reminded him of a brazier's shop. Somerset had the same thoughts, as he recalled, 'You might have fancied it was so many tinkers at work.'[20]

The two sides appear to have been evenly matched, as Elton described that his opponents, 'had every appearance of being picked men, extremely large & well mounted'.[21] Surgeon Slow of the Blues also witnessed this action:

> The clash of our horse against the picked mounted troops of Bonaparte was something I shall never forget. It made me hold my breath. For some minutes no one could tell how it was going to end. Neither side appeared to give way an inch. At last to our great joy the French right wheeled about and rode off in disorder, our men after them.[22]

In this first man-to-man action, it appeared the combination of fresh Household Brigade mounts versus blown French horses, surprise and possibly better swordsmanship weighed in the favour of the KDG and 1st Life Guards in this contest of the cream of the opposing armies' cavalries. The English cavalrymen were triumphant, with the French cuirassiers having been forced to turn tail and seek an escape towards their lines to the south.

Waymouth described the next stage of this charge. He said that after the initial shock of the right wing of the Household Brigade with the French cuirassiers had swung in favour of the former, the French cavalry could only escape by breaking to their right in a westerly direction. This was because of the press of their compatriots who were blocking their way south back to their lines. Waymouth went on to write that the 1st Life Guards, 'passed by the right of La Haye Sainte, and skirted round the fence of its orchard, which I think would bring them into the road a little before this hollow way'. Here he had reported Kelly having recalled:

[T]he 1st Life Guards made great slaughter amongst the flying Cuirassiers who had choked the hollow way, marked + – that its banks were then crowned by Chasseurs, who fired down upon the Life Guards in return killing great numbers of them, and that this road was quite blocked up by dead.[23]

Whilst the 1st Life Guards, and no doubt some of the KDG, were tied up with the cuirassiers west of La Haye Sainte and on the Charleroi road south of that farm, Graham's right-hand squadron charged on to the south without flank protection. No eyewitness accounts have yet surfaced from KDGs in Graham's right-hand squadron, although several KDGs, like Elton, described what they thought had happened to them:

What particular resistance they met with at first, I never could ascertain, but every officer belonging to them was killed. Owing perhaps to their going faster than the Life Guards who were, or ought to have been upon their right flank, the enemy flying & drawing them on without order & afterwards surrounding them with their very superior numbers of cuirassiers & lancers.

Graham's right-hand squadron probably left the 1st Life Guards and Blues to deal with the French around La Haye Sainte and tore on past them directly to the south, hot on the heels of the fleeing cuirassiers, to the west of the Charleroi road in the direction of La Belle Alliance. They would then have probably turned to their left, or to the south-east, just before or after the cutting halfway between La Haye Sainte and La Belle Alliance for two reasons. First, they were pursuing Dubois's men, who were presumably rushing back to their original brigade positions south-east of La Belle Alliance. Second, it would have been impossible for Graham's men to have gone directly south to the west of La Belle Alliance, as that location was where Bachelu's squares of infantry were placed. Hence they would probably have swung south-east towards the intermediate ridge to the south of La Belle Alliance, on the eastern edge of which were the three forward batteries of the French guns which were being attacked predominantly by the Greys.

We can deduce that as well as Bringhurst's 5th Troop, Graham's right-hand squadron also contained Battersby's 2nd Troop, given Elton's comments that, 'Major Graham, Bringhurst, Battersby, Brooke and Bernard were the officers of the right squadron.' From the radically different death tolls of the other ranks, it would appear these two troops did not take the same courses of action. Both troops were of similar sizes and suffered around the same number of wounded: twenty-six for 5th Troop and twenty-seven for 2nd Troop, which were slightly above the regimental average of twenty-four wounded per troop. However, 5th Troop suffered almost twice as many killed, with twenty-two dying to 2nd Troop's eleven; the regimental average was thirteen deaths of other ranks per troop. One plausible explanation was that the very high death rate suffered by Bringhurst's troop was a result of it having penetrated the French line. Here, those who had not yet been unhorsed or killed were either killed or captured and executed. Battersby, however, did not die in this first charge and was not killed until the last charge of the day, late in the evening. It seems likely he did not take his troop as far south as Bringhurst, managing to rally and recall most of his 2nd Troop.

Elton described the place where Bringhurst's men ended up along with their commanding officer, 'Scarcely a man belonging to the right of the regiment has returned. Colonel Fuller went with them at least a mile in advance of the Duke's position, behind the whole French army.' La Belle Alliance is almost exactly 1 mile south of Wellington's location at the Elm Tree Crossroads, so many of Bringhurst's troop must have ended up to the east of Bachelu's squares, possibly in amongst Lobaus' infantry, Milhaud's cuirassiers and Colbert's Red Lancers of the Guard. Bringhurst's death was described mournfully by his great friend Elton:

> Poor Bringhurst was seen lying dead on the side of the hill between the English & French position. It is reported that he killed four of the enemy's lancers, who seem to have attacked him [from] behind. He had a wound in the side near the loins from a lance or sword, which from the man's report who examined his body, must have been instantly mortal. Not a man has returned who can give [a] positive account of the precise manner in which he received his wound.

It would seem that this incident took place on Bringhurst's attempt to return to his lines, as he would have been surrounded by his men on his initial journey south on the first charge.

The details of Colonel Fuller's fate were not clear-cut, as there were three different versions of how he met his end. TSM Page stated Fuller's death had come early in the first charge, as he wrote, 'as soon as they showed themselves to our front the word charge was given for our Brigade by Col Fuller, who soon fell at our head – deeply regretted.' However, Elton stated that it was half a mile further to the south of La Haye Sainte and behind the French lines before, 'The colonel and all the men with him were entirely surrounded & cut to pieces.' Interestingly, Elton added that at the point of his death, 'He was heard calling his men to advance, without any support & not a squadron of the regiment together.' If this was the case, Fuller appeared to have not been content to reorganise his regiment and retire back behind the Allied lines, as his brigade and corps commanders had ordered; his intentions were to continue, true to his last words, 'On to Paris!', in a charge through and behind the French lines to the south.

The third theory on Fuller's death was that proposed by Hibbert, who suggested he was killed on the retreat from the French positions when he wrote:

> They were resolved either to get out of the scrape or die rather than be taken prisoners, so they attacked them, and three troops cut their way through them; about a troop were killed or taken prisoners. In this affair poor Fuller lost his life; his horse was killed by a lance, and the last time he was seen he was unhurt but dismounted. Of course the Lancers overtook him and killed him, for our men were on the full retreat.

It is reasonable to presume that Fuller's RSM had charged near him, and Barlow did state that, 'our brave Colonel advanced in our front'. In a letter home to his wife, Barlow described his part of the charge:

> [T]he charge was made in the most gallant style, the Enemy Cavalry ran away [and] we pursued them for about ½ a mile thinking the day was our own; but alas, dreadful fate was in reserve for many of our Brave Comrades; a body of the French Cavalry and Lancers surrounded us[.W]e took a flank movement to the left and cut our way through to them but with immense loss, how I escaped I can hardly tell[;] many of the French Infantry we had taken prisoners, now availed themselves of a favourable opportunity not only to escape but to fire at us – after the confused manner in which the Regiment retreated it could not reform.

Although Barlow did not mention where the KDG's commanding officer fell, his account of having been surrounded by French cavalry and lancers seems to chime with Hibbert's theory of how and where Fuller died. Derry explained what happened next:

> The Colonel and the Adjutant, Captains and Majors with Lieutenants and Cornets were killed with men and horses. Major Graham took command, gave the word loudly 'Kings Dn Gds threes about' - none returned and he swore, 'You may go to hell and be damned.' We went, cutting and slashing on all the way, till horses were spent & we began to return[,] in which the Major, neither watchful nor prayerful was pierced by a French lancer, fell down dead. Thus he went down to Hell.[24]

So some of the right squadron of the KDG went too far and pierced the French line, which gave elements of the enemy cavalry the time to get around to their north and surround and destroy many of them. But the right of the regiment had not in fact been annihilated, as Elton had stated. In the right squadron, thirty-six men were killed or died of their wounds, so at least two-thirds of them survived the battle.

Having either killed or chased off the French cavalry in the area of La Haye Sainte, the brigade commander called a halt to Elton's squadron, as he went on to explain:

> At length it [the area around La Haye Sainte] was tolerably well cleared & Lord Edward having heard that the greater part of the K[ing's] D[ragoon] G[uards] were broke & gone away without order into the enemy's lines ordered me to rally & halt as many as possible, which was done, but too late, as no one seemed to know what was become of the right squadron and other broken troops & the ground in the plain where they had so far advanced was covered with immense columns of the enemy.[25]

As discussed, Elton retired with his squadron in front of Picton's men to the north-east of La Haye Sainte.

The KDGs undoubtedly got muddled up, and the obstacles of the charge and the location of the French dictated where they went. It seemed Elton managed to rally his centre-right squadron and those KDGs who were still fighting or at rest in the vicinity of La Haye Sainte. Many in the right-hand squadron charged way to the south, some having got behind the enemy's lines. Probably two of the KDG's left-hand, or eastern, squadrons did the same, but 'the resistance there was not so great', as Elton described.[26] Naylor, and presumably many of his centre-left squadron, ended up behind the French lines to the west of Milhaud's cuirassiers and the Guard Light Cavalry Division. It can be assumed that many from Turner's extreme left squadron did likewise, with some soldiers having ended up behind the French lines.

The right-hand portion of the Household Brigade had remained west of La Haye Sainte. The 1st Life Guards and the most westerly squadron of the KDG had concentrated on destroying the cuirassiers in the vicinity of La Haye Sainte. The other regiment in this part of the brigade, the Blues, had also charged south. Uxbridge had intended that the Blues should have stayed in reserve behind the first line. However, many witnesses, including their commanding officer Sir Robert Hill, remembered this regiment as having been in the front line for the first charge. Sir Robert also recollected having seen Colonel Ferrior, the commanding officer of the 1st Life Guards, as having been shot to his right as the brigade was advancing to the charge.[27] Waymouth suggested the Blues undertook a mopping-up role, 'The impetuosity with which the front line swept over the Enemy must have left behind quite a sufficient number for the Blues to deal with when they came up, and even to lead them to imagine themselves quite in the front.' The Blues were held in hand better than the KDG, probably because they were seasoned troops who, unlike the KDG, had fought before in the Peninsular War.

So around three-quarters of the KDG charged to the left or east of La Haye Sainte, along with the 2nd Life Guards, who started on their left flank but probably blended together with them during their charge to the south. These KDG squadrons comprised Elton's right-centre squadron, Naylor's left-centre squadron and Turner's left-hand squadron. Waymouth of the 2nd Life Guards reported Naylor to have said that after the sounding of the charge, 'that the first obstacle they encountered was the road which runs along the top of the ridge, that it was too wide to leap, and the banks too deep to be easily passed, and that having crossed it, the next obstacle was the enclosure of the farm of La Haye Sainte'. Naylor had then made towards his left, or south-east, 'along with the current of our men, which was setting that way'.[28] From this statement, it can be assumed that early in the first charge the two left-hand KDG squadrons became intermingled with not only the 2nd Life Guards but also the Royals and the Inniskillings of the Union Brigade.

On beginning its charge, the right half of the brigade met those cuirassiers that had been driven east down the sunken road behind La Haye Sainte. The French horsemen were trying to turn south on the Charleroi road to regain their lines. Yet this road was cluttered with the dead horses and artillery carts that belonged to Ross's horse artillery troop, so many had to carry on east, in front of Kempt's brigade and up on to the Mont St Jean plateau. The French cuirassiers were then hit by the left half of the Household Brigade in the area to where they had been forced by the obstacle of the sandpit to the north-east of La Haye Sainte. Here, the cuirassiers had their escape blocked by the sandpit and the *abatis*, or obstacles of felled trees, which formed part of the 95th Rifles' defensive position. In that place, the cuirassiers were destroyed by the KDGs and 2nd Life Guards.

Having dealt with the cuirassiers and infantry around La Haye Sainte, the KDG's centre and left-hand squadrons, along with the elements of both the Union and Household brigades, streamed south. As Elton described, they, like Fuller and the right-hand KDG squadron, travelled around a mile to the south and had penetrated the French lines, as Sweny's actions proved, which will be described in the following chapter. The biggest threat these horsemen faced as they approached La Belle Alliance ridge was from the French infantry and artillery located there. Page explained, 'We lost but few men by their swords, it was the grapeshot and the musketry that cut us down before we got amongst them.'[29] Naylor corroborated this with his diary entry, 'Our attack was made under a very [heavy] fire of Artillery and Musketry.'[30]

But which French infantry and artillery? A comment by Page in one of his letters gave an indication of the direction from which this fire came, 'When the French lines broke and turned and ran, our Regiment being too eager, followed the French Cavalry while the cannon and musketry was sweeping our flank.'[31] The orthodox view was that this fire came from the infantry and artillery in Bachelu's 5th Division in Reille's corps located parallel to and west of La Belle Alliance.[32] Whilst the shells could well have come from Bachelu's cannons, it would not have been his shot as the British cavalry were unlikely to have charged infantry in square head-on. This French division contained the 18th Company of the 6th Field Regiment of Artillery, which had six 6 pounders and two 5.5in howitzers.[33] Some of these guns could certainly have been used to rake the front and flanks of the KDG and the other British heavy cavalry as they swung east and north-east across the Brussels–Charleroi road.

However, Bachelu's infantry it was not, as Somerset stated the KDGs crossed to the east of the *chausée*, out of the effective range of the French muskets west of the Brussels–Charleroi road:

> [T]he 2nd Life Guards and 1st Dragoon Guards, who ascending the position occupied by the Enemy's Infantry on the left of the high road, encountered a heavy fire, and sustained a very severe loss in their retreat. Colonel Fuller, commanding the 1st Dragoon Guards, and several officers of that Regiment fell in this attack. The 2nd Life Guards likewise suffered severely.[34]

The only men from Reille's infantry who could have fired on the charging KDGs would have been those men who lined the banks of the *chaussée*, as described by Sgt-Maj. Edward Cotton in his description of the battle.[35]

Another theory was that the heavy musketry that the KDG and the other British heavy cavalry suffered was from those units in d'Erlon's corps which had managed to form square during the first charge. In the KDG's case, these men could have been from Quiot's division on d'Erlon's left flank, or possibly Donzelot's division, which was immediately to the east of Quiot. This may have happened in a few instances but it was an unlikely scenario, as the French infantry would have had to be incredibly well disciplined to have heard words of command and managed to form square when under attack from cavalry.

The most probable route of the KDG's right-hand squadron was to have followed Dubois's men back to their initial positions north of Plancenoit, which would have led them east across the *chaussée* just north of the cutting that marked approximately the mid-point between La Haye Sainte and La Belle Alliance. This would have brought the KDG's right flank into range from one or several of Lobau's seven regimental squares that were situated on the intermediate ridge to the north-east of La Belle Alliance. This view that VI Corps was in this particular location was based on the evidence of eyewitness reports from members of Lobau's corps.[36] In particular, Lobau's Chief of Staff, Colonel Janin, who later wrote that his corps, 'advanced to support the attack on the centre' and that it took place, 'on the crest of the ravine that separated the two armies'.[37] This was the intermediate ridge where the guns attacked by the heavy brigades were located, and to where many of the KDGs headed in the first charge.

In fact there was an eyewitness report from a sergeant-major in one of Lobau's units, the 107th Regiment in Tromelin's brigade, who saw the arrival of the British heavy cavalry during their first charge. Francois Marcq later wrote that he had been in the 'middle of the battlefield' when, 'We were forced to form square because the English cavalry was near us who were fighting the French cuirassiers. Several times they shadowed our squares but had no success.'[38] The KDG must have got pretty close to Lobau's squares for the French infantry to have damaged them as badly as they did, as the maximum effective range of their Year IX muskets was only 100 yards.

So the KDG clearly charged too far, as Hibbert wrote in a letter home:

> Our brigade, never having been on service before, hardly knew how to act. They knew they were to charge, but never thought about stopping at a proper time, so that after entirely cutting to pieces a large body of Cuirassiers double their number, they still continued to gallop on instead of forming up and getting into line; the consequence was that they got among the French infantry and artillery, and were miserably cut up.[39]

The KDG was not the only regiment guilty of this act of folly and lack of control. As Elton mentioned, 'Every other regiment of cavalry engaged that day seem to have shown equal gallantry with as little judgement.'

The only regiments that seem to have not over-extended themselves were the Blues and the Inniskillings. The Blues appear to have been kept well in hand by their officers, reorganised early and helped to escort the remnants of the British heavy cavalry off the field after the first charge. Although many of the Inniskillings were not as disciplined and made it as far as the French guns, their losses were mitigated as halfway through their first charge they had been obliged to send a squadron back to the rear with the French prisoners.[40]

Notwithstanding having charged too far, the KDG and the British heavy cavalry had stopped and snuffed out Napoleon's first, main and probably his most dangerous attack of the day. Having gained the French lines after their first charge through the fierce musketry and cannon fire, the regiment and its fellow 'heavies' who had gained La Belle Alliance ridge were going to have an even rougher ride home at the hands of another arm of the French Army, her cavalry. Hasker certainly noticed a sinister development on his journey out on the first charge, 'I observed, however, that many of them on our right flank got behind us, and thus we were at once pursuing and pursued.' This could have been Ordener's ring of steel, whereby French lancers and cuirassiers managed to get behind, or to the north of, the British heavy cavalry on their way out south on the first charge. This manoeuvre was to cause the British heavy cavalrymen a huge headache on the return journey to their lines from the French guns.[41]

14

WATERLOO IV: THE JOURNEY BACK FROM THE FIRST CHARGE

TSM Page summed up the effects of this first charge and the bloody consequences of the KDG's return journey to the Allied lines thereafter:

> Many fell and our ranks suffered severely – the Duke of Wellington, with tears, it is said, when he saw us so far advanced among the French, himself said he never saw such a charge, but he was afraid very few of us would return – his words were too true.[1]

Many officers and non-commissioned officers, from the cavalry corps commander down, tried to get the Household and Union brigades to stop, rally and retire from the French positions. Uxbridge wrote, 'After the overthrow of the Cuirassiers I had in vain attempted to stop my people by sounding the Rally, but neither voice nor trumpet availed.'[2]

Somerset, too, tried to stop the KDG going too far, but with little success, as Elton recounted that it was all:

> … too late, as no one seemed to know what was become of the right squadron and other broken troops & the ground in the plain where they had so far advanced was covered with immense columns of the enemy.

However, as has been seen, on Elton's evidence quoted in the previous chapter, it does not seem that Fuller was intent on stopping his regiment and recalling it to the Allied lines. So it appears that when in the area of La Belle Alliance, he had still remained intent on his southward trajectory until the moment he was killed.

Once at the French lines, it appears that some like Fuller, Naylor and the 4th Troop Commander, Captain John Sweny, went further and penetrated into the enemy's rear areas. Here they were most probably surrounded and either killed, as in the case of Fuller, or captured, as was the case with Sweny. According to Sweny's wife, her husband had charged as far behind the French lines as Fuller.[3] Sweny, who had come through the ranks and was the last adjutant before taking over 4th Troop, was reported to have been captured having sustained seventeen lance and sabre wounds. On being brought before Napoleon for questioning, Bonaparte was reported to have ordered his surgeon, Larrey, to save Sweny's life as he was suffering from an immense loss of blood. Some months after his capture, Napoleon, who apparently had a great memory for faces, recognised John's image in that of his brother Mark, who was a lieutenant on board his prison vessel, HMS *Northumberland*. This was when Bonaparte was travelling to his second and final exile, this time on St Helena.[4]

However, not all Sweny's men in 4th Troop were killed or captured; his TSM, James Page, managed to escape from the lancers in or around the French lines. Page had probably used the same route back to the Allied lines as Naylor had taken when his troop had charged in the same south-easterly direction north of La Haye Sainte. According to Waymouth, who discussed the charge with Naylor afterwards, this KDG squadron commander had, 'made his way home again round the left of our line'.[5] However, before sensibly turning his horse north back to the Allied lines, Page clearly had been in the thick of it with the French lancers, as he described in a letter home:

> My mare carried me in famous style, she got a light wound in her off hind leg by a French Lancer. I was after a French Officer who was riding away from me, I came up to him and he thrust his lance at me, I turned it with my sword, it glanced down and cut my mare below the hock of the hind leg.

We can estimate his location was probably as far south as the French lines, as he had sustained musket fire from the French infantry squares. In all likelihood these were those of Lobau's men on the intermediate ridge just to the north of La Belle Alliance ridge. He described his lucky escape from this musketry:

> I was struck by a musket shot on the left thigh, but it was prevented from doing me harm in a singular manner, which was as follows. The day before my sabretasche [*sic*], which is a kind of pocket made of leather, had one of the carriages broken and in order to keep it safe it was taken up very short and lodged on my left thigh. The pocket being very full of books and other things prevented the shot from going right through when it struck me. This shot would have fractured my thigh-bone had not the sabretasche [*sic*] prevented it.

As discussed in a previous chapter, the lancers who harried the KDG and the rest of the heavy brigades on their return north from the first charge were reported to have attacked the British cavalry from the east. However, it seemed that the French must have simultaneously sent some of their party around to the north of the heavy brigades so as to have encircled them. This view was based on the statements by several French commentators, such as Sergeant Roy of the 7th Cuirassiers and de Brack of the Red Lancers, as well as eyewitness accounts from some of the KDGs. Barlow mentioned, 'a body of the French Cavalry and Lancers surrounded us'.[6] And Elton wrote, 'the enemy flying & drawing them on without order & afterwards surrounding them with their very superior numbers of cuirassiers & lancers'.[7] This view was also substantiated by Mauduit's map,[8] which showed the 7th and 12th Cuirassiers to have moved north and east of the Household and Union brigades, whilst Jacquinot's lancers were portrayed as having moved south of the British on their eastern flank to complete this encirclement.

For Elton's squadron, and those KDGs fighting alongside it around La Haye Sainte, the route home to the area behind the Allied infantry squares to the north would have been short and relatively hassle-free in comparison to most of the rest of the regiment who had charged too far south. The latter had to get back from behind the French lines and from the area lying to the south-east of La Haye Sainte and north of La Belle Alliance ridge, east of the Charleroi road. As well as the counter-stroke in their eastern flank and the encircling attack from their north by the French lancers, the British heavy cavalry also had to contend with masses of cuirassiers to their front in the south. As previously discussed, those heavy cavalrymen who had made it to the eastern edge of the French gun line would probably have faced Travers's 7th and 12th Cuirassiers.

Meanwhile the KDG and 2nd Life Guards would most likely have faced some or all of the 5th, 6th, 9th and 10th Cuirassiers of Delort's division. Although KDG sources talked about having fought cuirassiers to their front or to their south, one commentator believed they were also hit from the west, or in their left flank as they tried to return from the French lines.[9] This would fit with Roy's description of the ring of steel that the 1st Cuirassiers' commanding officer, Michel Ordener, had so skilfully thrown around the British heavy cavalry.[10]

The retreat back from the French lines was bad enough for those lucky enough to still be mounted. Hibbert described the end of the KDG's first charge and the dangerous journey back to their lines after getting among the French infantry and artillery:

They saw their mistake too late, and a few (that is about half the regiment) turned and rode back again; no sooner had they got about five hundred yards from the French infantry than they were met by an immense body of Lancers who were sent for the purpose of attacking them in the way. Our men [were] rendered desperate by their situation. They were resolved either to get out of the scrape or die rather than be taken prisoners, so they attacked them, and three troops cut their way through them; about a troop were killed or taken prisoners.[11]

Hibbert's record of the events corroborated the view that the main attack on the KDG by lancers were from those of Jacquinot's 3rd and 4th regiments. This is because he stated that the regiment was 'met' by the French lancers on its return from the French lines, and that they had to 'cut their way through them' to the north in order to regain the Allied lines. Barlow also mentioned the French lancers and likewise explained that the KDGs had to swing to their left or to the north-east and then north in order to escape the enemy lancers, and then to have proceeded north-west to regain their original position, just as Naylor had done:

> [T]he Enemy Cavalry ran away [and] we pursued them for about ½ a mile thinking the day was our own; but alas, dreadful fate was in reserve for many of our Brave Comrades; a body of the French Cavalry and Lancers surrounded us[.We] took a flank movement to the left and cut our way through to them but with immense loss, how I escaped I can hardly tell.[12]

This would explain why many of the KDG ended up east of La Haye Sainte and withdrew amongst the Royals, as was borne out by Captain Clark Kennedy of that regiment. He recalled, 'a small party of the King's Dragoon Guards that had joined in the charge on the other side of the Brussels road, retired on the *proper left* of my Squadron, and regained the position along with it.'[13] So even some of those KDGs in the more westerly, right-hand squadrons must have made their way back in the jumble of British heavy cavalry from the eastern side of the valley.

Hasker in 3rd Troop left a good description of his actions in the closing phase of the charge just before he attempted to make it back to the Allied lines. At one stage this devout Methodist nearly had a duel with a cuirassier:

> I was just in a charge of the whole brigade, and by some means, was opposed single-handed to one of the French cuirassiers; and, while brandishing swords, he muttered something which I did not understand, and I – thinking I must say something in reply – muttered in my turn, 'The sword of the Lord and Gideon!' … He very wisely turned his horse's head on one side, and rode off; and I as wisely turned my horse's head on the other side and rode off; and we have not seen each other since.

The ground was clearly a great problem for both sides, and in Hasker's case it caused him to have been unhorsed, which prevented him from getting back to his own lines and left him vulnerable to French soldiers of many different regiments:

On perceiving that I had lost time, and that the regiment had left me to settle the question with the French dragoon, I tried to follow; but, in crossing a bad hollow piece of ground, my horse fell, and before I had well got upon my feet, another of the French dragoons came up, and (*sans ceremonie*) began to cut at my head, knocked off my helmet, and inflicted several wounds on my head and face. Looking up at him, I saw him in the act of striking another blow at my head, and instantly held up my right hand to protect it, when he cut off my little finger and half way through the rest. I then threw myself on the ground, with my face downward. One of the lancers rode by, and stabbed me in the back with his lance. I then turned, and lay with my face upward, and a foot soldier stabbed me with his sword as he walked by.[14]

In the text of this Hasker biography, the dragoon who cut at his head was also described as a cuirassier. So clearly his squadron was engaged with cuirassiers and lancers. However, it is interesting that his troop captain, Robert Wallace, wrote, 'we were more in contact with the French Heavy Cavalry than with other troops'.[15] Notwithstanding the terrible time Hasker was having, Providence was on his side, as he went on to explain:

Very soon another man with a firelock and a bayonet, and, raising both his arms, thrust his bayonet (as he thought) into my side near my heart. The coat I had on was not buttoned but fastened with brass hooks and eyes. Into one of these eyes the point of the bayonet entered, and was thus prevented from entering my body. One of my fingers was cut before I fell; and there I lay bleeding from at least a dozen places, and was soon covered in blood. I was also at that time plundered by the French soldiers of my watch, money, canteen, haversack, and trousers, notwithstanding the balls from the British army were dropping on all sides as I lay there. The fighting went on with murderous effect until night.[16]

At the end of the battle, the KDG had by far the most men missing with 124; this was 44 per cent of the total missing in both heavy brigades put together, and over half that of all the men missing in the Household Brigade. The 2nd Life Guards also suffered very high numbers of missing, with ninety-seven men, which given the regiment was half the size of the KDG, was a far higher proportion. The number of missing from both these two regiments represented 90 per cent and 79 per cent of the total missing in the whole of the Household and in both heavy brigades respectively.[17] In fact, something very terrible must have happened to the east of the Brussels–Charleroi *chaussée* parallel to the ground between La Haye Sainte's orchard and La Belle Alliance. This was the point reached by many of the men of the KDG and 2nd Life Guards, but from which many of them did not return.

As there was a very large amount of men missing from these two regiments in comparison to other heavy cavalry regiments, it would appear that they had either disappeared once they were behind the French lines, or more likely were unhorsed and their deaths were not witnessed. These men would have ended up on foot, as they had lost their horses to the fire from the remnants of d'Erlon's men who had managed to form square or possibly also from Lobau's and Bacheleu's men. Or the muddy conditions meant they were forced to dismount, as Page explained, 'We had to charge to meet them so far over heavy ground that many of our horses were stuck in deep mud. The men were obliged to jump off, leave them and seek their safety away from the cannon fire.'[18]

Once on foot, however, they were fair game for the merciless French lancers. Hibbert described Fuller's fate: 'Of course the Lancers overtook him and killed him.' Some contemporary observers believed the French were instructed to give no quarter to the British cavalry in retaliation for the treatment some of them meted out to the young unarmed French gunners whom they put to the sword. However, this does not seem plausible as it seems impossible for words concerning the treatment of the French artillery boys to have travelled from their gun lines down to the lancers on the right flank or to the lancers to the south of La Belle Alliance ridge. Unless they actually witnessed any atrocities, it was unlikely the French lancers' mercilessness was retribution but was simply their *modus operandi*, as they had already been reported to have murdered prisoners a couple of days before at Genappe. One example was Major Hodge of the 7th Hussars, who was killed by lancers after he had been taken prisoner.[19]

Even if the KDGs and other British heavies were not murdered, it was an extremely unpleasant end for the individual or small clusters of dismounted KDGs and other British heavy cavalrymen who were put to death by those packs of lancers. These French horsemen would have closed in on the almost defenceless British dragoons and speared them to death or caused dreadful injury.

At least the French cuirassiers appear to have been chivalrous. A 2nd Life Guard eyewitness recounted how he had seen a cuirassier spare one of the trumpeters from his regiment, only to have been killed straight afterwards by another passing Life Guard.[20] However, one of the KDG troop commanders, Captain Robert Wallace, had grumbled that his gallantry had been abused by a French trumpeter. A friend of his recounted one of Wallace's Waterloo experiences:

When charging at Waterloo, a French trumpeter was passed lying on the ground. Few of the regiment forbore to have a slash at their fallen enemy, as they galloped past. But the kind-hearted old Colonel was more merciful. 'I did not slash at him,' he said, 'but the trumpeter slashed at me!'[21]

There were also several occasions witnessed where the French infantrymen lay prone in surrender to the British cavalry, and having been spared by them, then got up and shot at the horsemen's backs and mounts. Barlow described how, 'many of the French Infantry we had taken prisoners, now availed themselves of a favourable opportunity not only to escape but to fire at us'.[22]

For those 2nd Life Guards and KDGs who had escaped the lancers and had retreated back through the area of La Haye Sainte, the French infantry were waiting for them as they passed, as described by Cotton:

> Reille's troop fired down from the high banks [of the cutting south of La Haye Sainte] on Life Guards who had to get back to our lines as best they could. Most of the King's dragoon guards had dashed over the [Charleroi to Brussels] road and were falling back to reform; but they lost many men and some officers, by the enemy's fire from the little garden of La Haye Sainte.[23]

Some help was at hand from Vandeleur's light cavalry, which appeared from the east to engage the French lancers, and this enabled many from the heavy brigades to escape and regain the original positions where they had assembled before the first charge. The KDG returned to the Household Brigade position some 200 yards north of the Elm Tree Crossroads to the north-west of La Haye Sainte.

Yet the KDG had charged too far, as Somerset recalled with regret in a letter to his mother:

> [N]otwithstanding all exertions I could make, I could not restrain the King's Dragoon Guards who galloped on, till at length they arrived in the midst of the enemy's infantry, and a great part of them were cut to pieces. Almost the whole of their right squadron is missing … The other regiments went also further than was prudent, but I at length succeeded in withdrawing and forming them.[24]

Elton corroborated Somerset's failed attempts to recall the KDG as it charged on south to its destruction:

> At length it [the area around La Haye Sainte] was tolerably well cleared & Lord Edward having heard that the greater part of the K[ing's] D[ragoon] G[uards] were broke & gone away without order into the enemy's lines ordered me to rally & halt as many as possible, which was done, but too late, as no one seemed to know what was become of the right squadron and other broken troops & the ground in the plain where they had so far advanced was covered with immense columns of the enemy.[25]

Given that they had charged too far south, Somerset was unable to call back the two left-hand squadrons of the KDG and the 2nd Life Guards. With the exception of the one squadron of Inniskillings, which had escorted the French prisoners to the rear, the same fate befell the regiments of the Union Brigade, whose commander, Sir William Ponsonby, had been killed whilst he rode forward to try to recall his brigade.

It was now around 3.30 p.m. and the Household Brigade was in a terrible state. Survivors from the KDG and other heavy cavalry regiments struggled back to their reorganisation position, which was, according to Lieutenant Marten of the 2nd Life Guards, in 'a small orchard just out of Mont-St-Jean, and in the rear of our original ground'. He went on to state that after some time they, 'were marched up to the support of the right centre again on the slope of the hill'.[26] It had been a very costly charge for both British heavy brigades. In under an hour, more than a third of their horses and men had been killed, badly wounded or were missing.[27] The strength of the KDG at this point of the battle was not reported. From Hibbert's comments, it can be guessed that it was down to around three troops, or less than 40 per cent of its original strength.[28]

However, given that the KDG's casualties were some of the highest in proportionate terms, the regimental numbers still standing at that point were likely to have been considerably lower. In one of his letters, Barlow wrote, 'When I entered the field we could only muster 30 officers and men.'[29] This could have been evidence that there were as few as thirty KDGs who were available to fight after the first charge, prior to Turner's arrival later with thirty men.[30] This would seem plausible, given the facts that the Household Brigade, as a whole, was reduced to a single squadron of around 100 men by 4.30 p.m. and that the KDG suffered by far the highest numbers of men missing in the brigade. The vast majority of these men were found to have been absent after the first charge. Thereafter, the Household Brigade fought in a much tighter formation, where deaths were witnessed and soldiers could not have gone too far astray.

Yet the KDG, along with the rest of the Household Brigade and the Union Brigade, had together thwarted Napoleon's first, main and potentially most viable attack at the Battle of Waterloo. A brigade of cuirassiers and most of a French corps had been neutralised. Around 3,000 Frenchmen had been killed and around a further 3,000 captured.[31] Most importantly, some of the devastating French artillery had been put out of action for several hours; in fact it had been so reduced in capacity and in the will to fight, that some have argued that thereafter it ceased to have a significant impact on the day.[32]

WATERLOO V:
THE REST OF THE DAY

The Household Brigade, or what was left of it, ended up in its original location, just north-west of the Elm Tree Crossroads on the plateau above La Haye Sainte. Naylor mentioned in his diary that at this point, 'It was some time before we could collect our men. Turner with about thirty men joined the Brigade, he was wounded soon after by a cannon shot in the arm and I took the command of the King's Dragoon Guards.'[1] Turner, having commanded the far left squadron, had probably charged the furthest to the south-east and his was thus the last squadron to return, apart from the missing right-hand squadron. On having made it back to the brigade location, there was a short respite for the exhausted remnants of the KDG, many of whom carried wounds from the first charge and from the journey back to their lines. The badly wounded were moved to dressing stations in the rear and any prisoners the KDG had captured would have been escorted by the regimental farriers and other mounted members of the rear party to the holding areas behind the Allied lines.

From this stage of the battle to its conclusion, not much was written by KDG commentators. This was because the rest of the day was concerned with minor engagements compared to the memorable events of the first charge and so were not recorded. Also, few of those who kept a record of the battle were left mounted. Naylor and Barlow kept going the longest, the former until 7 p.m. and the latter being one of the only thirteen or so men who lasted the course of the day. Naylor's diary entry was very brief on the events from the first charge until he was invalided off the field. Elton, probably like the majority of the unwounded KDGs, was *hors de combat* due to the loss of his horse, as he described, 'And most of us who remained in the field till the evening, had canon shots through our horses.' Page probably suffered the same fate but, like Elton, was not badly injured. Hasker, however, was severely wounded and Hibbert had not been present at the battle.

Having reassembled into all they could muster as a fighting force, the heavy brigades then experienced Ney's massed cavalry attacks on the Allied infantry squares, which lasted from around 4 p.m. to almost 6 p.m. Ney, on seeing some movement to the rear by the Allied infantry withdrawing behind the crest of the Mont St Jean plateau, mistakenly appreciated this to have been a general retreat. He then unleashed the French cavalry in massed attacks on the Allied infantry squares at around 4 p.m., starting with the eight regiments of cuirassiers, the Red Lancers and the Chasseurs à Cheval of the Imperial Guard. The British artillery exacted a huge toll on this French cavalry with grape and canister, and the Allied infantry squares stood firm. Whilst this was happening, the KDG and the remains of the British heavy cavalry were mostly kept in reserve. They were held back in the rear by Uxbridge to attack any French cavalry that managed to penetrate the gaps between the Allied infantry squares.

Somerset recounted that his brigade had remained in its original location just west of the Charleroi road, 'until an opportunity offered of their acting offensively against a considerable force of the Enemy's Cavalry assembled on the reverse of the hill, and threatening our position'.[2] This was at about 4.15 p.m., when Uxbridge led a spirited charge against the first French cavalry assault. This charge had passed between the Allied infantry squares and came straight on for the second line of Allied cavalry. The KDG participated in this counter-attack, along with the rest of the heavy cavalry; the 7th and 23rd British Hussars, the 1st and 3rd Hussars of the KGL and two regiments of Brunswick cavalry, the Dutch-Belgian cavalry having been held in reserve. Although the French cavalry was disadvantaged by being mounted on fairly blown horses by the time they reached the plateau, the KDGs and British heavy cavalry still acquitted themselves well in what was more a series of duels, where horsemanship and swordsmanship counted, rather than a head-to-head clash.

During this series of engagements, the 1st Life Guards lost its commanding officer, Colonel Ferrior, and the Blues lost Major Packe. There then followed a series of ten small charges and counter-charges[3] between the remnants of the Household Brigade and the French cavalry in the area behind Kielmansegge's Hanoverian and Ompteda's KGL squares.[4] During these charges, the numbers in the KDG and the Household Brigade dwindled still further with significant losses. However, at this stage in the battle, the French cavalry had begun to lack some of its initial ardour. Uxbridge stated that after having been roughed up by the Household Brigade in the first charge, 'for the rest of the day, although the Cuirassiers frequently attempted to break into our Lines, they always did it *molle-ment*'.[5] The remains of the Household Brigade were then ordered to the right of the Allied position to near where the French were combining infantry and cavalry attacks to try and break the Allied line. The first of these attacks was repelled by the Allied artillery.

After the battle, Uxbridge's cavalry came under some criticism for its actions, or lack of action, during the massed charges of the French cavalry. Quotations criticising the British mounted regiments' inaction at this stage of the battle have been taken from two officers of the 1st Foot Guards to substantiate this assertion. Captain Stanhope has been quoted as having reported Uxbridge to have lamented that his cavalry had deserted him. Yet Uxbridge's reported reaction does not seem to stack up, as he appeared to have always intended to hold back what little cavalry he still commanded for use only when the French cavalry penetrated too far north beyond the Allied squares. By the later stages of the battle, the British heavy cavalry was so reduced in size and so outnumbered by the French cavalry that it could not be used effectively in any major counter-attacks on its mounted opponents.

The other 1st Foot Guards officer to have been often quoted for reporting Uxbridge's dissatisfaction with his cavalry was Lord Hill's ADC, Horace Churchill. There was a much-used excerpt from a letter he wrote straight after the battle, in which he quoted Uxbridge as having said, 'I have tried every brigade in the cavalry and I cannot find one to follow me!' Yet too often Churchill's preceding sentence is omitted, in which he wrote, 'Never was such devotion witnessed as the French cuirassiers. Our cavalry (with the exception of 2 Brigades) never would face them.'[6] Churchill was referring to the two British heavy brigades, and thus they were not included in his criticism of the British cavalry. In fact, Uxbridge has probably been taken out of context, as it appeared that his comments may have stemmed from his annoyance at some of his cavalry's performance at Genappe the day before Waterloo. This was when he had trouble destroying the French lancers in that village with the 7th Hussars and the 23rd Light Dragoons.[7] So accusations of the British heavy brigades having been unwilling to engage the French cavalry when ordered to do so appear not to have been based on any solid facts.

At around 5.30 p.m., Somerset hurled the tiny remnants of his brigade regardless against another French assault. Although they managed to stop it, they did not have the strength to push their enemies back off the plateau. In this action, Colonel Lygon, the commanding officer of the 2nd Life Guards and the senior officer in the brigade, had to leave the field with a wounded horse, and so Captain Naylor KDG took over command of the brigade under Somerset. This unit was now depleted to one super-squadron of around 100 men. After this costly charge, Somerset's men regrouped and were ordered back east to the original Household Brigade area to the north-west of the Elm Tree Crossroads just north of La Haye Sainte.

Just after this charge, Uxbridge decided to merge both heavy brigades into one under Somerset. This was because the Union, like the Household Brigade, had been reduced to just one squadron. So the 2nd Cavalry Brigade moved to join the KDG and the rest of the Household Brigade on the west of the Brussels–Charleroi road. In the front rank was stationed the composite Household Brigade squadron, and behind it, in the second line, was placed the remains of the Union Brigade. As the Union Brigade was reported to have lined up as it had done before the first charge, it is presumed that the KDG was in the centre of the Household Brigade line. Also, the 2nd Life Guards was recorded to have been located on the left as it had been just before the brigade had first gone into action. These battered remnants of the British heavy cavalry were augmented with a squadron of the 23rd Light Dragoons that had got separated from the rest of its regiment.

As a result of the ferocity of the musketry and artillery barrages that they had to face in that place, Uxbridge suggested to Somerset that he withdraw his force to seek cover behind the ridge to their north. However, according to one of Anglesey's ADCs, Sir Horace Seymour, it was apparent to Somerset that it would be risky for him to move his men to safety. This is because he perceived any move by his men to seek the shelter of the ridge to their north would unsettle the Dutch-Belgian cavalry located near them. Seymour explained that Somerset had thought them to have looked none too firm and liable to flight if the Household Brigade moved. As a result, Uxbridge acquiesced and both heavy brigades remained in that location and suffered the full attention of the French artillery, but bravely still 'retained their position until the end of the action'.[8]

Then, just before 6 p.m., Ney launched another assault on La Haye Sainte with men from the 13th Legère with some engineer support. The Prince of Orange, having seen La Haye Sainte was about to be taken, sent the 5th and 8th Line battalions of the KGL to save the farm from falling to the French. As the German units approached La Haye Sainte at around 6.30 p.m., the 8th was hit in the flank by cuirassiers. Whilst the 5th Battalion managed to form square and stave off the French cavalry, the 8th was scattered and lost its colour. The KDG, however, came to their rescue, as the 8th Battalion's Adjutant, Captain Julius Brinkmann, explained, "Few, if any of us would have survived if just at the right moment the English Dragoon Guards had not charged the French and thrown them back.' However, by 6.30 p.m. the French had finally taken La Haye Sainte.

At around this time, the Prussian cavalry turned up on Wellington's left flank, just to the north of Papelotte. Sir Hussey Vivian, who commanded the 6th Brigade of Light Cavalry near to where the Prussians had arrived, then appreciated he could move from the left, south-westwards to relieve the pressure on the Allied centre. He therefore proposed to the other British light cavalry commander, Vandeleur, who was his senior, and with whom he was located, that they should move their brigades in that direction. Vandeleur, nervous of disobeying orders from Wellington, insisted on staying put. Vivian, however, moved his brigade to the area of the Household Brigade concentration area just north-west of La Haye Sainte and the Elm Tree Crossroads.

Meanwhile, the remnants of the heavy brigades were still taking heavy artillery and musket fire whilst remaining static in the line. At around 7 p.m., Naylor received a wound which he said, 'compelled me to retire to Brussels where I met Macauly'. This man was one of the KDG's assistant-surgeons, James Macauley, who had evidently been left behind in the Belgian capital to establish a regimental hospital before the battle. As Naylor was retiring to the rear, Vivian's brigade arrived on the scene.[9] On passing his fellow brigade commander, Vivian asked Somerset, 'Where's your Brigade?' To which Lord Edward pointed to the ground around where he stood, which contained the bodies of many of the wounded British heavy cavalrymen who made up his brigade, and replied, 'Here.'[10] Almost half of the two brigades of British heavy cavalry were now casualties.[11] Vivian gave a detailed description of the state and predicament of the remains of the KDG and British heavy cavalry at that stage of the battle, which was just before the French retreated from the Mont St Jean plateau:

> Lord Somerset with the wretched remains of the two Heavy Brigades, not 200 men and horses, retired through me, and I then remained for about half an hour exposed to the most dreadful fire of shot, shell and musketry that it is possible to imagine. No words can give any idea of it (how a man escaped is to me a miracle), we every instant expecting through the smoke to see the Enemy appearing under our noses, for the smoke was literally so thick that we could not see ten yards off.[12]

Just half an hour later, five battalions of the French Middle Guard, supported by a further three battalions of the Old Guard, assaulted the Mont St Jean plateau. Within a quarter of an hour they were thrown back by the withering fire of the Allied infantry and gunners; of the latter, Krahmer's Dutch gun battery was particularly effective in helping stop this last-ditch assault. The fate of the Middle Guard was sealed thanks to a clever move by Sir John Colborne, who wheeled his 52nd Foot to the left to face east, supported by the 71st and 95th Foot, from where they were able to pour enfilade fire into the flank of the hapless French guardsmen.

By 7.50 p.m., it was all over; the French Guard had turned tail and was in full retreat. Apparently the cry of 'La Garde recule!' went up; this was reported as something no one present had ever heard before. The 52nd Foot, again in the centre of the action, led the vanguard of Adam's Brigade, supported by the Osnabrück battalion of Halkett's 3rd Hanoverian Brigade, in chasing the French to the south. Major Dorville described this last phase of the battle from the British heavy cavalry's perspective:

> [T]he heavy cavalry and the Royal Dragoons amongst the rest were for the most part reduced to a small number, so much so that several of the regiments were formed in an indiscriminate squadron; in front of them being some of the most distinguished officers of the different brigades. The heavy cavalry being, at that

period of the day so much reduced the light cavalry of Vandeleur and Vivian were brought forward and formed up with the heavy.[13]

According to Dorville, when Wellington ordered the advance, all that remained of the Household and Union brigades was just one squadron. The remnants of the British heavy cavalry were at that time stationed in a line some 300 yards below the crest of the ridge of Mont St Jean, and were about the same distance from the Brussels–Charleroi road. This squadron, with its handful of KDGs, joined in the Allied final charge in support of the infantry against the French, whose forces were by now falling into chaos and fleeing south on the Charleroi road. According to Captain Clark Kennedy of the Royals, this charge was a half-hearted affair:

> [W]e charged and were met half way. We were so tired that the shock was not that great and few were killed on both sides, after which we stood within 30 yards, firing our carbines at each other, both parties afraid to move for fear the infantry would give way.

Sadly, Captain Battersby KDG and his servant Thomas 'Trouser' Woodman, of Upton Grey in Hampshire, fell in this, their last charge of the day.[14] Woodman's father ran the Three Horseshoes pub in his home village and Thomas left a widow and five children.[15] Barlow described the scene thereafter:

> [O]ur small but courageous Squadron charged a body of Infantry but without any effect, about this time which was eight o'clock all the Prussians came up on our left[. W]hen the French retreated we followed them[;] it was an horrid sight to behold how many dead bodies covered the ground, the French especially.

All that stood firm against the Allied advance were four battalions of the French Old Guard, who made a stand just to the south of La Belle Alliance. The Imperial Guard's square was eventually split and they were slaughtered by the British 6th Cavalry Brigade.

Although he got his timings a little wrong, Lieutenant Hamilton of the Greys left a good description of the British heavy cavalry's last experiences of the battle:

> As it got dusk we could plainly perceive the flashes of the Prussian guns in the rear of the French army as we looked over it towards the left. This may give a tolerably good idea of the time at which the French retired: it was eight o'clock, and the victory to all appearances was then quite undecided … It was after nine o'clock at night when the French gave way, and our whole line advanced: we, as well as the first brigade of cavalry, were now such handfuls, that of course, we could do nothing, but followed slowly in the rear of the others.[16]

Just prior to the cessation of firing, Wellington and Uxbridge had been in the thick of it, rallying their men on to do further destruction. At this point, Uxbridge got hit by a cannon shot and exclaimed, 'By God I have lost my leg!' To which the Duke responded, 'By God, so you have!'

As the Prussians were relatively fresh in comparison to the other Allied troops, they were instructed to take up the pursuit of the French. Their dragoons slaughtered many of the French fugitives in their flight south. Some of the French made a last stand at Genappe, where 800 of them were destroyed. Napoleon, having sought refuge in one of his Guard's squares, realised that the battle was over and consequently fled south to Paris, escorted by the Red Lancers of the Imperial Guard.

Barlow had the last words on what the few remaining KDGs experienced that day, writing that, 'about ten o'clock we halted for the night when the Prussians and our Army gave many cheers'. This was when the one remaining squadron, which was all that was left of the two heavy brigades, was brought to a halt for the day in an area just south of La Belle Alliance. Their losses had been terrible, as Barlow mentioned in his letter, 'our two Brigades which before the action consisted of sixteen Squadrons were now removed to one Squadron and that only 32 files.'[17] So here the sixty-odd survivors, or around 3 per cent of the original compliment of the two heavy brigades[18], bivouacked on the spot where the Old Guard had made its last stand. This site is marked today by the Wounded Eagle Monument to the French Imperial Guard, which is located on the west side of the Charleroi road just south of La Belle Alliance. Here, the British survivors built camp fires from the wooden debris of battle and tried to cook some dirty lumps of fat using the cuirasses of the dead French cavalrymen.

RSM Barlow was one of the last of the KDG still present. It is still unclear exactly how many KDGs were left standing at the end of that momentous day. In Barlow's letter of 23 June 1815, he listed, 'two officers, myself 1 Sergeant and 9 men left in the field'. Eleven days later, on 4 July, he stated, 'the strength of the regiment that evening which was fifteen including officers'. However, the pitifully low number of KDGs remaining on the battlefield was not just a result of the rest of them having all been killed as, according to Barlow, 'the others were absent in consequence of their horses or themselves being wounded'.[19]

At the time of Waterloo, officers, sergeants, corporals and privates in the KDG ate separately; as they still do today in its descendant regiment, the QDG. However, as there were so few men left standing on the night of 18 June 1815, the KDGs all just mucked in and ate together. Ever since that evening, on every 18 June, war permitting, the officers and sergeants of the KDG, and now the QDG, have always dined together. This is an enduring regimental tradition. It had been a brutal day, and in one of his letters Barlow gave thanks to God that he had been saved in what he described as, 'one of the most dreadful battles that was ever fought, for twelve hours successively I was either exposed to the enemy's cannonading or charging the Enemy Cavalry who were clothed in steel armour'.[20] Altogether a pretty tough afternoon's work for the King's Dragoon Guards.

16

WATERLOO VI: AFTERMATH

To the more devout KDGs, the scenes that greeted them on the field of battle on 19 June were akin to a contemporary Armageddon. It had been such a day of carnage that the usual soldiers' questions on who had died from their regiment were replaced with who had lived. Corporal Stubbings described the aftermath:

> It is dreadfule to relate the seens I saw on the 18th. The field for miles around was covered with the wounded and slain and in some places my horse could not pass without trampling on them and I am sorry to inform you that Charles Stanley fell on that ever memorable day the 18th fiting manfully in the defence of his country.[1]

Derry stated simply, 'The Troop I belonged [to] told off in Nos. I was on left & last was No. 7. Thus me & my Horse Moses were saved.'[2] The fact that 8th Troop had been reduced to only seven men out of a troop that started the day with probably over sixty sabres underlined the devastation that was caused to the KDG on 18 June 1815.

However, straight after the battle, it did not seem that bad as only forty-three men were reported to have been killed. The KDG survivors knew they had lost Major John Bringhurst and Adjutant Thomas Shelver. Both men's bodies had been found close to the west gate of La Haye Sainte. Captain George Battersby was seen to die in the last charge of the day. Another forty of the regiment's rank and file had also had their deaths witnessed. So at first it appeared the death toll had not been that great. Fuller, the regiment's beloved commanding officer, was seen to have been severely wounded but alive, and was still missing. This was also the case for the rest of the officers of the right-hand squadron. These were Major Graham, Lieutenant Brooke and Cornet the Hon. Henry Bernard. The latter had been seen to have been severely wounded but was still alive. And there were a staggering 124 rank and file still unaccounted for. However, Barlow explained, 'the next morning many of our Brave Comrades joined us.'[3]

After a week had passed, more bodies had been found and pitifully few of the missing had rejoined the regiment. For the KDG survivors, the penny must have then dropped that most of their missing friends were actually dead.[4] The final reckoning was the largest sacrifice of all the British cavalry regiments at Waterloo. The official return of deaths was: seven officers, two sergeant-majors (along with Benwell, Tracy succumbed to his wounds in March 1816), eleven sergeants (in fact it was only ten, and may have been nine) and 109 (probably 110) privates, making a total of 129 all ranks. Tragically too, the number of KDG horses lost had been equally high, with 269 having been killed.[5] Around a quarter of the men who had charged with the KDG that day were to die. Of the official total of 129 deaths, ninety-nine had been killed and thirty had succumbed to their wounds. The regiment's casualties came to almost half of those of the Household Brigade and nearly a quarter of the total of both British heavy brigades together.[6]

In absolute terms, the total KDG casualties of 263 men were highest losses in the British heavy cavalry.[7] This size of the KDG's losses was understandable as it had fielded nearly twice as many sabres as the other regiments in its brigade and a third more men than in the regiments of the Union Brigade. In *The Digest*, Mann's account[8] and official returns, the KDG lost 129 men killed and 134 wounded. These numbers seemed to have been pretty accurate, but some soldiers' fates have been harder to pin down, so the figures may not be completely accurate.[9] Likewise, the number of wounded reported came down to subjective classification. If the men's records were to be used, there was a higher number of 191 KDG men wounded at Waterloo.[10] The KDG certainly had the worst mortality rate amongst the British heavy cavalry, in terms of the percentage of its casualties who had been killed at 52 per cent. The Greys were almost as high at 51 per cent and then the Royals at 46 per cent.[11] These statistics indicated the area in which the French were doing the most damage to the heavies, and it was that part of the battlefield where their lancers had been mopping up the dismounted and wounded dragoons.

In proportionate terms, the KDG had also been relatively hard hit. The KDG's casualty rate was 46 per cent, the third highest casualty rate in the British cavalry after the 2nd Life Guards and Inniskillings, which had casualty rates of 66 and 49 per cent respectively. In the British infantry, only the 1st Battalion of the 27th Foot and 73rd Foot had higher casualty rates, of 64 and 56 per cent respectively.[12] The historians who reported these statistics based the KDG casualty rate on a total regimental compliment of 595 men as having been present at Waterloo. However, the casualty rate was considerably higher if calculated on the total number who charged of around 540 men. On that basis, the KDG's casualty rate at Waterloo was over half of its fighting men.

One of the first publications that gave the British public some insight into what had happened on 18 June was *The Battle of Waterloo*, edited by John Booth and published just a few months after the battle. It was unequivocal as to what fate befell the four KDG officers who charged with the right squadron:

> Colonel Fuller of the 1st Dragoon Guards as also Major Graham and Cornet, Hon H.B. Bernard and another officer were taken prisoners in a desperate charge at the same time: for a long time their friends hoped they would return but though the particulars of their fate remains uncertain there can be no doubt that they were murdered by the enemy like many other brave unfortunate men.[13]

Hibbert echoed this accusation with bitterness in a letter written just over a month after the battle, 'None of our officers that were returned missing have as yet made their appearance; therefore there is no doubt that they were killed.'[14] Once Hibbert had realised the missing officers were dead, 18 June 1815 became a day to regret rather than to celebrate as he mourned, 'all our best and worthiest officers killed. It is very singular but really those officers who were the most respected and liked in the regiment are all killed; in fact the regiment will never be what it was.'[15] As tragic as the loss of the officers was, the fact that eighty-six more men had been killed than initially reported was awful and ensured the KDG topped the British cavalry's mortality tables.

The KDG suffered the highest amount of men missing as a regiment, with 128 unaccounted for. This number was around half of those missing in the Household Brigade. However, the 2nd Life Guards was also very hard hit, missing ninety-seven men, which was a higher proportion of its total sabres. The reason for this was probably that the left-hand KDG squadrons that charged to the east of La Haye Sainte with the 2nd Life Guards managed to penetrate the French lines and go further than the other squadrons in the heavy brigades. Private Joseph Lord of the 2nd Life Guards claimed in a letter home that he had got as far as 2 miles behind the French lines.[16] Many of the KDG who could no longer fight or gave themselves up were killed by the French after the first charge. Many historians consider 'murdered' to have been too strong a word to describe their fates fairly, and it will never be known what actually happened to these men. Suffice it to say that no one saw eighty-six of them being killed in action and they never returned to the Allied lines. It appeared that some who were taken prisoner died in captivity or were killed during the French retreat south.

Hibbert was convinced that many of the KDG prisoners were murdered during the French retreat:

What prisoners of our regiment were taken, we certainly believed to have been murdered in cold blood by the French on their retreat. A sergeant major of ours was taken prisoner at Waterloo and the other day he was discovered lying dead with his head split open, and about seven men of our regiment with him, in a small wood eight miles from this place. He was the fattest man in the regiment and we suppose he must have knocked up, for they used them shamefully, driving them on with their bayonets and giving them nothing to eat or drink the whole day. Added to this they stripped them of everything they had except their overalls and shirts, and some had nothing but [a] blanket to cover them. No wonder our poor fellow knocked up with this usage; we wonder how he got as far as he did, but he knew there was but one alternative and that when he gave in, he was to die.[17]

The poor sergeant-major was David Benwell of Kingsclere, who was the only KDG of his rank to have been returned dead in the fighting. The second TSM who was listed as killed was John Tracey, who died of his wounds some months after the battle. This murder of Benwell and the seven KDGs does not appear to have been an isolated incident, as borne out by other witnesses. One from the French side was Napoleon's ADC, Gourgaud, who recorded having seen a British dragoon being dragged out of a line of prisoners and bayoneted to death by a French infantry sergeant.[18]

Hibbert described one KDG officer's death to have taken place during this flight after the battle:

Young Bernard's body could not be found, but we know pretty well what became of him; he was taken prisoner after having been wounded and not being able to keep up with the French, they killed him on the road. They served a great many English Officers in the same way; their retreat was extremely rapid.[19]

However, some KDGs who died in captivity may have been killed by 'friendly fire' on the French retreat, as Hibbert also described: 'The Prussians kept up a continual fire on the retreating French and consequently killed as many English prisoners as French.'[20]

The hundred-odd wounded KDGs who had avoided being despatched by the lancers or taken prisoner, lay bleeding either in the relative comfort of Brussels, in the regimental medical aid station near Waterloo or, like Private Hasker, out on the battlefield. His account is the fullest we have for the night of 18 June and the following day by a KDG who had spent the evening in the fields north of La Belle Alliance:

The fighting went on with murderous effect until night when I heard the bugles sounding to march; and some dragoon regiment passed over the spot where I lay.

After that I saw some fires not far off, and endeavoured to rise, but staggered like
a drunken man, and soon fell. The dead and dying lay thick about me. Hearing
two men talking very near, I called them as well as I could to come and help me.
They said they could not for a while. Soon after this two foreigners passed by,
to whom I made signs; they came, and raising me up between them, took me
to one of the fires, and brought me a surgeon; they afterwards wrapped a cloak
about me, and left me there for the night.[21]

Hasker was lucky, as many a soldier from both sides was robbed and murdered
in the night by other soldiers, both French and Allied. In some cases it was the
locals looking for plunder. Hibbert recounted that the regiment could not help
its wounded that night:

The most melancholy thing is that no sooner were our poor men wounded than
the Belgic troops, who were without exception the greatest set of cowards and
rascals in the world, stripped them of everything but their shirts and left them
in this miserable way all night. Our officers were only known by the name on
the shirts; I daresay many died of cold in the night. Our brigade was so totally
cut up that a party could not be mustered that night to go over the ground and
consequently the wounded men and officers were left to shift for themselves.[22]

To most who had been left on the battlefield, 19 June was a relief. Those men who
had been used for prison escort duty and the less wounded were able to make it
back to where the remainder of the Household Cavalry Brigade had bivouacked by
the site of the last stand of the French Old Guard. As Barlow mentioned, 'the next
morning many of our Brave Comrades joined us'. However, if Hasker is anyone
to go by, many were left out on the battlefield for some time. At least Hasker, and
many others, made it to a makeshift dressing station by nightfall.

In his biography, Hasker described his day on 19 June:

The next day [19 June] I was kindly treated by some English soldiers, come to reinforce the army, and was laid, with many more on some straw near the road side. The
following morning several of my comrades were dead, and I prevailed on someone
to take the trousers off one of these, which I managed to put on. There was much
crying out for water, and some was brought. I requested to be allowed to taste but
finding there was blood in it, I could not drink. In the course of the day I saw two
or three wagons standing, and the wounded men getting upon them, I made an
effort, and succeeded in mounting one of these, and we rode on towards Brussels.[23]

The British Army medical services were not in the same league as the state-of-the-
art systems that the French Army had developed under barons Percy and Larrey.

However, there had been improvements with the army medical reforms brought about in 1806. Also, a commission in 1807 headed by James McGrigor had ameliorated the treatment of the wounded in the Peninsular War. At the time of Waterloo, all the medical staff each regiment would have been allocated was a regimental surgeon, who held a captain's rank, and two assistant-surgeons, who were ranked as lieutenants. The reforms had ensured these men were no longer glorified medical orderlies but were to be properly qualified. Notwithstanding the skills of the regimental surgeons, it was still a brutal time for the patient, with no antibiotics, pain killers or anaesthetics. Surgery conducted on or near the field of Waterloo was pretty rudimentary. The medical staff would have used sponges to clean the soldiers' wounds with water; employed bandages to dress and cover the wounds; and would have been equipped with a small bag of instruments with which to perform operations such as amputations where necessary. At that time there were not antiseptics, so sepsis was a great problem.

The main problem for the British wounded was not so much treatment, which was excellent given the contemporary state of medicine and the facilities available and conditions on the battlefield, but that there was no forward planning for casualty evacuation and triage at the battle. The poor process for the evacuation of the wounded led to many unnecessary deaths. This was because of the long time it took before the patient could have an operation, or the unsprung journey to the hospital that jolted many to their deaths. Hasker underlined this problem in the description he gave of his journey off the battlefield to Brussels: 'The stench of bodies was horrible. We stopped more than once, when some that had died from the shaking of the wagon were pulled off, and others who had travelled as far as they could on foot were taken up.'[24]

The wounds the KDGs suffered were from all manner of weapons. Most were injured by cannonballs and musket shot. They also suffered from the stabbing swords of the cuirassiers and the 9ft skewers of the lancers. One of the KDG troop commanders, Captain Wallace, remarked on, 'Many of our men having severe sabre wounds, particularly about the face'.[25] One of the contemporary experts on medical conditions at Waterloo, Mick Crumplin, released some noteworthy facts about the lance wounds experienced by the Greys, which would have pretty much corresponded to those experienced by the KDG. Of the twenty-nine dragoons who had been injured, forty-eight (62 per cent) of their wounds were from the lance, but of these less than a third had been body strikes – these French lancers were not, therefore, particularly accurate.

This was backed up by Lieutenant Wyndham of the Greys, who wrote, 'At Brussels some weeks afterwards, I found many of our men with 10 or 12 lance wounds in them, and one man, Lock, had 17 or 18 about his person, and lived afterwards to tell the story.'[26] This underpinned the view that many KDGs did not die from a swift *coup de grâce* but suffered the pain of a slow death caused by many inept jabs of the lance. Crumplin also mentioned another source of wounds that many historians have forgotten to mention, which were riding injuries. Seven out of twenty-nine of the Scots Greys soldiers' injuries were from severe bruising from falls from their horses. According to many of the KDGs' discharge papers, they were damaged with hernias and contortions from falls from their horses when their mounts were blasted from beneath them by the French artillery and musketry.

So, in all probability, the majority of KDG deaths were either outright from the musket and cannon of the French, or once dismounted by their lancers, who left few alive. The suddenness of death in the former case was likely to have been preferable to the longer drawn-out experience of being cornered, suffering multiple lance wounds and then passing away slowly, in most instances through the huge loss of blood.

The KDG was lucky to have the very experienced John Going as its regimental surgeon at Waterloo. He was helped in his herculean task of tending to over 100 wounded by his two assistant-surgeons, William Macauley and Richard Pearson. These men must have had a terrible time at, and for days after, the Battle of Waterloo. No statements made by the KDG's medical staff have yet been discovered, so we have to get an idea of what they went through by the writings of their peers in the other Household Brigade regiments. David Slow, a surgeon-major in the Blues, was still hard at it operating on his men three days after the battle, when he wrote on 21 June that he had not taken off his clothes since the battle and did not know how to stay awake.[27] However, it must be remembered that Going, with the same amount of surgeons as Slow, had to deal with at least one-and-a-half times the number of wounded. So the KDG surgeons must have been extremely stretched and should be remembered for their achievement.

The standard operating procedure would be for the senior assistant-surgeon to go into the field with his orderlies to tend to the wounded and retrieve them to the regimental aid post behind the front line. However, at Waterloo, given the proximity of the enemy and the density of the fighting, this was impossible to do. So the men simply had to wait until the next or the following days to be recovered. For those who were fortunate enough to make it back to the regimental surgeons, there was a good chance of survival. In the case of the KDG, it was Going and Pearson who operated on their men just behind the front line, whilst Macauley was back in Brussels receiving the regiment's wounded. Naylor mentioned in his diary that from Monday 19 June until Sunday 2 July he had been in command of the depot of wounded.[28] This meant the regiment probably had the foresight to have established facilities for its wounded in the Belgian capital before the battle.

We do not know where Going and Pearson operated, but it was more than likely to have been in or around the farm of Mont St Jean, as this was where several of the other regiments in its brigade had their regimental aid posts. George Steed, the Royals' surgeon, recorded that he was based in the farm of Mont St Jean. However,

David Slow, the Blues's surgeon, did not have it so good as he had to borrow a tent in which to operate and many soldiers had to remain outside, where most of his wounded were laid on horse cloths in a wheat field.

Going and his staff clearly did an excellent job on the basis of the KDG's survival rates. Assistant-Surgeon John Haddy James of the 1st Life Guards achieved a 76 per cent survival rate, having lost eleven out of forty-five wounded. Going did a little better, with a 78 per cent survival rate, as of the 134 men injured, only thirty KDGs eventually died of their wounds. The 2nd Life Guards's surgeon, Samuel Broughton, however, managed a 94 per cent survival rate, losing only four out of sixty-three men wounded.[29] As discussed, Going's achievement was all the more impressive given that he had to deal with over twice as many wounded, with the same amount of senior medical staff, as Broughton and the other cavalry surgeons would have faced. These survival statistics only applied to the soldiers who were retrieved, as many soldiers must have died on the battlefield due to exposure, loss of blood or to the murdering thieves of several nations who roamed the area, killing any wounded who resisted their attempts to rob.

The problem for the wounded KDG and others in the heavy cavalry at Waterloo was that their regiments were just too thin on the ground to go out and collect their wounded on 19 June. Also, the soldiers were left to fend for themselves as their regiments simply did not have time to hang around and look for their wounded. They had to press on the heels of the fleeing French, who were heading towards Paris. So it was down to fate whether many of the wounded KDGs, like Hasker, were helped in time before they died. Even then, those who were retrieved would have been slung on to one of the overflowing medical carts that made their way the 12 or so bone-bruising miles to Brussels.

Notwithstanding the general air of panic, many Bruxelloise were reported as having turned out to help tend the Allied and French wounded in the several hospitals set up in the city. As a result of the massive influx of wounded, there was a lack of capacity to house the victims, so many were placed on straw out on the city's streets. The KDG wounded were first taken to Brussels, where about half remained, and in due course the other half were paid for by the regiment to return to England. Those who were sent home appear to have been sent to three of the KDG's former regimental locations, at Northampton, Leicester and Warwick. A few of the overflow seem to have been sent on to Antwerp.[30] Naylor's diary recorded that the KDG officers were nursed in the comfort of some of Brussels's hotels. Naylor himself was nursed at L'Hôtel Grand Mirror, whilst Turner, Sweny and Irvine were tended to at L'Hôtel de la Coronne d'Espagne. Naylor wrote in his diary of, 'Sweney who arrived on 20 June having been made a prisoner as well as Irvine who escaped on the retreat of the French'.

Notwithstanding the tragedy of the day before, one of the things that preoccupied the officers on 19 June was the loss of their baggage. This event was mentioned by Hibbert, Barlow and Somerset. The latter wrote, 'I have been obliged to bivouac for two or three nights being without any baggage, and without anything to eat.'[31] However, Elton referred to the matter as 'trifling'. On a happier note, Corporal Stubbings got promoted in the field to sergeant, as he wrote to his parents:

> I take the first opportunity that lays in my Power of informing you that I ham in good health after the sharp engagement Which took place on 18th June and Dear father it is a wonder that I escaped without receiving any injury for whee was very much exposed to danger on both the 17th and 18th and a most dreadfule battle indeed and ham sorry to say our Regiment Suffered severely killed and wounded but thanks be to god who spared my life I came out of the field unhurt and I was in the hotest part of it and I Gained Great Praise for my Good and Coregous Beaver in the field and in consequence of wich I Ham Maid Sergeant. It is dreadfule to relate the seens I saw on the 18th.[32]

This was a pyrrhic victory for the KDG, as Barlow wrote, 'I often shed tears for the loss of my Brave Comrades, I could never imagine that men could fight as they did, they seem to have the strength and courage of lions rather than of men.'[33] Although Napoleon, the Corsican phoenix, had been defeated, he was still not yet destroyed. The British Army and her allies had to pursue Napoleon and the remnants of his army to Paris, occupy the French capital and exact terms for an enduring peace thereafter. The KDG then did as Fuller had bade them at the beginning of the first charge – they went 'On to Paris!'

17

'ON TO PARIS!': THE PURSUIT AND OCCUPATION

There was not to be any sort of celebration or chance to recover after this epic battle. The Allies had won the battle but not the war. It would be another exhausting nineteen days of pursuit before the KDG and the other British soldiers were to finally defeat the French. Wellington and the other Allied commanders knew that Napoleon could not be allowed to regroup, collect more men and materials in order to continue the conflict. They had all had enough of his reappearing tricks, and were determined to destroy his armies and capture and secure the scourge of Europe for good. So, early on the morning after the battle, Wellington sent his staff officers to the Allied divisional and brigade commanders to task them to pursue the French, who were currently being harried by the Prussians.

The remaining handful of KDGs were given a few hours' respite in their rough bivouacs south of La Belle Alliance. One of the few men still standing from the night before, RSM Barlow, recorded that, 'the next morning [after the battle] many of our Brave Comrades joined us'.[1] The KDG survivors had not eaten properly for three days, were mentally and physically shattered, and in many cases were still wounded. However, they did not rest for long, as that same day they were told to join the rest of their brigade in the pursuit of the French. On 19 June, they headed south-west and marched for 7 miles to Nivelles. Here they bivouacked for the night, as their tents had been lost along with their baggage on 18 June.

The march to Paris: the Allied armies' routes to the French capital. (Gareth Glover)

On 20 June, the regiment moved on from Nivelles to Valenciennes near Malplaquet, the site where the KDG had won one of its eighteenth-century battle honours. *The Digest* recorded that, 'Various small parties which had been separated from the regiment rejoined this day.'[2] Hibbert, who had caught up with the KDG 'a few miles from Genappe', recalled, 'The worst part of the business is not getting anything to eat, the Prussians having plundered all the villages before us.'[3] Later, when Hibbert had arrived in Paris, he explained the motive behind the Prussians' behaviour to his father: 'The hatred that exists between the two nations is astonishing; the French shudder at the very name of the Prussian, who plunder and burn wherever they go, and spare nothing. This retaliation is perfectly just, for the French committed much more atrocious when they were in Prussia.'[4]

Hibbert went on to bemoan the loss of their tents, but he was taking it all in his stride:

[W]e have been under going the greatest hardship since I wrote last. We march for twenty to thirty miles every day, up always at three o'clock and sleep all night in the fields, for we lost all out tents and most part of our baggage. I have done this now for some time and feel no inconvenience from it.[5]

Hibbert also confessed in his letter that he had not washed or changed his clothes since leaving Dendeleur a week before and that the KDG was by now a shabby bunch, but the regiment's halt at Valenciennes was its first proper break.

One of Hibbert's letters home gave a detailed description of the KDG's pursuit up to this point:

When we arrived near Valenciennes, we halted two days; the first day I dedicated entirely to sleep, the second I washed and made myself look as decent as possible, but I was a sorry figure after all my pains. You may conceive a person with a shirt of a weeks wearing on, a dirty brown handkerchief, for I cannot call it black, overall torn in eleven places, a jacket any colour but red, and to crown it all a beard that hung down to the breast, and a helmet without a tail. This was the costume of most of our officers. These two days we had a barn to lie in – a great luxury. It was the first we had had from the time we set out, for so great was the army in pursuit of the French that it was impossible to find quarters for them. The cavalry fared worse than the infantry for their baggage and tents could not keep up with them, therefore we were always obliged to bivouac excepting the instance which I mentioned.

In the same letter, Hibbert continued to describe that the weather had been kind but rations were still sparse and their daily routine tough:

All this time we had nothing to eat but biscuit and sometimes a bit of miserable cow that had been driven by dint of whip twenty six miles a day; the worst part of the business was that we could not get good water. We always marched about three in the morning or thereabouts and got to our bivouac about five, sometimes sooner.[6]

The following day, they arrived at Le Cateau-Cambrésis,[7] and by 22 June they had reached Le Forêt just north of Beaumont, some 4 miles from the French frontier. On 23 June, the King of France passed in front of them in the pursuit of Napoleon's men towards Paris.[8] In the next five days, they averaged 15 miles a day in their 76-mile march to Guyencourt, just to the north-west of Rheims, where they bivouacked on the night of 27 June. They then marched for another five days the 75 miles to the Château de Roissy, which they reached on 2 July. Hibbert described the weather at this point as having been extremely hot and thus he did not find life too unpleasant. Barlow described this stage of their march in detail and highlighted that the regiment's depleted ranks had been swelled by the return of some of the missing and wounded:

[W]e can now muster two Squadrons 40 file each so that our numbers are reduced one half – we have been advancing into France and are now within 14 miles of Paris, on the road to this place we found all the towns and villages deserted by the inhabitants and the houses plundered by the Prussians.[9]

The regiment was fortunate in that what fighting had been taking place was over before they closed with the French. The Prussians had defeated the French at Issy on the outskirts of Paris, and on 3 July the Prussian General von Ziethen's terms had been accepted by Davout, the Bonapartist marshal in charge of the defence of Paris. The main Prussian ultimatum was for the French to leave their defensive positions around the capital and to commence an armistice on the following day. As part of this agreement, the French had to move their army south of the River Loire and were not to station any troops in Paris. *The Digest* entry for 8 July quoted Wellington's proclamation which announced the French capitulation, and added that the Duke, 'congratulates the army upon this result of their glorious victory. He desires that the Troops may employ the leisure of this day and tomorrow, to clean their arms, clothes, and appointments, as it is his intention they should pass him in review.'[10]

After a couple of days' halt at Roissy, the KDG had made an early start and marched at 4 a.m. into the Paris suburb of Nanterre, crossing the River Seine at Argenteuil by way of a pontoon bridge. On 8 July, the regiment arrived at Rueil, or what is now Rueil-Malmaison, which the KDG commentators in their accounts have confusingly spelled in many different ways. Here the KDG found quarters which were to be its base for its occupation of the city. The KDG was clearly in a Household Brigade location, as Mercer recorded: 'The Life Guards, Blues &c., are at Nanterre, Rueil &c., hussars at Suresne & Puteaux &c.'[11] According to *The Digest*,[12] the General Headquarters was at Gonesse, which was some 15 miles to the north-east on the other side of the Seine.

Around this time, Naylor, who had remained in Brussels for twelve days after the battle in charge of the depot for the wounded, rejoined the regiment. He had made the journey with another KDG officer, Captain George Fairholme, whom Naylor reported was formerly in Fuller's troop but did not take part in the Battle of Waterloo with the regiment. They had travelled together from Mons and had taken various forms of transport to reach Paris. Naylor, like Hibbert, commented on the animosity felt by the Prussians towards the French, having described that, 'All the villages from Noyen were entirely deserted, having been pillaged by the Prussians, who had marched on that route. Windows broken, doors forced open, furniture destroyed – nothing but misery.'[13]

Notwithstanding the armistice, the soldiers still feared that they might have to fight again, as Hibbert described to his father in a letter dated 26 July 1815 how he expected:

… now to march every day to the Loire to subdue the remains of the Bony's army, who swear they won't give up. We have heard of Bony's capture long ago; we have not heard of it officially but it is generally supposed to be true. There certainly will be another battle, at least so it is asserted.[14]

Yet the KDG managed to shrug off these fears and, once ensconced in quarters in Rueil, life went from the ridiculous to the sublime, as Hibbert explained:

The weather is extremely hot and therefore we travel in cabriolets when we go to Paris, Versailles, St Cloud etc. for I have made it a point to see all these places, and likewise everything worth seeing in them. We are now in the height of luxury – nothing to do but eat, drink and sleep, pleasures [to] which we have long been strangers.[15]

In comparison to the privations, dangers and hard work of the previous couple of months, life for the KDG in occupied Paris was indeed a six-month holiday. Apart from the main events like parades, it seemed that there was not a strict routine, but generally there was a weekly morning parade, which fell on different days of the week. There were also church parades on most Sundays, and these seemed to escalate in frequency in September after the new commanding officer, Teesdale, had taken over. There were also mounted marching parades in July, and again in January, February and April 1816. Watering parades only appeared to have taken place once a month. Lord Edward Somerset held brigade field days every nine days or so in August and September, but these stopped in November. It is not known if the rank and file were housed in the former barracks of the Swiss Guard in Rueil, but the officers and senior NCOs were spread around in quarters, as Barlow wrote home on 11 July, 'I am now in country quarters and in a very genteel house with a very pleasant family.'[16]

On the evidence of Naylor's diary, not a lot of work was conducted by the regiment during its occupation of Paris. Naylor was diligent in writing to the next-of-kin of the officers who had died at Waterloo. Presumably this was his responsibility as the senior officer present, as Turner was still wounded and colonels Acklom and Teesdale had not yet arrived. Amongst those to whom Naylor wrote was General Fuller, probably the late commanding officer's closest sibling as he had appointed him as his executor over his two other brothers. Naylor also wrote to Battersby's brother, who was a captain in the Royal Navy. As well as the next of kin, Naylor wrote variously to the colonel of the regiment, Sir David Dundas, the regimental agent, Adair and the badly wounded officers who were still absent from the regiment, captains Turner and Sweny.

To judge by Naylor's diary, there was a lot of free time. He appeared to spend most of his spare hours sightseeing. Amongst the Parisian attractions he visited were the Jardins des Plantes, the Tuilleries, Montmatre, Les Invalides and the Catacombs. Naylor also visited a porcelain factory and the water works at Versailles. He even took a bizarre fascination in viewing 'the hemaphrodite' [sic], about whom he went into great detail describing this person's genitalia, bodily functions and desires. He recorded having visited this curiosity on more than one occasion. Other activities included riding his horses to Versailles and Saint Cloud, and dining, playing billiards and cards with his friends. He also mentioned his shopping trips, and amongst other purchases he bought a round and a cocked hat and silk for a waistcoat and breeches. He also bought himself *Napoleon's Campaigns in Italy* for his homework, snuffboxes and a gold chain.

Hibbert was less adventurous in exploring Paris, but managed a visit to the Louvre, which he described as:

[N]o longer worth a person going to see; the Allies have dismantled it terribly. The Venus de Medicis and the Apollo with many of the principal statues are on their return to their native countries; there are very few pictures left, however I saw it in its prime four days after the capitulation.[17]

One reason for Hibbert's lack of a sense of cultural adventure may have been that from his letters home he appeared to have been more of a countryman, having been raised in rural Cheshire, than the Londoner Naylor, and was clearly tiring of Paris. He had not been in the city a month when he wrote, 'I have seen everything in Paris worth seeing and have now devoted my time principally to shooting. The game is in great quantities here; I killed six brace and a half of partridges in less than two hours the other day.' So he might have taken to drowning his sorrows, as he described: 'Many of our officers have been ill; fevers are very common owing to the men eating quantities of grapes and drinking bad wine, for they can get claret of inferior quality here for five pence a bottle.'

Barlow had also had enough of Paris after just a few weeks: 'I am quite tired of France[.] I don't like the people nor their manner, [but] the country is certainly very beautiful and abounds with fruit and the climate is very warm.' The main reason for Barlow's weariness with Paris was that he was missing his wife Betsy, as he made it clear that if she were with him, things would have been just fine in France. Part of his disquiet was also that he was bored:

> I yesterday went to Paris to bring home some books to read as I have so much spare time and have no wish to associate in the gay exile as my situation nor incli-nation do not require it. I pass most of my time when not engaged regimentally in either reading, writing or walking with Mr Brown.[18]

Mr Brown was the quartermaster who had gained his commission by coming through the ranks. He was one of the oldest soldiers who had served the longest, and unusually for the KDG, he was a Scot. Barlow, like Naylor, enjoyed shopping, having bought, 'a blue Great Coat, two pair of Grey Pantaloons, a pair of short boots'. However, some of the racier outlets offended his Methodist sensibilities, as he remarked on some of the Parisian shops which were, 'very handsomely set out with good drawings but some of them rather offensive to a delicate mind. I judge from that, that their morals are greatly confused. Paris seems to be a place of dissipation.'[19]

However, there were some events that concerned the KDG during its six-month posting to Paris that were worth recording. The most significant event for the men's futures took place on their arrival in Paris. The Prince Regent, delighted with Wellington's victory, had decreed that those who had fought at Waterloo were to be given, the title of 'Waterloo Man', so that henceforth he should be recognised and respected in British society for his actions at the battle. More importantly for the soldiers, the Prince Regent added that, 'every "Waterloo Man" shall be allowed to count two years' service in virtue of that victory, in reckoning his services for increase of pay, or for pension when discharged'.[20] On 29 July, a War Office order confirmed this royal command.[21]

The other significant events of that month were parades. Just a few days after its arrival on 10 July, the regiment provided a squadron to attend to the Emperor of Austria and the King of Prussia. Then, just over a week later, a new commanding officer, Robert Acklom, arrived to take over from Naylor. On 22 July, the Household

Brigade was inspected by Somerset, ahead of a royal review of the British Army. This parade, according to Naylor, comprised 60,000 men and was attended by the Emperor of Austria, the King of Prussia, Marshal Blücher and Wellington in the 'Camp Elysie', or Champs-Élysées.[22] Naylor only reported one patrol in Paris, which he carried out with Captain Stirling and the Life Guards on 31 July.

August was a little less busy, and on the twelfth of that month, Brevet Lieutenant-Colonel Teesdale arrived to take command of the regiment. There was another inspection of the regiment, this time by Lord Combermere, on 15 August. During this period, missing and hospitalised KDG soldiers returned to the regiment in dribs and drabs; one significant arrival was TSM Wright, who had been imprisoned by the French for two months and reappeared on 22 August. August ended with the sale of the late John Bringhurst's chargers and an officers' dance at Rueil. There was yet another review at the beginning of September. This commenced at 4 a.m., where the KDG and the rest of the Household Brigade were reviewed, along with Lieutenant-General Beresford's brigade, which took place on the road to Saint Denis and was taken by the Emperor of Austria, the King of Prussia and Wellington. The pomp of this occasion had not made much of an impression on Naylor, who just complained in his diary that it had been a dusty day.

Around this time, the commanding officer's wife and son also arrived, along with Captain Wallace's wife. The appearance of officers' wives could have added to the discomfort felt by the other ranks, like Barlow and Page, who desperately wanted to get their wives out. The latter was later to describe how hard life was without his family in a letter written in January 1816:

My wife has not joined me yet, nor cannot do till I can get her a passport. She came as far as Dover, but was obliged to return, no more soldiers' wives being allowed to come over; the Duke of Wellington will allow only six to every hundred men. I am so fond of being in the Army in some respects that I should be sorry to leave it; my situation is it is a respectable one, but you see what troubles I am exposed to. No-one knows the soldier's troubles, fatigues and dangers but themselves. In regard to my wife and family, I could support them in a very comfortable manner, but cannot get them to me, but have to support them to so much disadvantage where the necessaries of life are so very dear to what they are in France.[23]

There was yet another royal review on 22 September, when the British and Hanoverian armies of 45,000 men were reviewed by the Emperor of Austria and Wellington. This show of strength was understandable, given the situation at the time did not appear to be that stable in Paris after four months of occupation, as Hibbert wrote on 25 October:

We all expect a devil of a kick-up soon, but if such a thing should happen, Paris will be burnt to a certainty; everybody says that this will be the end of that city, and very shortly. There have been very great disturbances lately. Every evening there is a crowd under poor Louis's window at the Tuilleries, and 'Vive l'Empereur!' sung out under his very nose … I believe if the Allies were to leave Paris, he would be murdered immediately, and if Bony was to make his appearance there is not a man who would not side with him, and really no wonder.[24]

Barlow made a similar observation: 'I don't think any force can make them forget Bonaparte, or rather erase from their minds the love they have for him[.] I don't think they are very fond of their present King.'[25]

Little happened in October, apart from the regiment sending three troops to Marly and two troops to Louveciennes. November and December were also relatively uneventful months. According to *The Digest*, a General Order Paris was issued on 29 November. This was Wellington's announcement that he was breaking up his army, in which he stated, 'The Field Marshall returns his thanks for their uniform good conduct. Whatever may be the destination of those brave Troops of which the Field Marshall now takes his leave.'[26] At this point Hibbert moaned that the KDG was being left behind:

Many dragoon regiments have received orders for marching homewards, among others the Life Guards and Blues, and where do you think they are going to send our miserable remains – to a village called Catoff [Cateau], on the frontier between Flanders and France, where it is likely we may remain some years.[27]

Yet only a month later, rumours were circulating that the KDG was to leave Paris, as Sergeant John Adams wrote to his mother on 17 January 1816:

Deare Mother you may expect to see me in a very short time as the armey is all coming home as sone as the National debt of France is paid, which will be in the month of March or April at the furtherest we can expect; you may expect us in England in the month of June at the furtherest.[28]

Hibbert and Barlow had had enough. Barlow simply wanted to get back to Betsy, for whom he pined. Hibbert felt foreign service was like being back at school and was incensed that Wellington had banned shooting. He and Hawley had tried and failed to get sent home on sick leave. Interestingly, they had been tripped up in their attempt by the Duke himself, as Hibbert wrote: 'Afterwards our colonel sent us two letters from the Adjutant General, in which we found that Lord Wellington had granted us each a month's leave, but where to? To St Denis.'[29]

Yet not all the KDG were having a miserable time. Adams was content, 'But now I am happy to inform you that we are in a paseful cunttrey and pervisions is very cheap all throw france, wine at 4 frs a bottle everything cheap in like manner … I have a very good reservation and like the armey varey well.'[30] The instruction to return home to England was finally given on 13 January 1816 by Deputy Quartermaster-General Sir Charles Broke.[31] Just before they left, the KDG's establishment was reduced by the staff at Horse Guards from twelve to eleven troops. The regiment left Rueil on 14 January on its march to Aix-le-Château in the Pas-de-Calais. This was to be to a holding area near the Channel ports prior to shipping the regiment home to England. Its route took it via Luzarches, Clermont, Breteuil, Amiens and Doullens. Regimental headquarters was located at Aix-le-Château on 4 February, and the rest of the regiment was stationed in cantonments in the surrounding villages.

A month after the regiment's arrival at Aix-le-Château, it was inspected by Lord Edward Somerset.[32] At the end of March, the regimental establishment was reduced yet again, from eleven to ten troops. The troop to be disbanded this time was the one commanded by Captain the Hon. William Bernard. The KDG then relocated to the area of Frevent. On 30 April, the men were awarded their Waterloo medals and were inspected a few days later by Lord Combermere. On 3 May they embarked for England on troop transport ships at Calais and eventually reached Dover on 7 May, their epic odyssey completed after almost a year on the Continent. On 18 May, the KDG was reviewed on Hounslow Heath by the Duke of York, and it was back to home duties once more.

FATES AND FORTUNES
OF SURVIVORS I:
THE OFFICERS

The KDG officers who survived the charge at Waterloo stayed on in the regiment for an average of around another seven years after 1815. Eight of those who had been present at Waterloo had left by 1821.[1] They left for a number of reasons, but the first batch to go were those who had been placed on half-pay, which was effectively a pension for those officers who had been made redundant. Their reduction was part of army-wide cuts for officers and soldiers now that a lasting European peace looked secure from 1816 onwards. The first two officers to leave the KDG were Lieutenant Thomas Middleton and Cornet William Huntley, who were both put on half-pay just after the regiment's return to England in July 1816. From the evidence of his having been cited in an Irish court case in 1839, Middleton appeared to have ended up in Ireland. Huntley managed to rejoin the army, having been put on half-pay after he had been promoted to captain, and subsequently joined the 9th Dragoons in 1818. He transferred to the 3rd Dragoon Guards in 1832 and ended up as a major. He married but did not have children, and appeared to have retired to Gloucestershire.[2]

Another officer to have left the KDG in 1816 was Assistant-Surgeon William Macauley. He left the regiment to get married and take his MD degree at Edinburgh University. He was followed by William D'Arcy Irvine, who retired, fairly soon after the regiment's return to England, in January 1817. He was only 24 years old and it appears that he had not joined the army as a career, but for a short stint prior to taking over his father's estate at Castle Irvine near Enniskillen in County Fermanagh. On his return to Northern Ireland, he married Maria Brooke, daughter of Sir Henry Brooke of Colebrooke. She was the sister of Francis, who had been in the KDG, and who sadly would not witness his sister marry his brother officer, having been killed at Waterloo. D'Arcy Irvine lived to the age of 64, dying in 1857. After Irvine, Regimental Surgeon Going left the regiment, having been put on half-pay in 1817.

The next officer to leave was William Stirling, who was put on half-pay in 1818. He did not hang around and seek re-employment, as he was rich and thus did not need the army for an income. He was from a wealthy aristocratic Scottish family and seems to have married well. On leaving the army, he had inherited his mother's Stuart family estate of Castlemilk, where he died at the young age of 36 in 1825. Robert Hawley was put on half-pay the following year in 1819. He quickly managed to be re-employed in the army, having found a job in the infantry the same year. He exchanged his commission with Lieutenant Dickens of the 14th Foot and 'received the difference'.[3] Presumably Hawley would have made some money out of this transaction, as a commission in the KDG was worth more than one in a line infantry regiment. He then appears to have moved around a number of infantry regiments before retiring as a captain in 1838. He lived to be one of the oldest Waterloo veterans, dying in Southampton in 1888 at the age of 93.

The eighth and last of these early leavers who had gone by the end of 1820 was James Naylor, the second most senior Waterloo survivor. In 1816, he was awarded the rank of brevet major for his actions at Waterloo by the Prince Regent. Little is known about Naylor after he finished writing his diaries, but he retired from the KDG as a brevet major in 1820. He returned to his native London, married and settled down in a house on Sloane Street, Chelsea. He had joined the regiment late, having first done a stint in the infantry, and was 54 when he resigned. This would have been a reasonable age to have called it a day. Naylor reached a good age and died aged 88, and was buried in the then fashionable London civil cemetery of Kensall Green.

Two more of the junior officers left in 1821. They were Lieutenant John Hibbert and Cornet Jonas Greaves, who changed his name to Elmsall. Hibbert, the useful contributor to KDG history through his letters, made it to captain in 1820 but left the regiment on half-pay the following year. He did not finally retire from the army until 1848, as a brevet major. In 1833, he married Jane Alexander and lived at Chalfont Park in Buckinghamshire, of which county he became high sheriff in 1837. Although he was a third son, he came from a very wealthy family that had made its money in Jamaica. He clearly lived comfortably, as the 1881 census reported him to have had fifteen staff. He lived to a very old age, dying at 90 in 1886. Jonas Greaves changed his name to Elmsall in 1817 and, like Hibbert, was promoted to captain in 1820. He left the KDG that year on half-pay and subsequently married Hannah Lawson in 1824. He stayed on the Army List until he died with the rank of major in 1851.

Interestingly, the two most severely wounded officers, Turner and Sweny, did not leave until after this first batch, moving on in the 1820s. The first of this pair to go was Michael Turner, who retired in 1823. Turner too had been awarded his brevet majority by the Prince Regent for his record at Waterloo. Remarkably, he had managed to soldier on another eight years in the army after Waterloo, even though he did not have the full use of his left hand, as his entry in the 1821 edition of *The List of Pensioners* described:

> He was twice wounded very severely in his left arm by the splinter of a shell which has deprived him in great measure of the use of his hand and arm and for which he receives a pension of £200 per annum. The other wound was from round shot, which grazed the fleshly part of his thigh, and carried off a considerable surface of the skin but without material injury.

Notwithstanding his serious injuries, Turner got on with life. In under a year after his return from France he got married. His wife was a vicar's daughter who came from around the corner from his home, Stoke Hall, near Ipswich in Suffolk. They went on to have four children, but his was not a happy ending as his 'beloved' wife Susannah died aged only 38 in 1832. Turner was left to bring up their children, then aged from 7 to 14. He subsequently moved out of Stoke Hall to live in Westgate Street, Ipswich. There he lived to a ripe old age of 89.

Lieutenant Edward Hamill was the next to have left in 1822 when he transferred into the 2nd West India Regiment, into which he was promoted to captain by purchase. He then exchanged the following year into the 66th Regiment of Foot, in which he served for four years before being retired as a captain on half-pay in 1827. He then faded into obscurity.

There must have been some cuts in the army in 1825, as four captains were put on half-pay that year. The most senior of these was another officer who had been badly wounded, John Sweny, whose wounds were not deemed as debilitating as Turner's, as his annual pension was half his brother officer's at £100 a year. Sweny had purchased Turner's majority when he retired in 1823. On leaving the regiment, Sweny promptly married Eliza Longden and they went on to have six children. In 1827, he joined the 2nd Ceylon Regiment as a major on half-pay and then retired to France. At the time of his death in 1841, aged around 63, Sweny was living near Finistère in Brittany. He was still on the Army List on his death. When he died, his naval officer brother Mark went over to France to bring back Eliza and her six children to London, where they lived with him.

The last of the Waterloo squadron captains, William Elton, also left in 1825. He, like Naylor and Turner, had been promoted to brevet major on 7 September 1815 by the Prince Regent as a reward for his actions at Waterloo. It seems that all the KDG squadron commanders who survived the battle were rewarded equally in this way for the regiment's performance at Waterloo. Elton was put on half-pay as a lieutenant-colonel on 5 November 1825. He died on 15 November 1847, aged 62. He was described as having served in the KDG all his life. He never married but had a son by a Mary Fuller. He ended up living at Mornington Place, St Pancras, near Regent's Park in London, where he died and was buried at All Souls, Kensal Green. *The Annals of the Elton Family* gave him a brief mention: 'He had a narrow escape at Waterloo when he was nearly cut down by French cuirassiers after his horse was shot from under him and his regiment scattered.' Captain James Leatham also left on half-pay in 1825. Apart from having had a fine portrait painted of him in KDG uniform with his Waterloo medal back to front, little is known of him after he left the regiment. He retired as a lieutenant-colonel in 1860, so must have lived to a reasonable age.

Another captain to have left in 1825 was Ralph Babington. He had taken time off in 1823 to become high sheriff of his home county of Donegal, where his family had its seat at Greenfort. Tragically, he died aged 35 of apoplexy in the same week as he was due to have been married. The younger Quicke, George, was the most junior officer to have left on half-pay in 1825. He then transferred on purchase to gain his captaincy in the infantry as an unattached officer. He, like Babington, died young and unmarried, having passed away in Southsea in 1838. George Quicke's elder brother, Thomas, was discharged on half-pay in 1827 as a captain. He had married Sophia Evered in 1823 and they had one son, Nutcombe. George ended his days in Bath, dying at the young age of 37.

Robert Wallace left a year later than Thomas Quicke, as a lieutenant-colonel on half-pay. Wallace, like Quicke a troop captain at Waterloo, had been promoted to major and then lieutenant-colonel in 1828, whereas Quicke senior had the same rank on leaving the regiment as he had held at Waterloo. Wallace was the fourth of the officers to have received an award for Waterloo, having been made a Knight of the Third Class of the Royal Hanoverian Guelphic Order. In 1834, he was living in York as an unattached lieutenant-colonel.[4] He died in 1863, aged 73, and was buried in the cemetery of Christchurch in Worthing. Assistant-Surgeon Richard Pearson was the next to go, leaving the regiment in 1830. He had left the KDG on a sabbatical to study medicine at Glasgow University, where he got his MD in 1828. He returned to the KDG for a couple of years before he was promoted to be surgeon of the 87th Foot. He remained in that regiment until he retired from the army on half-pay in 1847.

The old Scottish war horse John Brown, the quartermaster, achieved an impressive forty-five years with the regiment. He was put on half-pay and retired in 1838. He lived on for another thirteen years and died in 1851. The prize for the 'Waterloo man' amongst the officers who lasted the longest in the KDG after the battle was Thomas Brander, who beat Brown by one year, leaving the regiment in 1839. Brander was still a lieutenant, aged 45, that year when he transferred to the

15th Light Dragoons and was at last promoted to the rank of captain. He remained one year in his new regiment before retiring on half-pay in 1840. He was still collecting his half-pay in 1853, aged 58, and died aged 66 at Somerford Grange near Christchurch in 1861.

Little is known of what happened to the officers' widows and orphans. The commanding officer, William Fuller, was married and his wife was probably well provided for. This can be supposed as she was the sole-beneficiary of a man who came from a wealthy banking family. There is also no evidence to suggest that she had needed the widow's pension, as had the widows of the second-in-command, Henry Graham, and the 5th Troop captain, John Bringhurst. Maria Graham received £100 per annum, as she had been left 'unprovided for', and Frances Bringhurst was paid £80 a year, 'in consideration for her being left with two children in distressed circumstances'. Yet things turned out well for Bringhurst's daughter, as in 1835 she married Major Sir Richard-Frederick Hill of the 53rd Foot, who was the nephew of the then commander-in-chief of the British Army, Lord Hill. There is no information on the other officers to indicate that they were married. It seems unlikely that the subalterns Brooke and Bernard were, and no evidence has come to light as to Battersby's or the Adjutant Thomas Shelver's marital statuses. Rank and number of children clearly had an influence on the amount paid to the widows, as the wife of Union Brigade commander Sir William Ponsonby was paid £300 a year, whereas Susan Grant, the widow of Captain William Charles Grant of the 92nd Highlanders, who died of his wounds at Quatre Bras, only received £60 per annum.[5]

FATES AND FORTUNES OF SURVIVORS II: THE SOLDIERS

The soldiers' discharge papers have given some indication as to where the KDG non-commissioned officers and privates ended up after their service in the regiment. From looking at those records that show both their origins and their final residences, it can be seen that whilst only 16 per cent of the men returned home, 40 per cent ended up living in the large industrial towns of the regions from which they came. Presumably the majority of those from rural locations could not find work in their old villages, and like many of their civilian peers, had to migrate to the larger towns for work, which was reflective of the urbanisation of English society in the nineteenth century. Of the remainder, 20 per cent had elected to live in towns where the KDG had been posted during their time of service. And no doubt, in many cases, these were men who had met and married local women and thus returned to the areas from where their wives hailed. The few men listed as having lived in London seemed to have ended up there as a result of having spent time at the military hospital in Chelsea.[1]

However, more details on the lives of the other ranks after Waterloo are hard to find. In many of the soldiers' cases, literacy was necessary for success, which in turn bred biographies. Most of the material available was on the same soldiers whose accounts of Waterloo have already been used to tell the regiment's story in that conflict. It was significant that all three of the other ranks who have left behind detailed accounts of their time at Waterloo were strong-minded, literate Methodists, and their post-army lives are probably not a representative sample of the KDG rank and file. Luckily some nuggets of information on other soldiers' destinies have been provided to the QDG Regimental Museum by their descendants.

The most senior other rank in the regiment, Thomas Barlow, not only left a record of the KDG's Waterloo campaign through his letters to his wife Betsy, but his life after the army was eventful enough to have been recorded. One of his descendants has collated enough information to provide a snapshot of his post-KDG life.[2] Barlow was commissioned after Waterloo and in 1818, when he transferred to the 23rd Light Dragoons. The following year, he became a cornet in the Prince Regent's 2nd Regiment of Cheshire Yeomanry. He remained in Cheshire with his first wife Betsy, who bore him five children before she died in 1830. In 1833, at the age of 48, Barlow then retired from this yeomanry regiment and the army and married his second wife, Sarah.

For the next sixteen years, he brought up his family and, as a strong Methodist, became a full-time preacher in Deansgate, Manchester. He was described as, 'a bold soldierly man, who spoke in a very pompous style. His remarks from first to last were of a cutting and slashing nature.'[3] Instead of enjoying his retirement, the couple emigrated to Australia in 1841, probably as a result of their evangelical zeal. They were both employed by the commissioner for emigration, Barlow as a schoolmaster and his wife as a matron. The Barlows irritated the ship's master and their fellow passengers on board the ship in which they travelled to Australia with their proselytising and noisy hymn-singing. The Barlows settled in the Collingwood district of Melbourne, where Thomas ran a school in Nicholson Street. This school was run by the Wesleyan Association and Barlow subsequently got involved in litigation with two of the school's trustees over a £10 loan. Nothing appeared to come of this court case, and Barlow died in Collingwood aged 73.

Thomas Hasker's biographer has also given some insight into his life after Waterloo. On the day after the battle, he had been taken to Brussels where, he told his biographer, they were 'receiving great kindness from the ladies who ministered to the patients with abounding generosity'. He was then sent to rejoin the regiment in Northampton as a 'disabled man'. Shortly afterwards he was transferred to Chatham, where he worked for eighteen months as a hospital attendant. He then returned to Northampton to receive his discharge with a pension.

He then tried to marry Eleanor, the widow of his old Methodist friend James Curtice, who had been killed at Waterloo. Hasker had promised Curtice that should anything befall him, he would oversee his wife and their son Robert's welfare. However, Eleanor's mother burned the letter without informing her daughter. So Hasker settled down in Northampton as a boot block maker and married another woman, who died giving birth to his daughter in 1818. He then fired off two more letters to Eleanor's mother, who finally acquiesced to Hasker's request for permission to propose to her daughter. The couple were married in Newcastle in 1819 and returned to Northampton for seven years.

However, lack of employment forced the Haskers to move to Newcastle in 1826, where they brought up the four children they had between them. As he could not find work making boot blocks, Hasker established a school in Byker that failed. He then got inspiration from God, when walking on the beach at Tynemouth, to make his living from the sea. His Methodist friends subsequently set him up with a job selling salmon from Mr Muir's fishery on the River Coquet. Finding the Sandhill fishwives, with whom he had to deal, too bawdy for his moral sensibilities, he set up his own fishmongers with help from his Methodist friends. 'This business ultimately so prospered that he was enabled, in good time, to retire from it, and devote the closing years of life to occupations agreeable with strong religious pre-dilections.' So, notwithstanding almost going bankrupt with a bank failure in 1845, becoming deaf and breaking his leg in old age, Hasker's was a happy ending. He died a financially stable, spiritually fulfilled and happy man at the age of 69 in 1858.

There seemed to be a common theme of muscular Christianity demonstrated by those KDG Waterloo survivors who recorded their actions, as Private John Derry's Methodism and demeanour seemed to have been similar to that of Barlow and Hasker. Derry's first wife was one of the few allowed to follow the regiment to Flanders in 1815. He referred to his wife as having been, 'sickly and how this complicated matters for soldiers on the march'. Leaving his wife 'with bed in a cart', Derry marched towards the battlefield, whilst the women and baggage went on to Brussels. He never saw his first wife again. It was only once he had arrived at the regimental base in Rueil near Paris that, 'his man [the regimental paymaster, Webster's clerk] told me she was dead and buried'.[4] Apparently she had died whilst looking for him amongst the wounded.

Derry was promoted to corporal and found his second wife in Manchester. More accurately, Elizabeth found him, as his papers recalled she and a friend had come to the gates of his barracks and had enquired after those men who had lost their wives. They were married in the old church, now Manchester Cathedral, and their first child John Junior was born in York in 1817. In that year, Derry, whose piety had already been demonstrated by his recitation of prayers at Waterloo, properly found God when, 'his wife urged him to seek religious fellowship in a Methodist church'.[5] On Derry's return to Ireland with the regiment, 'he became active as a co-worker with fellow Methodists in the [King's Dragoon] Guards.'[6] In 1819, the regiment was back in Dundalk and the leader of Derry's Methodist group was William Shirley, a corporal in his troop. Apparently many KDGs joined their ranks, as Derry wrote, 'it is not uncommon for 15 or 20 to be converted "under a sermon".'[7] As a general observation, not based on hard evidence, it appears that whilst the Church of England was the religion of the officers and privates, many non-commissioned KDGs were, or became during their military service, non-conformists, and especially Methodists.

Derry was discharged six years after Waterloo, at Ballinrobe in Ireland in 1821. The reason given was 'reduction', or redundancy, but there may have been a vol-untary element to this as at that time he had reported in his letters that his mother was in a dire financial situation and he needed to support her. He returned to his home town of Leicester and worked as a book salesman. He also spent much time as a missionary to the boatmen of the town. He and his wife had five children, but they were very poor and close to bankruptcy on one occasion in 1834. Elizabeth pre-deceased her husband by eighteen years, having died in 1851. When John eventually died in 1869, at Leamington, his body was taken to Leicester to be buried alongside that of his wife.

Of the other KDG commentators who served in the ranks, little is known of the fate of TSM James Page. He clearly had a good Waterloo, as he replaced Barlow as RSM straight after the battle, having been promoted over TSMs Fairclough, Wright and Linton, who were all senior to him.[8] He held that position for seven years, before being discharged from the army in 1823, aged 41. However, there is information on John Stubbings, who had been praised for his, 'Good and Coregous Beaver [behaviour]' at Waterloo, where he had lost his friend Charles Stanley. Stubbings, unlike the other KDG rank and file who left accounts of their Waterloo experiences, was not a Methodist. Thus his life after the KDG was somewhat different from those of the soldiers already described, and probably more reflective of the majority of soldiers who left the regiment.

Stubbings, known to his friends in the KDG as Jack, was reputed to have been the shortest man in the regiment at 5ft 6½in. Yet, according to records of the KDG soldiers' discharge papers, there were several men who were half an inch shorter than him. For his good work at Waterloo, Stubbings was promoted in the field to sergeant. However, not long after this, during the pursuit of the Bonapartist soldiers south to Paris, Stubbings went missing for a couple of days. He was eventually found straddling a barrel of brandy in a French cellar! He left the regiment in 1816, aged 28, after completing ten of his twelve years' service.

Stubbings had his travelling expenses paid to proceed from the regiment's location in Manchester to Mansfield Woodhouse in Nottinghamshire, where he had grown up as the son of a sawyer on the Warsop estate, and from where he had been recruited back in 1806. From that village he walked the 3 miles or so to his home in Market Warsop, where he was reunited with his family for the first time in ten years. The Market Warsop village register recorded an endearing story for 1818, when Stubbings was reunited with the charger that had carried him at Waterloo, 'the meeting between the two was most affecting; the detachment halted in front of the "Hare and Hounds"; and villagers turned out to a man to see the one-eared horse on which John Stubbings rode at Waterloo'. In one of the duels he had fought with French cuirassiers, Stubbings's horse's ear had been slashed, but both man and his mount survived. Stubbings did not reach a great age and died at 61 when he fell from a roof which he was trying to repair in November 1849. He was buried and is remembered by a plaque in his local parish church of St Peter & St Paul in Church Warsop, Nottinghamshire.[9]

Apart from those whose lives after the army were recorded or for whom there are records which have been kept by descendants, there is little known about what trades these men turned to on their release from the army. Some like Joseph Fairfax returned to the job they had carried out before joining up. In his case it was as a framework knitter back in his native Leicester. When discharged in 1838, Fairfax's report had stated that he, 'is unfit for service and is likely to be permanently incapacitated for military duty[,] his constitution being broken and having chronic difficulty of breathing'. He died twenty-one years after his discharge, in 1859. Many KDGs could not return to the jobs they left to enter the regiment, as several of their trades, like that of framework knitters, had effectively died with mechanisation.

Private Thomas Nicholson, who left the regiment as sergeant-major when he was 50 years old, could not carry out heavy manual labour as he suffered from pains in his limbs and loins which had disabled him. He also suffered from the effects of having been run through with a sword at Waterloo. However, he managed to find a good job to suit his abilities and ran the Light Horseman Inn on the Fulford Road in York. Nicholson died there at the age of 60, on 28 September 1850. Private Leonard Helps from Frome returned to his native Somerset. He had married Ann Roberts, whom he had met when the regiment was stationed in Sussex in 1804–07. He was discharged aged 33 in 1816 as he had been wounded in his left arm. Helps and his wife went on to have eight children, and in 1837 he was recorded as being a baker and his wife Ann a confectioner. In addition to his wages, he earned 9d a day from his pension. He died in Bath, aged 76, in 1858.

As well as Barlow, a few former KDGs had a go at emigrating. Ulsterman Robert Ringland had been a sergeant at Waterloo but had been reduced to a private. He had emigrated to Canada before the KDG went there, but did not stay the course. He was discharged for length of service in 1821, aged 40, at Ballinrobe, Ireland. He subsequently emigrated to Canada and settled in Eldon Township in northern Canada, where he tried his hand at farming. However, he could not survive there as it was difficult to farm in the barren wilderness. He returned to Britain and had to seek assistance from the Chelsea Hospital. He died in around 1855. More successful at staying put in Canada was Sergeant Richard Hollis. He had made it to RSM and was promoted through the ranks to become the adjutant in 1836, when the regiment was stationed in Canada, and here he was discharged as a lieutenant in around 1842. He then joined the Royal Canadian Rifles as a lieutenant in 1845, retired as a captain in 1856 and died in the same year. Private Richard Herdsman was discharged in St Catharines, Western Canada, in August 1842, when he was 46 years old. His papers, dated 10 January 1843, stated that he wanted to live and draw his pension in St Catharines, Western Canada. Corporal Robert Gripton also emigrated to Canada. Having left the KDG aged 48 in 1823, he returned to his native Staffordshire. In 1831, he requested his pension to be transferred from Lane End, Staffordshire, to York in British North America.

However, a lot of unfortunate former KDGs were too damaged to get a labouring job to support themselves after their military service. Yet some pensions were available, as this petition to the Royal Hospital at Chelsea on behalf of Private Bellinger highlighted:

> Sir, your petition Benjamin Bellinger having been so disabled by his wounds as to render him incapable of doing any heavy labouring work, and having served His Majesty for the period of twenty years and twenty two days as is more fully specified by the enclosed discharge is quite unable to maintain a wife and five children who depend on him without the assistance of said pension and therefore trust that your honour upon consideration of the length of his service and the wounds he has received see next to continue the pension which his Majesty was so graciously pleased to confer upon him.

Yet many of the injured former KDGs did not get a pension, found it impossible to support themselves and no doubt some ended up in the workhouse, like Private Thomas Bottoms. He was discharged from the regiment, aged 40, in 1817 for an unfortunate combination of 'Chronic Catarrh, Weakly habits and injured testicles'. He probably found it hard to find a job at that age and in a reduced physical state. His first residence on leaving the army was listed as Brighton. He left there to return home to Leicester, where he was recorded as having been a special constable in 1830. In 1847, he died in Leicester's Union Workhouse.

Little is known of what happened to the widows and orphans of the other ranks. The support they received was less than that bequeathed to officers' widows. They were more of a regimental responsibility as there was no government bounty set aside for them. What often happened was the widow remarried another soldier in the regiment. This was seen in the case of Thomas Hasker, who married the widow of his friend in 3rd Troop, James Curtice, and took on his fatherless son. In one case, when there was no groom forthcoming, the KDG took on two sons of a soldier who had died. These were 11-year-old George and 9-year-old John, the sons of Corporal Richard Watts, who had died of cholera in 1833. Both boys served in the regiment, with John later becoming its bandmaster.

In absolute terms, life after the army for the vast majority of ex-KDGs was less than rosy. However, life for the working class in mid nineteenth-century Britain was still tough, and those retired soldiers would have been relatively better off, given they were 'Waterloo Men' who were entitled to an extra two years towards their pensions; this was to be a useful boost to the men's meagre finances. Some men who were entitled could increment their incomes with a pension. Yet life would still have been tough for those with physical or mental issues, as other than their pensions there would have been no form of financial or moral support. The last line of defence was the workhouse. Although often not a pleasant place, at least it offered a lifeline to those who could not support themselves.

So the fate of the KDG officers and soldiers once they left the regiment was relatively kind. They may have faced a rougher time as a civilian than their ordered, well-fed and comfortably housed existence in quarters or barracks, yet they were probably no worse off than their equivalents in the gentry and the working class at that time. We will not know whether they were happy but, on the basis of a fairly rudimentary analysis, they were certainly healthier and tougher than their civilian peers. The average length of life for those KDG survivors for whom we have records was 70 years. This was in sharp contrast to their working-class peers in England, who had a life expectancy of only 40 years in 1850.[10] What was remarkable was that, notwithstanding their relatively worse diets and living conditions, the ex-KDG soldiers lived on average just one year less than their officers. It was also interesting that those who left the KDG because of wounds sustained at Waterloo lived on to the same age as those who did not.[11] Of the KDG Waterloo men, Robert Hawley was the officers' longest-liver, at 93 years of age on his death. However, he was comfortably beaten by the other ranks' champion, Corporal Robert Gripton, who died aged 96 in the Canadian town of Katesville, Ontario.

20

WHAT HAPPENED
TO THE REGIMENT?

With the exception of its initial actions in Scotland and Ireland, for the first 130 years of its existence the KDG had just fought on the Continent. After the Allied victory at Waterloo, peace more or less prevailed in Western Europe for the rest of the nineteenth century, and all the KDG's actions and battle honours were won outside of that continent. However, for much of the first half of that century the regiment was occupied in assisting the civil power in quelling riots at home and controlling unrest in Ireland. In the second half of the century, the regiment's focus was in defending the nation's interests in or on the borders of her empire, as well as in China. The nineteenth century for the KDG was divided into roughly four twenty-two-year cycles of peace (1816–38), then action (1838–60), peace (1860–79) and then action again (1879–1902).

Once the KDG arrived back in England from the Continent in 1816, it embarked on twenty-two years' service which alternated between policing Ireland and controlling anti-social behaviour by the unions in England. As a result of the latter activity, it gained the nickname 'The Trades Union'.[1] Poignantly, in 1833, the last surviving Waterloo horse, No. 22 of H Troop, was retired to one of the royal parks, which marked an end of the era of the 'Waterloo Men', as there only remained a handful of these men in the KDG after that date.[2]

The prospect of some real action finally materialised in 1838, when the KDG was sent to Canada to help suppress the Lower Canada Rebellion by the mainly French-speaking *Patriotes*, who sought independence for Quebec from British rule. The KDG was first sent to the city of Quebec and then progressed to Trois Rivières. At this time, Lieutenant-Colonel Cathcart took over command of the KDG from Sir George Teesdale, who retired. In 1840, whilst the regiment was in

Canada, Lord Hill offered the colonelcy-in-chief of the KDG to Prince Albert, who declined the 1st Dragoon Guards in favour of the 11th Hussars, who had provided his escort on his arrival in England. Finally, after five years of counter-insurgency work, the KDG left Canada. For its part in defeating the *Patriotes*, the KDG won the battle honour 'Canada', its first since Waterloo.

On their return to England in 1843, the three squadrons which had been in Canada were joined by the Depot Squadron from York. It was the first time the whole regiment had served as one unit since 1828, fifteen years before. Lieutenant-Colonel Cathcart retired and was replaced by Lieutenant-Colonel Hankey. In 1848, the KDG returned to Southern Ireland, and in 1850, the colonel of the regiment, General Sir William Lumley, died and was replaced by Lieutenant-General the Earl of Cathcart.

Five years after returning from Canada, the KDG returned to active service in 1855 when the regiment left for the Crimea. It was based in Kadikoi, where it and the Carabiniers reinforced the original regiments of heavy brigade. These were the 4th and 5th Dragoon Guards, the Royals, the Greys and the Inniskillings. Major Briggs commanded one wing of the KDG at the Battle of the Tchernaya. However, there was little for the regiment to do in the summer of 1855, as Sevastopol was being besieged, so the KDG officers indulged in race meetings with the French officers. Those KDG who went on this campaign were awarded the Crimean War Medal with a clasp for 'Sebastopol'. The regiment returned to England in 1856, only having lost twenty-five men killed or died of disease and won another battle honour for 'Sevastopol'.

In 1857, the regiment sailed for action to help thwart the Indian Mutiny. But it was to be disappointed as there were no horses available to enable it to enter the fray. So the KDG took no part in the suppression of the mutineers, and instead its role was limited to peaceful patrolling operations in the south of India around Madras.

There then came the KDG's major action of the mid-nineteenth century, when it fought in the Second Opium War against China in 1860. The regiment, commanded by Lieutenant-Colonel Sayer, went as part of an Anglo-French force which comprised the follow-up attack after a failed British amphibious assault. This attack had been on the Taku forts that protected the mouth of the Pei-Ho River, which flowed east from the direction of Beijing to the sea. Shortly after having landed, the KDG was engaged with hordes of Tartar cavalry, and although hugely outnumbered, put them to flight with just one trooper slightly wounded. The Taku forts were then taken and the regiment moved west along the Pei-Ho River to Beijing. Just prior to entering the Chinese capital, the KDG participated in a remarkable charge against the Tartar cavalry, for which they were commended by the British commander, Major-General Sir James Hope Grant, who stated, 'I should wish most particularly to bring to notice the very excellent service of the

King's Dragoon Guards.'[3] The regiment was thereafter instructed to take part in the destruction of the Imperial Summer Palace in Beijing. This course of action was decided upon for two reasons. The first was as an act of retribution for the Chinese torture of Allied prisoners, one of whom was KDG private John Phipps, who had displayed great stoicism until his death at the hands of his captors. The second reason was to bring the war to a rapid end. According to the Minister of War, Sydney Herbert, the Chinese would not have signed the peace treaty if this destruction had not taken place.[4] For this campaign, the KDG was awarded the battle honours of 'Taku Forts' and 'Pekin'.

After another period of peace lasting almost twenty years, the KDG was sent to another continent, Africa, where it spent much of the last quarter of the nineteenth century. With the crushing defeat of the British at Isandlwana in January 1879, the army needed to send reinforcements to defeat the Zulus. The KDG was to be part of that force and was instructed to leave for South Africa a month after that reverse. The regiment arrived in Durban eight weeks later and advanced from that port north-east and then north into Zululand. It had reached the heart of the country by May, when it arrived at the battlefield of Isandlwana and interred the sun-dried and hence curiously preserved British dead that had been strewn around that eerie rock, unburied, for some three months. The next month, D and H troops found the remains of Napoleon III's son, the Prince Imperial, next to the Ityotosi River.[5]

By July 1879, elements of the KDG and the rest of General Lord Chelmsford's force, that also included the 17th Lancers, colonial troops and around six British infantry battalions, reached the Zulu's royal kraal of Ulundi, where they defeated King Cetshwayo once and for all. The decisive battle had been won but the war was not over, and there ensued a desperate hunt to track down the Zulu king, who had fled into hiding. There then started a bit of a contest between Lord Gifford, one of Wolseley's ADCs, and Major Marter KDG as to whom could track down Cetshwayo first – a race that Marter won. The KDG was rewarded for its part in this British victory with the battle honour 'South Africa 1879'.

After the Zulu War, most of the KDG were posted to India, but a detachment of two troops, under Major Brownlow, were kept on in South Africa as they were intended to be sent back to England to form the regimental depot. However, the First Anglo-Boer War started before they could embark on their passage home. At the end of January 1881, the KDG took part in the Battle of Laing's Nek a month before the British disaster and defeat at Majuba. In this battle, the KDG, along with the other British troops, attacked the Boers, who were dug in on the high ground around the nek. Brownlow had his horse shot from under him and was saved from the Boers by his servant, Private Doogan, who won the Victoria Cross for this act of bravery. Notwithstanding the British loss of this battle and the war, the KDG was awarded another battle honour, that of 'Laing's Nek'.

An important event took place for the KDG in 1896, when the Emperor of the Austro-Hungarian Empire, Franz Josef II, was made colonel-in-chief of the regiment. As a result of his appointment, he granted the regiment the privilege of wearing his family's Hapsburg double-headed Eagle as its cap badge, collar badge and sergeants' arm badge. The Emperor also ordered that a set of band parts be sent to the regiment. This was the *Radetzky March* composed by Johann Strauss in 1848 in honour of Austrian Field Marshal Count Josef Wenzel Radetzky. It was made the regimental quick march of the KDG, and on amalgamation that of the QDG. It is of interest that in 1915, because of anti-Austrian feeling during the First World War, when they were Britain's enemies, the KDG reverted to the Garter Star cap badge. It was not until 1937 that the Hapsburg Eagle was restored. Today, the Hapsburg Eagle is still proudly worn as the cap badge of the KDG's descendant regiment, the QDG.

The regiment returned to South Africa in February 1901 to fight in the Second Anglo-Boer War. The war had by then moved from the pitched battles of the opening stages to a war of movement in which the British Army tried to bring the Boer commandos to bay. The KDG's first task was to pursue Boer general de Wet, who was then operating in the Orange Free State. This was frustrating and unremarkable work, and took the form of several 'drives' to track down the elusive Boer leader, who disappeared with his men into the vastness of the South African veldt. Some Boer equipment was captured but not de Wet, whom the KDG was still seeking when peace was signed at Vereeniging in May 1902.

The KDG was in India at the outbreak of the First World War and came to France as a part of the Indian Expeditionary Force. The regiment fought as infantry in the trenches at Festuburg, Ypres, on the Somme and at Morval. In October 1917, it returned to India. The regiment gained the following battle honours for the Great War: 'Festubert', 'Hooge', 'Somme 1916' and 'Morval'.

In 1919, the Third Afghan War broke out and the KDG was by then serving on the Northwest Frontier. It was ordered to advance into Afghanistan, and at Dakka made the last recorded cavalry charge of a horsed British cavalry regiment. For its actions, the regiment received the battle honour 'Afghanistan 1919'. Just prior to the Second World War in 1939, the regiment made the momentous transition of being re-roled from cavalrymen who fought on horseback to becoming tank soldiers. The KDG lost its ranking as cavalry of the line and then became the senior regiment of the newly formed Royal Armoured Corps, as the Household Cavalry regiments were still mounted at this time.

At the outbreak of the Second World War, the KDG was equipped with the Mark VI Light Tank but it did not form part of the British Expeditionary Force that was sent to France. The KDG was posted to North Africa and re-roled as a reconnaissance regiment, equipped with the South African-built Marmon-Herrington armoured cars. The KDG arrived in the Western Desert in time to take part in the last battle of Wavell's campaign at Beda Fomm. The regiment was the first unit to come into contact with the German Afrika Corps under Rommel and took part in the Siege of Tobruk. It was engaged in all the major desert battles, including the relief of Tobruk, Gazala, Bir Hacheim, the defence of the Alamein line, Alam Halfa and then the advance to Tripoli, the Tebega Gap, El Hamma, Wadi Akarit and the final push to Tunis.

The KDG then moved across the Mediterranean to take part in the Allied invasion of Italy. It landed at Salerno in September 1943 and was the first Allied force to enter Naples. The regiment fought on the River Volturno, at the Battle of Monte Camino and at the crossing of the River Garigliano. During the advance up Italy during 1944, it took part in the capture of Perugia and Arezzo, moved through Florence and fought on the Gothic Line. Whilst in the Po Valley in December 1944, it was ordered to Greece to combat the communists' attempt to take over that country.

In 1945, the KDG was based in the Middle East to keep the peace in Lebanon and Syria. In September it moved to Palestine in aid of the civil power. The regiment returned to Britain in 1948. The KDG was ordered to Malaya in 1956, and served there during the 'Emergency'. On 1 January 1959, 1st The King's Dragoon Guards ceased to exist as it was amalgamated with the 2nd Dragoon Guards, or Queen's Bays, to form the present descendant regiment, 1st The Queen's Dragoon Guards. The QDG is unique in the British cavalry as it is fortunate to be the product of just one amalgamation. Hence its roots have not been obfuscated by a series of regimental combinations, and much of the substance and spirit of the KDG and its Waterloo traditions are still visible.[6]

★★★

The historical phenomenon of the twenty-year cycle in terms of the location and the responsibilities of the regiment continued after its amalgamation with the Bays to form the QDG. The 1950s and 1960s were all about colonial wars as part of Britain's withdrawal from her empire. In the 1970s and 1980s, the QDG alternated mainly between its Cold War role in protecting Germany as part of NATO and tours in support of the civil power in Northern Ireland. There was the odd UN tour to Cyprus, and Lebanon was also visited in a peacekeeping role. After the dismantling of the Berlin Wall and the Warsaw Pact, the regiment's attentions turned to the Middle East and Afghanistan.

The QDG's first posting after its creation in 1959 was a move to West Germany to become one of the armoured car regiments of the 1st British Corps. It was stationed in Wolfenbüttel, a strategically important town close to the inner German border. After six years in Germany, the regiment moved to Omagh in Northern Ireland for a brief period before being placed on standby to send a squadron to

Cyprus to support the United Nations, as well as sending troops to Borneo. The QDG's next move was to Aden, where it again saw active service in a reconnaissance role from August 1966 to 1967. During this period, one squadron was detached to Sharjah on the Persian Gulf. The regiment was involved in the defence of and eventual withdrawal from outposts in the mountainous hinterland close to the Yemeni border, combating rioters and suppressing the mutiny of the local police.

In January 1970, the regiment was posted to Catterick Camp in Yorkshire, where it became the Royal Armoured Corps Training Regiment and provided an armoured squadron for the Berlin brigade. After two years in Catterick, the QDG moved to Hohne, West Germany, as an armoured regiment equipped with the Chieftain main battle tank, where it served for the next eight years. It took part in many Cold War deterrent exercises across northern Germany, as well as deploying to Northern Ireland to serve in an anti-terrorism role. In November 1980, after nearly eight years in West Germany, the regiment moved to Lisanelly Barracks in Omagh, Northern Ireland. Here, the QDG operated in an infantry role, assisting the Royal Ulster Constabulary in combating terrorism in the province. During its two-year tour, the regiment was mainly responsible for County Tyrone but also operated in parts of Fermanagh and Armagh.

In November 1982, the regiment returned to England to Carver Barracks in Wimbish, Essex. Its role once again reverted to armoured reconnaissance, and it was equipped with the Combat Vehicle Reconnaissance Tracked (CVRT) family of vehicles. These included the Scorpion tank armed with a 76mm gun and the Scimitar tank, equipped with a 30mm RARDEN cannon, whilst D Squadron was equipped with Striker, a Swingfire wire-guided missile platform. In February 1983, C Squadron was sent to Cyprus to undertake a six-month tour as the Scout Car Squadron of the United Nations Forces in Cyprus (UNFICYP). It patrolled the green line or buffer zone between the Turkish-occupied north and Greek-controlled south. Whilst in Cyprus, and at short notice, a large element of the squadron was sent to Beirut in the Lebanon to form the British contingent of the Multinational Peacekeeping Force. C Squadron was later relieved by A Squadron, who witnessed some of the worst fighting there. In subsequent years, both B and D Squadrons fulfilled the UN Scout Car role in Cyprus.

In 1985, the regiment celebrated its Tercentenary. A parade was held that June on the old airfield of Carver Barracks. The salute was taken by Colonel-in-Chief Her Majesty Queen Elizabeth, the Queen Mother. In February 1987, the Queen Mother held a reception at Clarence House to mark her fiftieth anniversary as colonel-in-chief of the Bays and the QDG. Later that year, the regiment moved from Wimbish and returned to Wolfenbüttel, where it formed a part of the 1st Armoured Division in the same reconnaissance role in which it had been employed on its previous tour based in the Lower Saxon town.

In September 1990, in response to the Iraqi invasion of Kuwait, A Squadron was deployed to Saudi Arabia on Operation GRANBY with 7 Armoured Brigade. By the time the ground offensive had started, over half the regiment had deployed. During this war, A Squadron led 7 Armoured Brigade into Kuwait. After the First Gulf War ended, the regiment moved to Assaye Barracks at Tidworth in Hampshire. C Squadron undertook a reconnaissance squadron role in the Ace Command Europe (ACE) Mobile Force (LAND), in which it undertook exercises in Norway. The QDG also sent a composite squadron in support of 1 Royal Regiment of Fusiliers in Northern Ireland.

In the summer of 1991, the government announced *Options for Change* and the QDG was one of only three cavalry regiments to survive amalgamation, along with the Royal Scots Dragoon Guards and the 9/12th Lancers. The regiment then re-roled to the Challenger tank and moved to Athlone Barracks in Sennelager, Germany, in September 1992. The QDG then spent a six-month tour in Bosnia and Croatia as part of the NATO force (IFOR). The regimental commitment consisted of two armoured squadrons (C and D Squadrons) and Regimental Headquarters (RHQ), forming the lead regiment in an armoured battlegroup. B Squadron was also deployed as a mechanised infantry company with the Royal Green Jackets, equipped with Saxon armoured vehicles.

The regiment then moved to Northern Ireland and in 1998 it was tasked to cover the Troubles in Belfast during the famous Drumcree stand-off. In August 1998, after a twenty-six-year absence, the QDG returned to Cambrai Barracks in Catterick. A year later, the regiment deployed to Kosovo for a six-month tour. The initial deployment for this included one armoured squadron (A Squadron) and one light-role squadron (B Squadron). C Squadron was deployed in the light role in January 2000 for six weeks. In 2000, the QDG re-roled back from armour to formation reconnaissance.

Later in 2000, the QDG participated in Colonel-in-Chief the Queen Mother's 100th birthday celebrations. The regiment went on to commit two squadrons to operations in Bosnia. They were primarily involved in locating and seizing illegally held weapons, detaining war criminals and assisting in the maintenance of the ceasefire. In 2001, B Squadron and Regimental Headquarters were deployed to the South West of England to help tackle the foot and mouth disease epidemic. Also, for the first time in the regiment's history, both snipers and forward air controllers were included in its order of battle.

In March 2003, the QDG deployed to Kuwait with the 1st (UK) Armoured Division as part of the US-led force gearing up to invade Iraq. A Squadron was attached to 7th Armoured Brigade, B Squadron was used as divisional troops, C Squadron was attached to 3 Commando Brigade and HQ Squadron was tasked to build and man the first POW handling camp just inside the Iraqi border. The QDG served once again in Iraq on Operation TELIC. On its return from Iraq, the regiment moved to Imphal Barracks, Osnabrück, Germany. In 2004, after being stood down from Northern Ireland training because of the success of the peace process there, the QDG was sent on another tour of duty in Iraq with the 4th Armoured Brigade on Operation Telic 5. Shortly after arriving in Basra, B Squadron was detached to deploy on Operation Bracken with the Black Watch Battle Group to support US operations in the notorious 'Sunni Triangle'. It then rejoined the remainder of the QDG in time for the whole regiment to deploy to Al Muthanna Province, where it undertook a relief in place with the Dutch Battle Group.

On the regiment's return from Iraq in 2005, Brigadier Rose of 3 Commando Brigade presented the QDG with the Commando Dagger in recognition of the superb relationship between C Squadron and the Royal Marines during the liberation of Iraq. It is of note that this squadron had the distinction of spending one of the longest periods of constant contact with the enemy, for around twenty days, during this operation.

In 2006, the QDG deployed again in Iraq, this time on Operation Telic 8 with the rest of 20 Armoured Brigade, and oversaw the successful transfer of Al Muthanna province back to Iraqi control. At the end of 2007, the regiment left Osnabrück and moved to Dempsey Barracks in Sennelager, where it trained for a six-month deployment to Afghanistan as part of 3 Commando Brigade. RHQ, A and HQ Squadrons formed the core of Battlegroup South, responsible for holding the strategic Garmsir District in the south of Helmand Province, with C Squadron detached in support of 2nd Royal Gurkha Rifles in Musa Qala.

In early 2009, the QDG returned from this, its first tour in Afghanistan. In July that year, the regiment paraded at Cardiff Castle in front of Colonel-in-Chief His Royal Highness, The Prince of Wales, who had succeeded his grandmother in that role after her death. This parade was part of the Golden Jubilee to mark fifty years of loyal service by 1st The Queen's Dragoon Guards. In late 2010, the regiment faced its most significant threat for almost thirty years as the army was asked for massive cuts following the 2010 Security and Defence Review. The strength of this small family regiment and the effective campaign it mounted, as well as the loyal cross-party support given to it by MPs from the regiment's recruiting areas of Wales and the English Border Counties, convinced the government that there were better alternative regiments to combine rather than one that would involve the loss of a cap badge and the disappearance of Wales's only cavalry regiment.

The QDG took part in two further tours of Helmand in Afghanistan in 2011 and 2014. The regiment participated in both of these as part of its parent, the 20th Armoured Brigade. Its job was principally to train the Afghan security forces, although the regiment also provided the Brigade Recce Force. The QDG then packed its bags and left Germany for the very last time, after a fifty-five-year association with the British Army of the Rhine. Its next home was at Swanton Morley in Norfolk in its new light cavalry role. Despite having experienced over a decade of intense campaigning in Iraq and Afghanistan, and after coming within a hair's breadth of having been amalgamated in 2010, it was fitting that the QDG survived long enough for the 200th anniversary of its most important battle, Waterloo. The commemoration was held at Cardiff City Hall in September 2015. The Battle of Waterloo was celebrated at dinner in the same way it has been every year since those thirteen survivors shared a modest meal just south of La Belle Alliance in 1815, in that the officers and the sergeants messed together. The KDG's Waterloo spirit lives on in the QDG.

THE KDG AT WATERLOO: THE CAVALRY THAT BROKE NAPOLEON?

The title of this book is a bold statement with which many would disagree. However, one could argue it was a fair assertion based on Waterloo expert Mark Adkin's opinion that, 'the KDG were at the forefront of the cavalry charge that smashed into D'Erlon's corps at their most vulnerable moment. It was the charge that defeated what was arguably the best chance Napoleon had of breaking Wellington's line that day.'[1] The first charge of the British heavy brigades at Waterloo shattered the French emperor's plans for a quick and decisive victory at the only point in the battle when it was, more than likely, his to take. This feat of arms, therefore, cost him not only the battle but his cause with it. The KDG, having contributed the largest regimental presence to that charge, could thus lay claim to having been the cavalry that broke Napoleon.

Yet, in the process of shattering the French emperor's grand design, the KDG and the rest of the British heavy cavalry were destroyed. So, whilst these men may have stopped d'Erlon's corps's attempt to break the Allied line, Napoleon was far from beaten after this reverse. As the events of the rest of the day showed, his army was still a potent force that could have beaten Wellington at several points later in the battle. One example was seen during the series of massed cavalry attacks. Had the French used more infantry and artillery in conjunction with their horsemen, they would have had a very reasonable chance of breaching and destroying Wellington's squares. This in turn should have enabled them to have taken the Mont St Jean plateau and in the process to have destroyed Wellington's army, which was Napoleon's main objective rather than that of taking territory.[2]

Probably the clearest example of Napoleon's continued potential for victory after the heavies stopped d'Erlon's initial assault came with the fall of La Haye Sainte around 6.30 p.m. Sir James Shaw Kennedy, an assistant to the adjutant-general of Alten's 3rd British Infantry Division, and hence close to the action around La Haye Sainte after its fall to the French, described this critical time for the Allies:

> Ompteda's brigade was nearly annihilated, and Kielmansegge's so thinned, that those two brigades could not hold their position. That part of the field of battle, therefore which was between Halkett's left and Kempt's right, was unprotected; and being the very centre of the Duke's line was consequently that point, above all others, which the enemy wished to gain. The danger was imminent.[3]

Interestingly, Shaw Kennedy was describing the small area in the Allied defences that a military expert described as the 'vital ground', the occupation of which he felt was the key to the outcome of the battle.[4] And it was to this very spot that Dubois's cuirassiers had been advancing earlier in the day when they were repulsed by the Household Brigade.

So from Shaw Kennedy's comments it can be seen that, in addition to d'Erlon's attack, there had been another crisis that day when the French had come within a whisker of victory. Thus Napoleon's potency at that later point in the battle had not been significantly diminished; and thus he had clearly not been totally broken by the first charge of the heavy brigades, as he would not otherwise have been able to have threatened Wellington's position.[5] In fact, the Household and Union brigades did not destroy d'Erlon's men. The evidence of the French I Corps's recovery was seen throughout the remainder of the battle. Durutte's 4th Division resisted the Prussians on the eastern flank. Donzelot's 2nd Infantry Division succeeded in taking La Haye Sainte at approximately 6.30 p.m. And this corps was still fighting into the evening when it joined the Imperial Guard's attack on the Allies. D'Erlon's men had been stopped but not broken by the British heavy cavalry, and did not lose more than around a quarter of their numbers in that charge.[6]

Yet clearly Napoleon had broken the British heavy cavalry, as after their first charge they ceased to be a significant weapon in Wellington's arsenal. Although the majority of the British heavies had been destroyed, they were not superfluous players for the rest of the battle, as some have argued. Later in the afternoon, they made several counter-attacks against French infantry and infantry supported by cavalry. Although too weak to drive back the French, they had stopped them from advancing. The heavy brigades also bolstered the Allied lines and ensured some of the more flimsy non-British infantry remained in the line. Also, at another stage of the battle when in the Allied infantry squares, they provided a vital back-stop that prevented any unsteady infantry from having leaked out of the back of the squares.

Most significantly, they held the Allied line when it was at its greatest peril after d'Erlon's initial assault, as referred to previously by Shaw Kennedy. This was that period of time just after La Haye Sainte had fallen to the French at around 6.30 p.m., when Napoleon was given his second great chance to penetrate the Allied centre. Although Uxbridge gave the order for the Household Brigade to retire to avoid the terrible cannonade it had been suffering, Somerset insisted on keeping it in its single line on the same ground to prevent what he perceived to be the wavering Dutch cavalry from withdrawing.[7] Had the heavies not remained in that location, there was a good chance the Allied centre could have collapsed at that point of the battle. So it was true that after the first charge, the British heavy cavalry was no longer potent enough to have been a relevant offensive force. Yet they still continued to contribute to the defence of the Mont St Jean ridge, even if it was just a show of strength, until the Allies moved south from the defensive to the offensive.

Notwithstanding their continued contribution after the first charge, Napoleon well and truly broke them. Having started the day with two brigades of nineteen squadrons, the British heavy cavalry were reduced by the French to just one squadron at the end of the day. Not only were they destroyed, but some saw their performance as having fallen short. One of those who liked to quote detractors of the British cavalry was Rees Gronow, a 1st Foot Guards officer attached to General Picton's staff, who kept a detailed record of his time at Waterloo. In one of his books, he quoted the French cavalry general Exelmans's verdict on Uxbridge's men's first charge, 'I need not remind you of the charge of your two heavy brigades at Waterloo: this charge was utterly useless and all the world knows they came upon a masked battery, which obliged a retreat, and entirely disconcerted Wellington's plans during the rest of the day.'[8] There was some truth that the destruction of the heavy brigades constrained Wellington's ability to fight the rest of the battle. However, Exelmans's labelling of their first charge as useless was absurd in the light of its success in stopping d'Erlon's first assault.

It must also be remembered that these words quoting Exelmans were from the pen of the man who was responsible for trotting out some of the famous Wellington quotes against the British cavalry. Gronow was one of those who had reported the Duke's famous lines that the British cavalry had, 'invariably got me into scrapes'. Although his opinions seem to reflect those of other detractors of the British cavalry in the 1st Foot Guards,[9] he has been dismissed by one historian as a gossip who busied himself in 'low-level regimental complaining'.[10] Notwithstanding Gronow's bile, there was some truth in the accusation that the KDG especially, and most of the British heavy cavalry, the Blues excepted, displayed a poor lack of command and control during the first charge at Waterloo.

Far more important to the legacy of the heavy brigades than the words from a subaltern's pen was the belief of some that Wellington was dissatisfied with the Household and Union brigades at Waterloo. This perception has been based on the often quoted remark he made to Uxbridge after the first charge of the British heavies, 'Well Paget, I hope you are satisfied with your cavalry now.'[11] Yet this was probably not so much a back-handed compliment to the heavy cavalry but was more about Wellington giving a dig in the ribs to their chief, Uxbridge, for having moaned about his men's abilities, which he appeared to have done to his boss since the various cavalry actions at Genappe the day before.

Uxbridge had felt doubly let down by his cavalry at Genappe, as some of the officers of his old regiment, the 7th Hussars, had baulked at his order to make a possibly suicidal charge against French lancers in an unassailable position with their flanks protected by the village's houses. Then, once the hussars had been badly cut up in their attempt to assail the lancers, he had turned to the 23rd Light Dragoons. Its commanding officer had, understandably, shown no enthusiasm to repeat the 7th Hussars' experience with his own men. So Uxbridge had to resort to the Life Guards, who did not refuse him. So what the Duke probably meant by his question concerning Uxbridge's satisfaction with his heavy cavalry after their first charge was, 'after that magnificent feat of arms, can't you now stop grumbling about your men?' It appears that Uxbridge must have relented, as Somerset reported in a letter to his mother that, 'Lord Uxbridge made a speech and declared that the heavy cavalry had took his heart.'[12]

The view that Wellington was actually pleased with the Household Brigade is supported by Uxbridge's recollection of the Duke's and the *Corps diplomatique Militaire's* reaction to their first charge, that he had never seen, 'so joyful a group as was this *Troupe dorée*'.[13] Probably the best piece of evidence that Wellington was pleased with the KDG, the Life Guards and the Blues was that they were the only three regiments (the two Life Guards having been referred to as one) of all Wellington's Allied army that were singled out for praise for their actions on 18 June 1815 in his Waterloo Dispatch, when they were lauded for having 'highly distinguished themselves'.[14]

Yet several observers have pointed out quite reasonably that Wellington felt strongly enough about the British cavalry's lack of command and control at Waterloo that he had felt obliged to issue strict guidelines to correct this inadequacy. Shortly after Waterloo, Wellington attached a memorandum to his *General Orders* that set out his 'Instructions to Officers Commanding Brigades of Cavalry in the Army of Occupation', which was a set of five key points of cavalry management that he insisted were adhered to.[15] However, these instructions did not address the KDG's and the other heavy cavalry regiments' inability to stop and rally when instructed at Waterloo. They were aimed to correct the errors of those heavy cavalry regiments that had been ordered to remain in reserve, namely the Blues and the Greys, but which had ended up charging with the first-line regiments at Waterloo. It still remained a fact that, with the exception of the disciplined Blues, the accusation of poor discipline amongst the British heavy cavalry during the first charge was a fair one. Yet the Household and Union brigades' records at Waterloo should not have been judged on this factor alone.

The Union Brigade had clearly charged too far, and the Household Brigade's prime suspect for lack of command and control was the KDG. One person to have made this accusation was Lord Greenock, who was assistant-quartermaster-general to the cavalry at Waterloo:

> On the right of the Haye Sainte, the Household Brigade had charged at the same time with the other heavy cavalry Brigade when one of its regiments, the King's Dragoon Guards, having likewise been too eager in the pursuit had almost been annihilated; the Life Guards and the Blues having been kept better in hand, had then suffered (comparatively speaking) but little loss.[16]

He was not the only senior British officer to have identified the KDG's fault, as Somerset lamented:

> It happened unfortunately (as is too often the case with cavalry, particularly with young troops) that they do not know when to stop. That occurred on the present occasion, notwithstanding all the exertions I could make, I could not restrain the King's Dragoon Guards who galloped on, til at length they arrived in the midst of the enemy's infantry, and a great part of them were cut to pieces.[17]

So yes, it was true that the KDG and most of the other British heavy cavalry regiments had charged too far. There has been some debate as to whether the Blues and Greys had been ordered by Uxbridge to remain in reserve. Had they done so, it would have helped matters greatly as had they stayed behind, they could have helped to recover the first lines after the initial charge. The Blues actually achieved this to some degree, notwithstanding having charged around the same time as the two regiments of Life Guards and the KDG. Uxbridge regretted for the rest of his life that he had charged with the first line instead of having remained behind with a second line. Had he done so, he would have been better placed to support the first line with other units of his cavalry when it was trying to extricate itself from the French lines after the first charge.[18]

Yet to have assessed the performance of the British heavy cavalry at Waterloo solely on its lack of command and control during the first charge, which led to its almost total destruction and subsequent impotency, would be to miss the most important point in an assessment of their performance at that battle. They did their job that day, and that job was to either defeat Napoleon or at least to stop him from winning at Waterloo. Clearly the British heavy cavalry and the KDG did not totally 'break' Napoleon, but they broke him sufficiently at a vital moment which denied him a likely victory at that point in the battle. Yet how significant were their actions? Was the destruction of d'Erlon's combined arms assault by the heavy brigades the only event that saved the day for the Allies?

Clearly this was not the case, as there were several other events that also stopped
Napoleon that day. Of these, there were probably three actions that were crucial in
denying the French victory. To Wellington, the ultimate act of defence at Waterloo
was clear, as he said, 'the success of the battle turned upon the closing of the gates
at Hougoumont'.[19] Without doubt, the successful defence of Hougoumont contributed hugely to the Allied victory. It ensured that Wellington's right wing did
not collapse, and it also prevented the French from outflanking and rolling up the
Allied line in the west. It has also been argued that it sucked just under 13,000
French infantrymen from the 6th and 9th Infantry divisions in Reille's II Corps
into a diversion from an assault on the Allied main front line.[20] These troops could
have tipped the balance in favour of the French elsewhere on the battlefield. Yet it
must also be remembered that the net effect of sucking in troops to this engagement was neutral. In other words, almost as many Allied soldiers were committed
to this action as there were Frenchmen. Although there were never more than a
couple of thousand British, Hanoverian and Nassauer soldiers directly involved
in defending Hougoumont, Wellington rotated 10,000 Allied troops through the
fight for this fortified château.[21]

The Prussians clearly saved the Allies from defeat. Their agreement to provide
two corps was the reason Wellington was prepared to give battle at Waterloo.[22]
From when they were first sighted at around 1 p.m., Bonaparte was obliged to
lose a whole corps that he could and probably would have used against the Allied
centre. This was Lobau's VI Corps, which had to be transferred to the south-east
to meet the Prussian threat in that area. Napoleon later haemorrhaged ten more
battalions of his vital infantry when his precious Old Guard had to be moved to
his right flank to stem the advance of the Prussians in and around Plancenoit. In all,
Blücher's men had diverted around 23 per cent of Napoleon's strength in infantry.[23]

The last of the three decisive actions that probably denied Napoleon the key
to unlocking the Allied line and destroying Wellington's army was the defence of
La Haye Sainte and its environs. This was carried out by the KGL in the farm and
in its proximity by the men of Alten's and Picton's divisions. Shaw Kennedy was in
no doubt that this area was the 'vital ground' that Wellington had to hold at all costs:

> No one can doubt, who knows the circumstances, that Napoleon's plan of attack
> was that of breaking Wellington's centre at La Haye Sainte, overthrowing the left
> of the Allied line, and thus going far to ensure the defeat of the Anglo-Allied
> army; to separate it entirely from that of Blücher: and to gain command of the
> great road to Brussels.[24]

In returning to the other candidates for the key action that prevented the Allies'
defeat, Shaw Kennedy reflected on, 'the attack on Hougoumont, which attack was
only an auxiliary operation to the main one [the breaking of the Allied centre] by

which he hoped to gain the battle'.[25] Although a thorn in the side of the French, Hougoumont was eventually bypassed by Ney with his massed cavalry attacks on the Allied squares. By taking Hougoumont, Napoleon was not guaranteed victory. To have attained this, Bonaparte needed to have smashed and passed through a hole in the Allied line, to have established himself on the Mont St Jean plateau and then rolled up and destroyed Wellington's army. As far as the arrival of the Prussians was concerned, some historians have argued that after d'Erlon's failed assault, the French lacked the three-to-one superiority in infantry to have shifted Wellington's rock-like squares of infantry and, in all probability, the Duke would have held on until nightfall. If this had been the case, the outcome of 18 June would have been a tie. However, given the reduced and exhausted state of Wellington's army at the close of the Battle of Waterloo, the Prussians would almost certainly have been a necessary contributor to any subsequent Allied victory. As mentioned by one of the British generals consulted during the writing of this book, whilst Wellington was the Allies' right fist, so Blücher was their left.[26] So on 18 June 1815 it would, therefore, seem that the defence of La Haye Sainte and the area around that farmhouse could qualify as the most crucial of several key actions that denied Napoleon victory.

Yet it is probably futile to argue the significance of one event over another, as that would be an objective call. A better approach might be to ask whether the British heavy cavalry stopped Napoleon and how crucial was their role in his defeat? Given that the author is understandably open to accusations of bias as a former officer in the KDG's descendant regiment, the QDG, it is more helpful to present readers with the opinions of two groups of relevant experts with different perspectives, and then leave them to decide on the answers to those questions.

The first group of experts comprised two senior British Army officers, acclaimed for their tactical ability and with a good knowledge of the Battle of Waterloo. The reason for having consulted them is that a tactical problem is not necessarily influenced by time. So a modern informed opinion can be as relevant as that of a historian, or maybe more so, as an anonymous 'General Officer' wrote in the nineteenth century, 'When civilians write military history, and venture to advance opinions of their own technical points of which the Profession alone are able to judge, they generally talk nonsense.'[27] This was a harsh, and in many cases an unjust, view. So whilst it was clearly helpful to have sounded the opinions of two up-to-date senior professional soldiers on these questions, it was also extremely useful to have a balanced view and to set out the judgements of two contemporary historians who are esteemed for their knowledge of this battle.

Neither of the British generals consulted served in the British cavalry or the Foot Guards, so can be accepted as not having had regimental axes to grind. If anything, their infantry backgrounds could have made them harsher judges of the performance of the British cavalry at Waterloo than a civilian would have been.

A potted version of their view was that whilst the heavy cavalry did stop Napoleon, it did not do so in isolation, such that it could be claimed to have saved the day. In their opinions, the heavy brigades did indeed stop Napoleon, but only as part of Wellington's all-arms repulse of d'Erlon's assault. This defensive action comprised: the crucial holding of La Haye Sainte by the KGL; the holding of the Allied line in the area of the French assault by Picton's division; the heavy brigades' second echelon counter-stroke; and the support provided by the Allied artillery. Their belief was that the Household and Union brigades only stopped Napoleon in terms of having brought him to a temporary halt, rather than having brought his ambitions to an end at around 2.30–3 p.m. on 18 June 1815. One of these generals also stressed that there was no reason to suppose Wellington could not have dealt with d'Erlon's men on the Mont St Jean plateau by using his reserves and other troops, had the heavy brigades not repulsed the French I Corps.[28]

Of the historians consulted, Mark Adkin, another former British infantry officer and a 'neutral', was consulted as he has been considered by many to be one of the leading authorities in the study of this battle, based on his *Waterloo Companion*, which is one of the most comprehensive guides to that event.[29] He named the half an hour or so before the first charge of the heavies, 'the crisis of the entire battle'.[30] Adkin has also pointed out that this particular threat to the Allies came at the only time when Napoleon could have used his reserve of Lobau's corps to back up an assault on Wellington's line before it was employed to the south-east to face and engage the Prussians. In his view, d'Erlon's assault was, 'the nearest Napoleon got to winning as they had almost got over the road [the *Chemin d'Ohain*] and had they been supported, it would have probably been all over for Wellington'.[31]

The other historian consulted is an Italian who has written one of the most acclaimed of the recent accounts of the Battle of Waterloo. He is Alessandro Barbero, and whilst he did not want to identify one particular action that stopped Napoleon, he was prepared to state:

> I believe that the result of a battle is the sum of so many events that it is not always possible, or necessary, to single out one of them as the most important; but if I should indulge in that game, I'd say the cavalry charge which effectively broke d'Erlon's attack. Although Chandler and other historians didn't always stress this fact, most contemporary witnesses attest that the attack was being successful and Wellington's left wing was all but broken itself when the cavalry appeared and saved the day.[32]

So did the KDG and the British heavy brigades break Napoleon, as the title of this book suggests? As discussed, they certainly did not destroy him. Yet in stopping d'Erlon's assault they inflicted on the French the first in a series of significant reverses that eventually led to the breaking of Boneparte at Waterloo. The emperor's destruction was an Allied all-arms team effort, and of their cavalry component, the British heavies surely played the most decisive part. The British heavy brigades were certainly guilty of lacking command and control and charging too far. Nonetheless, that first charge, which reflected the British cavalry's hallmark of exuberant impetuosity, was probably the vital ingredient that ensured them success. A measured charge *à la manière française* and without the British hunting vigour might well have been insufficient to have overturned d'Erlon's corps.

Not only did the British heavies stop d'Erlon with this first charge, but the Household Brigade took part in and won probably the best example of a massed cavalry-on-cavalry duel to have taken place in modern European history, as Shaw Kennedy attested:

> Somerset's brigade, meeting the French heavy cavalry on the slope from the Allied position, defeated the French cuirassiers in the most brilliant manner; and crossing the road, assisted Kempt's brigade in clearing their front. I believe this to have been the only fairly tested fight of cavalry against cavalry during the day. It was a fair meeting of two bodies of heavy cavalry, each in perfect order.

Many of the participants in this contest were KDGs. Their achievement was all the more remarkable when one considers that this was their very first taste of action. Their inexperience was in sharp contrast to both their peers in the Household Brigade and their cuirassier enemies on the field.[33]

As the British heavy cavalry were destroyed in the process, their first charge at Waterloo was therefore a pyrrhic victory, but it was a victory nonetheless. The British heavy cavalry's achievement was very much a team effort; all the seven regiments that it comprised should be recognised for that first charge, with no more emphasis being placed on the contributions of either the KDG or those regiments fortunate to have been the focus of authors and artists. In conclusion, those KDGs who charged at that battle of all British battles could have quite reasonably laid claim to have been a part of the cavalry that helped to break Napoleon. On a regimental basis, the KDG played the major part in that first charge, having comprised nearly half of the Household Brigade and almost a quarter of both heavy brigades. It also made the biggest sacrifice in the British cavalry that day, having lost the most men at Waterloo. To put those losses into perspective, the regiment suffered more deaths in that battle than the whole of the Light Brigade did in its fabled charge at Balaclava some years later. Most of the KDG officers have been remembered with memorials, yet only a few of the men have been commemorated. These soldiers, therefore, need a monument to help raise awareness of their awesome achievement and to preserve their memories for posterity. All net proceeds from this book will go towards that aspiration, and you, by buying this book, will have helped to attain that tribute to the men of the 1st or King's Dragoon Guards who charged at Waterloo.[34]

APPENDIX I

THE BATTLE OF WATERLOO

By Samuel Wheeler, trumpeter in His Majesty's 1st or King's Regiment of Dragoons [sic]

On the sixteenth of June my boys that was the very day
When we received orders for to march away,
To face the tyrants army my lads then we was bound
That on the plains of Waterloo encamp'd was all round.

We espied our foes next morning as in a wood they lay,
And like Britons we advanced to shew them British play,
Our grape shot flew among them and put them to the route
But still those cowardly raskals refused to come out.

When Duke Wellington saw their cowardness he ordered a retreat,
Which orders was comply'd with and his design it was complete
We retired through the village of Genap as you soon shall hear
Followed by a large body of the enemies launceers.

And in our retreat the horrid thunders began to roar,
And rain like unto rivilets upon the ground did pour,
But our brave English heroes endured both heat and cold,
And caused our foes to rue the day the truth I now unfold.

The first that charged was the Life Guards the enemy to subdue,
They charged a column of the launceers and caused them to rue,
Full half an hour a hard fighting these heroes did endure,
And left three hundred launceers a bleeding in their gore.

When they returned from their work our regiment was call'd out,
For to face those French dogs and put them to rout.
But the noble Earl of Uxbridge some danger did espy,
King's Dragoon Guards threes about he loudly then did cry.

The cunning French three field pieces had placed in the town,
Thinking as we advanc'd to cut our heroes down,
But our brave commander soon ordered us away
And then brought up some English guns and on them began to play.

Then we again retir'd and enticed them on the plain,
And gained a good position which we was determined to maintain.
But the night being fast advancing we could no longer see,
And neither of the armies could claim the victory.

Then we lay by that night with our horses by our side,
To tell the sufferings we endur'd no pen can e'er describe,
For the rain descended in torrents the light'ning flash'd so blue,
Still each Briton kept his spirits up his foes for to subdue.

Then early the next morning our out piquets did espy
Napoleon and his army that was advancing nigh,
Our army being ready the cannon began to roar,
And musquet shot into their lines so quickly we did pour.

About ten o'clock in the forenoon our cavalry in a body lay,
Their shots and shells into our column so briskly they did play.
Two heavy brigades then formed a line in readiness to advance,
To charge the tyrants curiseers that was the pride of France.

Lord Somerset commanded the household brigade,
And led us on to victory thro' the hottest cannonade,
So well the brigade then play'd their parts and charged their foes so free,
Which was the cause my British boys of gaining the victory.

O when we came up with them the slaughter it was great,
Our gallant troops so boldly led soon caused their lines to break,
We charged them so boldly and made them for to run,
And cut them down with our broad-swords like moths in the sun.

General Ponsonby's brigade charged next, and I am bound to say,
They done their duty manfully all on that glorious day,
They charged them so valiantly and caused them to rue,
That ever they fought for Bonaparte on the plains of Waterloo.

But now the painful task comes on I'm sorry for to say,
We lost many a noble officer although we gained the day,
Besides some thousands of our men lay bleeding on the plain,
And on the minds of Britons their deaths will long remain.

So now the battle's over the victory we have won,
Fill up a bumper and drink a health unto Duke Wellington,
Likewise the Earl of Uxbridge Lord Somerset also,
That led us on like heroes on the plains of Waterloo.

Date: between 1815 and 1819. Printed & Sold by J. Pitts, 14 Great St Andrew Street, Seven Dials, London. Price One Penny. Source: ballads.bodleian.ox.ac.uk/search/round/1922. Edition – Bod18789. Round Number: 1922.

REGIMENTAL ROLL OF KDG WHO FOUGHT AT WATERLOO

First Name	Last Name	Rank	Troop	Casualties (K: Killed/ DOW: Died of Wounds/ W: Wounded)
James	Abbotts	Pte	1	
John	Adams	Cpl	3	W
John	Adams	Sgt	4	
John	Allen	Sgt	6	K
John	Andrews	Pte	2	W
William	Appleton	Pte	4	
John	Archbold	Pte	7	W
John	Arlett	Pte	6	DOW
William	Arlingstall	Pte	8	
William	Armstrong	Pte	6	W
Robert	Ashley	Pte	7	
John	Ashton	Pte	1	W
John	Ashton	Pte	4	K

Thomas	Ashworth	Sgt	1	K
George	Aspinall	Cpl	3	W
William	Aston	Pte	8	W
Benjamin	Atha	Pte	1	W
Henry	Babb	Pte	4	
Ralph	Babington	Lt	★	
Charles	Bagley	Pte	5	W
Benjamin	Ball	Pte	5	
Thomas	Ball	Pte	8	W
John	Banks	Sgt	6	
Alexander	Baptie	Pte	2	
John	Barber	Pte	2	W
Thomas	Barlow	RSM	1	
John	Barnes	Pte	6	W
Charles	Barnett	Pte	5	
Joseph	Barnett	Pte	6	W
William	Barrack	Pte	8	DOW
Richard	Barrell	Pte	4	
Thomas	Barrett	Pte	2	K
John	Barron	Pte	8	
Thomas	Bartlemore	Pte	3	W
Charles	Bateman	Pte	1	K
William	Bateman	Pte	8	
George	Battersby	Capt.	2	K
John	Battie	Pte	4	W
Thomas	Battie	Pte	1	W
James	Bearder	Pte	8	
James	Beardsley	Pte	1	
Thomas	Beerson	Pte	7	
Samuel	Beeston	Pte	7	W
John	Bell	Pte	7	
Benjamin	Bellinger	Pte	7	W

William	Benton	Pte	4	K
David	Benwell	TSM	6	K
Francis	Berkshire	Pte	2	
Hon. Henry	Bernard	Cor.	★	K
Hunter	Bewley	Pte	2	W
Robert	Binder	Pte	1	W
John	Birch	Pte	2	W
Samuel	Birchill	Pte	5	K
Thomas	Bird	Pte	5	K
Henry	Blackburn	Pte	2	
Ralph	Blackhurst	Pte	2	
Thomas	Blake	Pte	4	W
Stephen	Blanch	Cpl	2	
Edward	Bodill	Pte	5	W
Edward	Bond	Pte	4	W
Richard	Bonser	Pte	4	DOW
John	Booth	Pte	3	W
John	Booth	Pte	8	W
John	Bosson	Pte	5	K
Thomas	Boswell	Pte	8	W
Thomas	Bottoms	Pte	3	
James	Bourne	Pte	2	W
Stephen	Bowen	Pte	4	K
Samuel	Bower	Pte	3	
Emanuel	Bradbury	Sgt	3	
George	Bradbury	Pte	1	
John	Bradbury	Pte	1	K
Stamford	Bradshaw	Pte	4	W
Thomas	Brander	Lt	★	
Thomas	Bray	Pte	7	
Thomas	Brew	Sgt	2	
Bury	Bridge	Pte	5	W

James	Bridge	Pte	4	
William	Bridgeman	Pte	1	K
Abraham	Briggs	Pte	8	
Charles	Bright	Pte	1	
John	Bringhurst	Capt.	5	K
Joseph	Briscoe	Cpl	5	
John	Brittney	Pte	1	DOW
William	Brockett	Pte	3	
Francis	Brooke	Lt	★	K
Benjamin	Brooks	Pte	4	DOW
Thomas	Brotherton	Pte	5	K
Francis	Brown	Pte	2	
James	Brown	Pte	1	K
James	Brown	Pte	8	W
John	Brown	QM	★	
John	Brown	Pte	1	
John	Brown	Pte	7	K
John	Brown	Pte	7	
Richard	Brown	Pte	8	
William	Brown	Sgt	4	
John	Bull	Pte	4	K
Samuel	Bull	Pte	4	
George	Bullman	Cpl	8	K
William	Bunny	Pte	4	
John	Butcher	Pte	3	
Edmund	Butterworth	Pte	8	K
James	Buxton	Pte	1	K
William	Caplin	Pte	8	K
Henry	Capon	Pte	1	
Patrick	Carr	Pte	7	K
Isaac	Carter	Pte	2	
John	Carter	Pte	2	K

Joseph	Carter	Pte	7	
Joseph	Castle	Sgt	1	
George	Chantry	Pte	2	W
William	Chaplin	Pte	3	
Henry	Chapple	Pte	8	
John	Chelton	Pte	4	
John	Chiney	Pte	6	W
William	Chivers	Sgt	5	
Samuel	Chorley	Pte	5	K
Joseph	Clapp	Pte	4	
John	Clark	Pte	4	K
John	Clark	Cpl	7	W
William	Clark	Cpl	6	W
James	Clegg	Pte	7	K
Thomas	Clements	Pte	1	
Thomas	Cockburn	Pte	2	K
James	Collingham	Pte	7	
John	Cook	Pte	4	K
Joseph	Cook	Pte	2	W
Samuel	Cook	Pte	2	W
James	Cooper	Sgt	7	
Jeremiah	Cooper	Pte	1	
George	Copley	Pte	4	
Thomas	Coult	Pte	2	W
William	Cousens	Pte	3	
Robert	Cracknell	Pte	6	
Robert	Craig	Pte	8	K
John	Crane	Pte	5	K
William	Crosby	Pte	1	
John	Crosswell	Pte	2	W
George	Cullam	Pte	3	W

William	Culley	Pte	5	W
Charles	Cumner	Pte	6	
James	Curtice	Pte	3	K
James	Custobody	Pte	1	
Thomas	Dakin	Pte	4	W
Thomas	Dale	Pte	4	
Robert	Dalrymple	Pte	4	
Adam	Davenport	Pte	8	
Thomas	Davenport	Pte	4	
George	Davis	Pte	7	
James	Davis	Pte	5	W
Richard	Davis	Pte	5	K
Robert	Deacon	Pte	3	W
Thomas	Deakin	Pte	3	W
James	Death	Pte	7	W
William	Death	Trumpeter	2	
David	Denner	Pte	7	
John	Derry	Pte	8	K
George	Dixon	Pte	7	
William	Dixon	Trumpet-Maj.	1	
John	Docker	Pte	7	W
William	Dolton	Pte	7	
John	Downham	Pte	8	
Frederick Dillon	Downing	Pte	1	W
Joseph	Drake	Sgt	8	
John	Dry	Pte	2	W
Thomas	Dudgeon	Cpl	2	K
John	Dymes	Pte	5	K
Ely	Dyson	Pte	3	
Thomas	Eckley	Pte	2	W
William	Elliott	Pte	8	W

Esau	Ellis	Pte	3	W
Thomas	Elson	Pte	7	
William	Elton	Capt.	1	
John	Emerson	Pte	7	
Joseph	Englefield	Pte	4	
James	Evans	Pte	6	W
Luke	Evans	Pte	3	K
William	Evatt	Pte	7	K
William	Fairbrother	Pte	4	
James	Fairclough	TSM	1	
Joseph	Fairfax	Pte	2	
John	Falconbridge	Pte	5	W
Samuel	Fieldhouse	Pte	2	
William	Fitch	Pte	8	W
James	Fletcher	Pte	7	
William	Folkes	Pte	7	
John	Frankum	Pte	3	
William	Fray	Pte	3	W
Joshua	Freeman	Pte	6	
John	Fulbrook	Pte	2	K
John	Fuller	Pte	2	
William	Fuller	Lt-Col		K
William	Gadsby	Pte	7	
Timothy	Gardiner	Pte	7	
Thomas	Garratt	Sgt	2	K
Thomas	Gaskill	Pte	3	
Peter	Gee	Pte	2	
Samuel	Gibbons	Pte	8	
Henry	Gieves	Pte	4	
Charles	Gillon	Pte	5	DOW
John	Glover	Pte	2	K
Henry	Godber	Pte	6	DOW

John	Going	Surgeon		
William	Goodacre	Cpl	4	
Charles	Gordon	Pte	1	K
Henry	Graham	Capt.		K
John	Grayshon	Pte	6	W
Jonas	Greaves	Lt	★	
Jeremiah	Green	Pte	2	W
Richard	Green	Cpl	2	
James	Greenhalgh	Pte	1	
James	Greenhalgh	Pte	7	
Richard	Greenhalgh	Pte	1	W
Joseph	Gregory	Pte	3	
Thomas	Grimshaw	Pte	8	W
Robert	Gripton	Cpl	7	
Edward	Groves	Pte	4	K
William	Groves	Pte	3	
Thomas	Guilford	Pte	4	W
George	Hasite	Pte	3	W
Richard	Hale	Pte	2	DOW
Francis	Hall	Pte	2	DOW
Richard	Hall	Pte	8	
Robert	Hall	Pte	4	W
Edmund	Halson	Arm.-Sgt	1	
Edward	Hamill	Lt	★	
John	Hancock	Pte	2	K
Charles	Hansler	Pte	7	
Joseph	Harfield	Pte	4	K
Benjamin	Harriman	Pte	8	W
Lewis	Harris	Pte	6	DOW
Richard	Harris	Pte	5	W
Samuel	Harrison	Pte	4	W
William	Harrison	Pte	3	DOW

Thomas	Hasker	Pte	3	W
William	Haslam	Pte	1	
Joseph	Hawkins	Pte	8	W
Thomas	Hawkyard	Pte	6	
Robert	Hawley	Lt	★	
Charles	Haynes	Pte	6	
Matthew	Haynes	Pte	5	K
Charles	Haywood	Cpl	2	
John	Headings	Pte	8	K
Robert	Headley	Pte	8	
William	Heap	Pte	7	W
Leonard	Helps	Pte	5	W
Edward	Hemming	Pte	5	
William	Hemming	Cpl	3	
Thomas	Herbett	Pte	1	
Richard	Herdsman	Pte	1	
Matthew	Hewett	Pte	1	
Thomas	Hewkin	Pte	8	K
William	Hickman	Pte	5	
George	Hill	Pte	8	K
James	Hill	Pte	3	W
Ramage	Hill	Pte	3	
Robert	Hill	Pte	7	
William	Hillier	Trumpeter	4	
Samuel	Holdknow	Pte	2	
Richard	Hollis	Sgt	3	
Moses	Holloway	Pte	1	
James	Holmes	Sgt	4	K
John	Holmes	Pte	6	W
Samuel	Horobin	Pte	7	
Joseph	Houghton	Pte	3	W
Richard	Houghton	Pay-Sgt	1	

Charles	Howarth	Pte	6	
William	Howett	Pte	7	
William	Huntley	Cor.	★	
Robert	Hurford	Cpl	6	
William	Hurford	Pte	8	
Robert	Hutchins	Pte	6	DOW
James	Hutchinson	Pte	4	W
William	Irvine	Lt	★	W
Francis	Jacques	Pte	5	
George	James	Pte	8	
John	James	Pte	2	W
John	James	Pte	5	
William	James	Pte	5	W
John	Jennings	Cpl	6	
Joseph	Jepson	Pte	7	
Emmanuel	Johnson	Pte	5	
Moses	Johnson	Pte	6	DOW
William	Johnson	Pte	5	K
William	Johnson	Pte	5	
John	Jones	Pte	4	K
Richard	Jones	Pte	7	W
Thomas	Jones	Pte	2	
William	Jones	Pte	7	
John	Kay	Pte	3	W
John	Kay	Pte	4	W
Richard	Kennett	Sgt	1	
Samuel	Kibble	Pte	8	K
Thomas	Kibble	Cpl	5	W
William	Kilband	Pte	3	
Joseph	King	Pte	4	DOW
Thomas	Kisbie	Pte	6	
Robert	Kitchen	Pte	8	K

George	Knights	Pte	6	W
George	Ladd	Pte	5	W
John	Lamport	Pte	5	W
William	Lancely	Pte	4	W
Henry	Lawdemore	Pte	8	K
Jonathan	Lawson	Pte	4	W
William	Lawson	Pte	7	
James	Leadley	Pte	5	K
James	Leatham	Lt	★	
John	Lee	Pte	3	K
Thomas	Lee	Pte	5	W
William	Lee	Pte	6	
John	Leek	Pte	8	
William	Lenton	Pte	7	W
Timothy	Levers	Pte	6	W
Isaac	Levitt	Pte	7	
John	Levitt	TSM	3	
John	Lewis	Pte	1	K
Joseph	Lewis	Pte	2	
Thomas	Linton	TSM	5	
Thomas	Lloyde	Pte	2	W
James	Lock	Pte	6	W
Henry	Lockey	Pte	8	W
Joseph	Lomax	Pte	6	W
William	Lomax	Pte	3	W
Joseph	Long	Pte	4	K
William	Longfield	Pte	4	
Charles	Lord	Pte	6	
James	Lord	Pte	5	K
John	Loughton	Pte	1	K
Thompson	Lynn	Pte	5	K
Joshua	Lywood	Pte	3	W

John	Maiden	Pte	1	
Joseph	Makin	Pte	1	
Michael	Marnham	Pte	6	DOW
George	Marsden	Pte	6	
George	Marshall	Pte	3	W
James	Martin	Pte	4	
William	Marvin	Pte	6	W
Thomas	Mason	Pte	3	K
Thomas	Mason	Pte	6	W
James	Mather	Pte	1	
Robert	Mathews	Pte	4	
Richard	May	Pte	7	
Alexander	McKay	Pte	6	W
James	McKenna	Pte	7	K
John	Meyrick	Pte	4	W
Thomas	Middleton	Cor.	★	
John	Millett	Pte	3	W
Robert	Missett	Saddler–Sgt	1	
Joseph	Moass	Pte	3	
Joseph	Monger	Pte	3	
Joseph	Morley	Pte	2	
William	Morley	Pte	6	DOW
Emmanuel	Morton	Pte	7	
Benjamin	Moss	Pte	5	W
James	Musson	Pte	4	
Henry	Mutton	Sgt	1	
James	Naylor	Capt.	6	W
William	Newbold	Pte	6	DOW
Mark	Newell	Pte	6	DOW
Edward	Newman	Pte	4	K
William	Newton	Pte	2	
Henry	Nicholson	Pte	5	

Thomas	Nicholson	Pte	5	W
John	Nickson	Pte	1	
Nathaniel	Norman	Sgt	8	K
John	Nosely	Pte	2	W
Thomas	Novis	Pte	1	W
Septimus	Noyes	Pte	8	W
James	Nuttall	Sgt	7	
John	Nuttall	Pte	2	K
John	Nuttall	Pte	5	W
Robert	Nuttall	Sgt	6	W
William	Oliver	Trumpeter	5	W
James	Orme	Pte	6	
William	Osborne	Trumpeter	6	W
George	Ovendale	Cpl	7	
Joseph	Owen	Pte	8	W
John	Ozwin	Cpl	1	
James	Page	TSM	4	
James	Page	Cpl	7	
John	Parker	Pte	6	DOW
John	Parr	Cpl	4	
Thomas	Partridge	Pte	3	W
William	Pattinson	Pte	8	
John	Pearson	Pte	7	K
Richard	Pearson	Asst-Surgeon		
John	Peet	Pte	8	
William	Peet	Pte	1	
Joseph	Pegg	Pte	2	
Thomas	Pemberton	Pte	1	
Nathaniel	Perkins	Pte	6	W
Thomas	Perkins	Cpl	5	
John	Perry	Pte	3	
John	Picton	Pte	3	W

William	Pigg	Pte	5	W
James	Pilgrim	Pte	7	
John	Pinder	Pte	3	K
Charles	Pink	Pte	3	
William	Pink	Pte	6	
Isaac	Piper	Pte	1	K
William	Piper	Pte	2	
Richard	Pizzey	Pte	1	
Joseph	Platt	Pte	1	
Thomas	Pointon	Sgt	4	
William	Pointon	Pte	7	W
Charles	Pomfrey	Pte	6	
John	Poole	Pte	4	W
James	Pope	Pte	5	
Richard	Porter	Pte	4	
William	Porter	Pte	8	
John	Postell	Pte	5	
Joseph	Poultney	Pte	6	
James	Powell	Pte	1	W
Benjamin	Preece	Pte	4	
Thomas	Preece	Pte	2	W
Edward	Price	Pte	8	W
Philip	Priece	Pte	3	W
Thomas	Priece	Pte	2	
Giles	Purham	Pte	2	
George	Quicke	Cor.	⋆	
Thomas	Quicke	Capt.	7	
James	Ramsden	Pte	5	K
Thomas	Ramsden	Pte	6	DOW
George	Raynor	Pte	5	
James	Reed	Pte	4	
John	Reeves	Pte	5	W

Thomas	Reeves	Pte	8	W
Edmund	Rhodes	Pte	6	
Abraham	Richards	Pte	8	
John	Richardson	Sgt	2	W
John	Richardson	Pte	7	K
William	Richardson	Pte	8	W
John	Rider	Pte	5	W
John	Rider	Pte	7	
Thomas	Rider	Pte	5	W
James	Ridge	Pte	6	
James	Rigg	TQM Sgt	2	
Robert	Ringland	Sgt	1	W
John	Robinson	Pte	4	W
Thomas	Robinson	Pte	8	
Thomas	Robinson	Pte	8	
William	Robinson	Pte	2	
Samuel	Roe	Pte	1	
James	Rollinson	Cpl	4	W
Ralph	Roper	Cpl	1	
Elias	Ross	Pte	6	DOW
Edward	Rosthorne	Pte	3	W
Henry	Rosthorne	Pte	5	K
Charles	Sacker	Pte	5	W
William	Sanderson	Pte	6	DOW
Thomas	Sands	Sgt	2	
William	Sarson	Pte	1	W
James	Saunt	Pte	3	K
John	Schofield	Pte	3	W
William	Schofield	Pte	3	W
James	Scott	Pte	6	
William	Seagrave	Pte	5	W
Stephen	Seaman	Pte	1	W

John	Serjeant	Pte	7	DOW
William	Settle	Pte	7	
James	Sharp	Pte	6	DOW
John	Sharpless	Pte	6	W
James	Sharpley	Pte	8	W
John	Shaw	Pte	1	W
John	Sheffield	Pte	4	W
Thomas	Shelver	Lt (Adj.)	3	K
William	Sheward	Sgt	1	
John	Shipman	Pte	8	
William	Shirley	Pte	8	W
Joseph	Sikes	Pte	3	
Silas	Sims	Pte	5	W
Henry	Simpson	Pte	3	
James	Simpson	Cpl	8	W
John	Simpson	Pte	5	W
Thomas	Simpson	Pte	1	K
John	Sims	Pte	4	DOW
John	Sisson	Cpl	1	W
Samuel	Sisson	Pte	7	W
George	Slater	Pte	2	
Nathaniel	Smallwood	Sgt	2	K
John	Smith	Pte	3	
Joseph	Smith	Pte	5	
Samuel	Smith	Sgt	5	W
Samuel	Smith	Pte	6	
Thomas	Smith	Pte	5	
William	Smith	Sgt	5	K
John	Snutch	Pte	5	
Robert	Soper	Pte	1	
James	Speller	Cpl	5	
James	Stacey	Pte	5	K

Rueben	Staniland	Pte	5	K
Charles	Stanley	Pte	1	K
Joseph	Starbrook	Pte	8	
Charles	Starkey	Sgt	8	K
Richard	Starkey	Pte	8	
James	Steel	Pte	7	
George	Stevens	Pte	5	
Leonard	Stevenson	Pte	2	
William	Stirling	Lt	★	
John	Stokes	Pte	2	W
John	Stoneystreet	Pte	8	W
James	Storey	Pte	6	
John	Street	Pte	7	
Thomas	Stringer	Cpl	8	W
John	Stubbings	Cpl	1	
Joseph	Sutcliff	Pte	7	W
John	Sutton	Pte	6	W
William	Sutton	Pte	2	
John	Sweny	Capt.	4	W
Stephen	Syer	Pte	7	K
Francis	Tanner	Pte	6	W
John	Tasker	Pte	5	
George	Taylor	Pte	1	
Thomas	Taylor	Cpl	4	
William	Taylor	Pte	3	
John	Tebbs	Sgt	5	K
John	Temple	Pte	1	K
John	Thomas	Schoolmaster–Sgt	1	
George	Thompson	Cpl	2	W
James	Thompson	Pte	4	
James	Thornton	Pte	7	

John	Thwaites	Pte	5	
Samuel	Tilley	Pte	6	
Thomas	Timpson	Pte	6	DOW
James	Towers	Pte	4	
John	Tracey	TSM	7	DOW
William	Tressler	Cpl	8	W
George	Trilloe	Pte	7	K
John Lewis	Tucker	Sgt	8	
Samuel	Tucker	Pte	8	W
James	Tudman	Pte	7	W
John	Tune	Pte	6	W
Michael	Turner	Capt.	8	W
William	Turner	Sgt	3	
Thomas	Tyers	Pte	1	
William	Valance	Pte	5	W
William	Varley	Pte	5	
Thomas	Vent	Sgt	6	K
James	Vickers	Pte	2	
William	Vickers	Pte	8	
John	Vincent	Pte	3	
Hinman	Wainford	Pte	1	
Thomas	Wakefield	Pte	7	DOW
John	Waldron	Pte	5	
John	Wale	Pte	7	
William	Wale	Pte	1	W
Adam	Walkden	Pte	1	Died 1816
Charles	Walker	Pte	2	W
Edward	Walker	Pte	7	K
George	Walker	Pte	2	
John	Walker	Pte	2	W
Thomas	Warbutton	Pte	5	DOW
James	Warcop	Pte	8	

John	Ward	Sgt	7	W
Matthew	Ward	Pte	8	
Nathaniel	Ward	Pte	2	W
Samuel	Ward	Pte	3	
William	Ward	Pte	4	W
Edward	Warren	Pte	7	K
John	Warren	Pte	2	W
Richard	Warren	Pte	6	W
Josh	Watkins	Pte	4	K
Richard	Watts	Cpl	6	
Robert	Watts	Cpl	3	
William	Watts	Trumpeter	7	
Richard	Webster	Pte	7	K
Samuel	Webster	Pte	8	
Job	West	Pte	1	
John	West	Pte	2	
Joseph	Westroop	Pte	6	
John	Wheatcroft	Pte	3	
Samuel	Wheeler	Trumpeter	3	
Henry	White	Pte	3	
John	White	Pte	7	W
Joseph	White	Pte	3	
Samuel	White	Pte	4	W
Thomas	White	Cpl	1	W
William	White	Pte	8	W
Richard	Whitehead	Pte	7	
William	Whitehouse	Pte	3	W
Edward	Wild	Pte	7	W
Robert	Wilkins	Trumpeter	8	W
Thomas	Wilkins	Pte	3	K
William	Williams	Pte	3	K
Richard	Williamson	Pte	2	W

William	Wilshee	Pte	4	K
Jonathon	Wilson	Sgt	6	W
John	Witton	Pte	1	
Joseph	Wood	Pte	6	W
Richard	Wood	Pte	6	W
William	Woodburn	Pte	3	
Thomas	Woodman	Pte	2	K
James	Woodward	Pte	1	
William	Woodward	Pte	2	W
Thomas	Woon	Pte	4	W
Edward	Wright	TSM	8	W
John	Wright	Pte	1	K
John	Wright	Pte	3	W
Jonathon	Wright	Pte	6	
Athen	Wyatt	Pte	8	W
John	Young	Pte	2	
William	Young	Pte	6	

Notes

1 There were 604 KDG all ranks present at Waterloo, according to the regiment's paylist. This comprised twenty-four regimental officers, one officer on the staff (Dawson), two sugeons, seven regimental non-commissioned officers, seven TSMs, thirty-four sergeants, thirty-four corporals, seven trumpeters and 488 men.

2 Note 1 listed 604 KDG all ranks present at Waterloo, yet the Regimental Roll shown in this appendix only lists 603 names. The missing man was Major the Hon. George Dawson, who, whilst he was present at Waterloo, did not serve with the regiment but as the quartermaster-general to the Prince of Orange.

3 Officers have been shown with their regimental and not their army rank. For example, Fuller was a full colonel in the army but a lieutenant-colonel in the KDG. Both Graham and Bringhurst were majors in the army but captains in the regiment.

4 Awarded the Waterloo Medal but absent from the battle were Lt John Hibbert, who was sick, and presumably his servant, Pte William Oliver, who would have stayed and attended him and therefore was not counted on the regimental strength for 18 June 1815. Asst-Surgeon Macauley was in Brussels on

18 June 1815 when Naylor arrived wounded and was, therefore, not actually present at Waterloo. However, he was counted as having been present on the Army Strength and was awarded a Waterloo medal. Paymaster Webster was not present at Waterloo and therefore not included.

5 The numbers reported killed in *The Digest* and those NCOs and men as listed in the *Waterloo Pay Return* tally. The only discrepancy was that *The Digest* listed eleven sergeants to have been killed, when there were only nine who were unequivocally killed, as Mann reported Sgt Nathaniel Smallwood to have 'later returned'. However, the total of eleven men killed is explained by counting sgts Smallwood and Chivers, both of whom had been listed as missing.

6 The total number of KDGs killed was probably 128 not 129, as Moses Johnson, recorded to have been 'killed in action', was still being paid in 1816. The author believed the misconception over his death may have resulted from a comma having been put in the wrong place in the reproduction of Naylor's diary. This was reproduced as, 'Died of Wounds: Robt Hutchins (returned after), Moses Johnson, Michael Marnham'. Hutchins died and did not return, and Johnson reappeared.

7 The total numbers reported as killed may have been lower. Pte Benjamin Brooks, who was listed in the *Waterloo Pay Return* to have died of wounds, was reported by Mann to have been subsequently discharged. Pte Adam Walkden, who died on 18 July 1816, may have not died as a result of Waterloo and his death has, therefore, not been associated with Waterloo.

8 Officer's army and not regimental rank was shown here to facilitate tallying this list with official records. Both capts Graham and Bringhurst were brevet majors, and referred to by this rank in the regiment at the time of Waterloo.

9 After Waterloo, lts Irvine and Greaves changed their names respectively to D'Arcy-Irvine and Elmsall.

NOTES

Introduction

1   I have been in communication with the following officers' and soldiers' descendants/relations: Tricia Datené (Capt. Michael Turner); the Hon. Julia Elton (Capt. William Elton); John Quicke (Thomas and George Quicke); Viscount Brooke (Lt Francis Brooke); Canon Anthony Hawley (Lt Robert Hawley); Anthony D'Arcy Irvine (Lt William D'Arcy Irvine); Robert Lowry (Assistant-Surgeon William Macauley); John Shead (Sgt John Stubbings); and Peter Derry (Pte John Derry).

2   The following men served with the KDG at Waterloo and were christened in St Mary's Church, Kingsclere: TSM David Benwell, Pte James Brown, Pte Richard Hale, Pte George Hill, Pte Joseph Long and Pte Samuel Tucker.

Chapter 1

1   William Siborne, *History of the War in France and Belgium, in 1815: Containing Minute Details* (Cambridge, 2012), p.505. According to Siborne, Uxbridge's ADCs were Major Thornhill 7th Hussars and Captain H. Seymour 60th Foot. His extra ADCs were captains T. Wildman and J. Fraser of the 7th Hussars.

2   Elizabeth Longford, *Wellington: The Years of the Sword* (London, 1971), p.454.

3   Haythornthwaite in a letter to the author dated 26 January 2016 confirmed that Uxbridge was regimental colonel of the 7th Hussars until his death, according to N.B. Leslie, *The Succession of Colonels of the British Army from 1660 to the Present Day* (Society of Army Historical Research, 1974), p.22.

4   The Marquess of Anglesey, *One Leg: The Life and Letters of Henry William Paget, First Marquess of Anglesey* (London, 1961), p.121.

5   Ibid.

6   Ian Fletcher, *Galloping at Everything, The British Cavalry in the Peninsular War and at Waterloo 1808–15* (Staplehust, 1999), p.226. And see note 8 to this page that gives more details of Wellington's attitude to Uxbridge.

7   Alessandro Barbero, *The Battle: A New History of the Battle of Waterloo* (London, 2003), p.15.

8   Henri Lot, *Les deux généraux Ordener* (Paris, 1910), p.91.

9   TSM James Page KDG, letters held by 1st The Queen's Dragoon Guards Heritage Trust.

10   Page, op. cit.

11   Rank can be confusing as the officers could have had different army and regimental ranks. For example, in the regiment Henry Graham was a captain but in army terms he was a major. Hence he was not classified as the senior captain in the regiment. The same was the case for John Bringhurst, who was a brevet major in the army but still a captain in the regiment. William Fuller was a colonel in the army but a lieutenant-colonel in the regiment. For consistency, the regimental ranks of the officers have been used in this book except when quoted.

12   RSM Thomas Barlow KDG, letters held by 1st The Queen's Dragoon Guards Heritage Trust.

13   Capt. William Elton KDG, letters held by the National Army Museum (NAM) 1963–10–36.

14   Michael Mann, *And They Rode On* (Salisbury, 1984), p.1.

15   Maj.-Gen. H.T. Siborne, *Waterloo Letters* (London, 1891), p.37.

16   Capt. James Naylor KDG, diaries held by 1st The Queen's Dragoon Heritage Trust.

17   Elton, op. cit.

18   George Luckley, *The History of Thomas Hasker, Soldier and Methodist: With His Letters* (London, 1875).

19   Page, op. cit.

20   Gregory Fremont-Barnes, *Waterloo 1815: Britain's Day of Destiny* (Stroud, 2014), p.11.

21   Page, op. cit.

22   Elton, op. cit.

23   N.L. Beamish, *History of the King's German Legion, Vol. II* (London, 1837), pp.360–1.

Chapter 2

1   Gareth Glover, *Waterloo Archive, Vol. IV*, doc. 12, letter from Private Thomas
     Playford, 2nd Life Guards, undated.

2   Ibid.

3   Gordon Corrigan in *Waterloo: A New History* (London, 1992), opined that, as
     Wellington did not usually delegate, it was highly unlikely in this case that this vital
     decision would have been made by anyone but himself. This sentiment echoed
     Jac Weller's comments in *Wellington at Waterloo* (London, 1992), p.102, note 1.

4   Siborne, op. cit., p.4.

5   Siborne, op. cit., p.8.

6   John Lee in an email dated 12 February 2016 commented that this force
     was not finished for the day and that one battalion remained in line, whilst
     the remainder re-formed in the Allied rear. They took part in a subsequent
     counter-attack in which van Bijlandt was wounded by a French bayonet.

7   Anglesey, op. cit., p.138.

8   Anglesey, op. cit., p.121.

9   Rees Howell Gronow, *Reminiscences of Captain Gronow* (London, 1862), p.108.

10   Sir Herbert Maxwell, *The Life of Wellington: The Restoration of the Martial Power
     of Great Britain* (London, 1899), II: p.138-9.

11   Lt-Col John Gurwood, *The Dispatches of Field Marshal the Duke of Wellington:
     During His Various Campaigns in India, Denmark, Portugal, Spain, the Low Countries,
     and France, Volume VII*, p.412. Wellington's letter to Beresford, 30 March 1811.

12   Fletcher, op. cit., p.137.

13   Mann 1984, op. cit., p.2 from Crofton.

14   Siborne, p.46.

15   Page, op. cit.

16   Barlow, op. cit., letter dated 7 July 1815.

17   Naylor, op. cit.

18   Siborne, op. cit., p.8.

19   Playford in Glover, op. cit.

20   *Two Generations, John Derry (1792–1869) and John Derry Junior (1817–1838)*,
     private papers held by the Derry family.

21   Anglesey, op. cit., p.139. Map 12 shows, 'Probable position of UXBRIDGE
     at start of charge.' This was represented by a star located to the west of the
     Brussels–Charleroi road, in front and to the south of the 2nd Life Guards and
     behind and north of the KGL.

22   Barlow, op. cit., letter dated 4 July 1815.

23   Elton, op. cit.

24   Page, op. cit.

25   Longford, op. cit., p.543, and Barbero, op. cit., p.149.

Chapter 3

1   John Harold Wilson, *Court Satires of the Restoration* (Ohio, 1976), p.40. In this note to an anonymous court satire, the author of this collection of satires explained that the word 'beau' referred to a lover of the promiscuous Mary, Countess of Arundel, who was the Hon. Henry Lumley.

2   Richard Cannon, *Historical Records of the British Army, 1st Dragoon Guards* (London, 1837), p.12.

3   Michael Mann, *The Regimental History of 1st The Queen's Dragoon Guards* (Norwich, 1993), p.15.

4   Mann 1993, op. cit., p.21, from State Papers, 1691; 'De Ginkel's Despatch'; Records of The King's Dragoon Guards.

5   Haythornthwaite's letter to the author dated 26 January 2016 stated the first battle honour to have been awarded to British regiments was authorised for Waterloo on 18 December 1815. It was only subsequently that the Alison Committee of 1882 made retrospective awards of battle honours that pre-dated Waterloo.

6   Haythornthwaite's letter to the author dated 26 January 2016 stated that on the evidence of a painting of Capt. William Pritchard Ashurst, yellow facings were still being used by the KDG in 1722–23 when this officer served in the regiment.

7   Cannon, op. cit., p.53.

8   *The London Gazette*, 16 July 1743.

9   Sir Francis Skrine, *Fontenoy and Great Britain's Share in the War of the Austrian Succession 1741–48* (London, Edinburgh, 1906), p.163.

10   David Ramsay, *Military Memoirs of Great Britain: Or a History of the War, 1755–1763* (Edinburgh, 1779), p.286.

11   Mann 1993, op. cit., p.127.

12   Cannon, op. cit., p.84.

13   Mann 1993, op. cit., p.150.

14   Sir John Fortescue, *British Campaigns in Flanders 1690–1794 (Extracts from Volume 4 of A History of the British Army)* (London, 1918), p.310.

15   *The Digest of Services (The Digest)* was the regimental diary of the King's Dragoon Guards from its creation in 1685 until its amalgamation with The Queen's Bays in 1959. It recorded the major events that affected the regiment and is available online at www.qdg.org.uk/digest.php.

16   Lt John Hibbert KDG, letters held by 1st The Queen's Dragoon Guards Heritage Trust. In a letter dated 11 June 1815, Hibbert wrote, 'I believe Colonel Fuller is made Major General, and therefore we shall lose him I am sorry to say.'

Chapter 4

1   The places of birth for over 60 per cent of the KDGs who fought were in just the five counties of: Leicestershire, Lancashire, Hampshire, Yorkshire and Nottinghamshire.

2   Luckley, op. cit., p.7.

3   'Enquiry into the General State of the Poor, 1795', *Hampshire Repository*, I, 1799, p.19.

4   T.L. Richardson, *Agricultural Labourers' Wages and the Cost of Living in Essex, 1790–1840*; Gordon Mingay, *Land, Labour and Agriculture, 1700–1920*, Appendix 4.1, p.90. Agricultural workers' wages in 1805 were 9s per week.

5   Bob Burnham and Ron McGuigan, *The British Army Against Napoleon, Facts, Lists and Trivia 1805–1815* (Barnsley, 2010), p.235, Table 5.13, Daily and yearly pay for soldiers in 1805. And Table 5.15, Yearly pay for an infantry private after deductions, p.237. From *A Treatise in Military Finance Vol. 2*, Appendix 1. The KDG private's weekly pay in 1805 was 1s 3d a day, with an additional 1s 4d a day in additional allowances (see note 6).

6   Philip Haythornthwaite, *British Cavalryman 1793–1815* (London, 1994), p.8.

7   Bryan Fosten, *Wellington's Heavy Cavalry* (London, 1982), p.17.

8   Ibid.

9   Ibid, p.6.

10 *The British Military Library or Journal, Vol. II* (London, 1798), p.275, stated, 'The average height of the men [KDG troopers] is five feet ten inches.'

11 KDG soldiers' records compiled by Clive Morris, Curator of 1st The Queen's Dragoon Guards Heritage Trust.

12 Fosten, op. cit., p.15.

13 Haythornthwaite, in a letter to the author dated 26 January 2016.

14 Haythornthwaite, in a letter to the author 26 January 2016, stated that the recruit could not be taken before the magistrate within twenty-four hours of agreeing to enlist, 'presumably so that drunks would have time to sober up before they were presented, and thus [be] capable of renouncing their declaration if it were made under the influence of alcohol'.

15 Haythornthwaite, op. cit., p.7.

16 Hibbert, op. cit.

17 Burnham and McGuigan, op. cit., pp.167–9, Table 4.8, Daily and yearly pay for officers from *The Army List 1810*, p.107.

18 This was calculated by using Burnham and McGuigan's Table 4.16, Deductions in pay for an ensign in the Foot Guards in 1810 on p.174 of *The British Army Against Napoleon, Facts, Lists and Trivia 1805–1815,* and substituting the cornet's £146 per annum pay for the £106 listed for the ensign.

The cornet was left with net daily pay of 2/7d, thus 2s a day better off than the ensign, who was left with 7d a day after deductions.

19   Haythorthwaite, op. cit., p.7 reported that of the 329 troop officers in the British cavalry at Waterloo, 'there was only one peer ... 13 sons of peers, 17 sons of baronets'.

Chapter 5

1   Fosten, op. cit., p.6.
2   Philip Haythornthwaite, in a letter to the author dated 20 December 2015, based his comments on Col H.C.B. Rogers, *Wellington's Army* (London, 1979), p.46.
3   Mann 1993, op. cit., p.169.
4   Sir Barney White-Spunner, *Horse Guards* (London, 2006), p.303.
5   1st The Queen's Dragoon Guards website, http://www.qdg.org.uk, History and Research, *The Digest of Services 1815*.
6   Ibid.
7   Dundas had held this post from 1809–11 as a stopgap whilst the then commander-in-chief, the Duke of York, had been obliged to stand down over the accusations against his mistress Mary Anne Clarke of having offered influence over officers' promotions in return for money.
8   Philip Haythornthwaite, letter to the author dated 20 December 2015.
9   *The Digest*, op. cit.
10   Burnham and McGuigan, op. cit., p.153, Table 3.44, Regimental Agents for the cavalry regiments from *The Army List 1812*.
11   Fosten, op. cit., p.13.
12   Col W. Johnson, ed. Lt-Col H.A.L. Howell, *Roll of Commissioned Officers in the Medical Service of the British Army ... 20 June 1727 to 23 June 1898* (Aberdeen, 1917), letter from Haythornthwaite, op. cit.
13   Fosten, op. cit., p.12.
14   Ibid, p.162.
15   Fosten, op. cit., p.14.
16   Fosten, op. cit., p.25. Fosten lists the Field Calls, which were: March, Trot, Gallop, Charge, Halt, Retreat, Rally, Turn our Skirmishers, Cease Firing and Call in Skirmishers.
17   Fosten, op. cit., p.12.
18   Fosten, op. cit., p.6.
19   Article No. 16 of *The Standing Orders King's Dragoon Guards* published 1819 stated, 'Each Troop is to be divided into squads according to their strength.'

20 *General Standing Orders for Third, Or Prince of Wales's Dragoon Guards* (Edinburgh, 1803), p.90. Article I stated, 'Every troop must be divided into as many Squads as there are Serjeants.'

21 *The Standing Orders King's Dragoon Guards*, op. cit.

22 Ibid.

23 Fosten, op. cit., p.11.

24 Fosten, op. cit., p.12.

25 Fosten, op. cit., p.13.

26 Margaret Elton, *Annals of the Elton Family* (Stroud, 1994), p.133.

27 Haythornthwaite letter, op. cit., 'at the time of Waterloo a commission in a dragoon guard regiment or dragoon regiment, for a cornet, cost £755; a Foot Guards ensigncy £900. (Statistics taken from Army List).'

Chapter 6

1 For a complete list of 'Appointments', 'Accoutrements' and 'Necessaries', see Fosten, op. cit., p.15–17, and Haythornthwaite, op. cit., p.60.

2 Cannon, op. cit., p.92. In 1812, 'cloth pantaloons and short boots were adopted'.

3 Cannon, op. cit., p.93. In December 1812, 'gauntlets were replaced by short leather gloves'.

4 Philip Haythornthwaite, letter to author 20 December 2015, 'gauntlets were supposed to be worn only when the white dress breeches and long boots were worn; otherwise short gloves. The white breeches and long boots were discontinued in September 1815 in favour of ankle-boots and overalls similar to those worn on active service.'

5 Ibid.

6 Apart from the cuffs and officers' facing material, the KDG uniform was identical to that of the 1st Royal Dragoons at Waterloo. As a result, one of the Royals officers mistook a group of KDG s for men from his regiment, as he was quoted in Siborne, op. cit., p.77.

7 Haythornthwaite letter, op. cit.

8 Ibid.

9 Philip Haythornthwaite, telephone conversation with author, 10 December 2015.

10 Fosten, op. cit., pp.36–7.

11 Fosten, op. cit., pp.26–30.

12 Haythornthwaite letter, op. cit. In this he drew attention to the fact that only Household Cavalry officers would have worn a frock coat, 'as they were unique in the cavalry in having two styles of uniform for officers: the laced

jacket as worn by the KDG, and a much plainer, almost unlaced, single-breasted jacket which was worn on campaign.'

13   Charles Martyn, *The British Cavalry Sword from 1600* (Barnsley, 2004), pp.78–83.

14   Philip Haythornthwaite and Adam Hook, *Napoleonic Heavy Cavalry & Dragoon Tactics* (Oxford, 2013), p.13.

15   *The Digest* is shown on the QDG website, www.qdg.org.uk.

16   Siborne, op. cit., Letter No. 19 from Major S. Waymouth, p.44.

17   Mark Adkin, *The Waterloo Companion* (London, 2001), pp.224–5.

18   'An officer of dragoons', *United Services Journal* (London, 1831), quoted in Haythornthwaite, 1994, op. cit., p.26.

19   Martyn, op. cit., p.83.

20   Siborne 1891, op. cit., p.11.

21   Haythornthwaite 1994, op. cit., p.32.

22   QDG website, op. cit.

23   Paul Dawson, *Boots and Saddles* (Stockton-on-Tees, 2014), p.30.

24   Dawson 2014, op. cit., p.27.

25   *The British Military Library or Journal, Vol. II* (London, 1798), p.275, stated, 'The average height of the men is five feet ten inches; the horses fifteen hands one inch and a half.'

26   Ibid, p.35.

27   Ibid, p.157.

28   Naylor, op. cit., diary entry for 7 May 1815 mentioned that he, 'Received of Webster [the Paymaster] 30 Napoleons for Troop Bat horse'.

29   Dawson 2014, op. cit., p.198.

30   Shown in print in Charles Hamilton-Smith, *Costume of the Army of the British Empire, 1812–14.* Quoted in Haythornthwaite letter, op. cit.

31   Fosten, op. cit., p.17.

Chapter 7

1   *The Standing Orders King's Dragoon Guards* was published in 1819 but was probably based on the previous set of regimental standing orders in force at the time of Waterloo.

2   Burnham and McGuigan, op. cit., pp.233–5.

3   Ibid, p.235, from Thomas Reide, *A Treatise in Military Finance Concerning the Pay and Allowances in Camp, Garrison and Quarters of the British Army, Vol. 1* (London, 1803), p.249.

4   Haythornthwaite 1994, op. cit., p.8.

5   Ibid, p.133–4.

Chapter 8

1   Dawson 2014, op. cit., p.113.
2   Ibid, p.232.
3   Ibid, pp.129–30.
4   Ibid, p.113.
5   Ibid, p.116.
6   Ibid, p.120.
7   Lt-Col John Gurwood, *The Dispatches of Field Marshal the Duke of Wellington: During His Various Campaigns in India, Denmark, Portugal, Spain, the Low Countries, and France, Volume II*, pp.678–9.
8   J.E. Cookson, *The British Armed Nation 1793–1815* (Oxford, 1997), p.31.
9   Adkin, op. cit., p.230.
10   Siborne, op. cit., No. 21 from Lt Waymouth, p.46. In this letter, Waymouth wrote that Naylor, 'distinctly remembers that he commanded the central squadron of the King's'. He went on to write that Naylor, 'remembers that on advancing, Colonel Fuller placed himself by him'.
11   Siborne, op. cit., p.44. Letter No. 19, Major S. Waymouth late 2nd Life Guards.
12   Gen. Sir David Dundas's *Instructions and Regulations for the Formation and Movements of the Cavalry* (London, 1796), pp.31–5.

Chapter 9

1   Hibbert, op. cit., letter dated 12 April 1815.
2   Ibid, letter dated 15 May 1815.
3   Mann 1984, op. cit., p.1.
4   Hibbert, op. cit., letter dated 15 May 1815.
5   Barlow, op. cit., letter dated 30 April 1815.
6   Naylor, op. cit.
7   Mann, 1984, op. cit., p.2. Quoted from Sir Morgan Crofton, 'Household Cavalry and the Waterloo Campaign', *Household Brigade Magazine*, 1911.
8   Hibbert, op. cit., letter dated 15 May 1815.
9   Ibid, letter dated 28 May 1815.
10   Barlow, op. cit., letter dated 30 May 1815.
11   *The Digest*, 1st The Queen's Dragoon Guards, www.qdg.org.uk.
12   Ibid.
13   Mann 1984, op. cit., p.1.
14   Hibbert, op. cit., letter dated 28 May, 1815.
15   Hibbert, op. cit., letter dated 1 June, 1815.

16 Mann 1984, op. cit, p.4. From Sir Morgan Crofton, 'Household Cavalry and the Waterloo Campaign', *Household Brigade Magazine*, 1911.

17 Barlow, op. cit., letter dated 30 May 1815.

18 Barlow, op. cit., letter dated 14 June 1815.

19 Private Charles Stanley's letter to his cousin Christopher Alvey, dated 15 May, in the Nottinghamshire Archives Office, reference DD191/1.

20 Burnham and McGuigan, op. cit., p.233, 238.

21 Paul L. Dawson, *Charge the Guns!* (Stockton-on-Tees, 2015), p.42.

22 Barlow, op. cit., letter dated 16 May 1815.

23 Naylor op. cit., 5 and 11 June 1815.

24 Hibbert, op. cit., letter dated 11 June 1815.

Chapter 10

1 Hibbert, op. cit., letter dated 1 June 1815.

2 Dawson 2015, op. cit., p.45.

3 Barlow, op. cit., letter dated 14 June 1815.

4 Mann 1984, op. cit. p.11.

5 Barlow, op. cit., letter dated 4 July 1815.

6 Haythornthwaite, in a letter to the author of 26 January 2016, pointed out that Naylor had omitted the 44th Regiment from his description of the composition of Picton's Division.

7 Naylor, op. cit.

8 Dawson 2015, op. cit., p.47. From William Hay, *Reminiscences 1808–1815: Under Wellington* (London, 1901), pp.159–60.

9 Gen. Alexander Cavalié Mercer, *Journal of the Waterloo Campaign, Volume I* (London, 1870), p.238.

10 Mercer, op. cit., p.240.

11 Mercer, op. cit., p.242.

12 Dawson, op. cit., p.46, from W. Siborne, *Waterloo Letters*, op. cit.

13 Mercer, op. cit., p.243.

14 Mercer, op. cit., pp.246–8.

15 Barlow, op. cit., letter dated 14 June 1815.

16 Naylor, op. cit.

17 Barlow, op. cit., letter dated 4 July 1815.

18 Mann 1984, op. cit,. p.14.

19 Page, op. cit.

20 Barlow, op. cit., letter dated 4 July 1815.

21 Dawson 2015, op. cit., p.66, from National Library of Scotland, MS15379.

22   Ibid, from John Edgecombe Daniel, *Journal of an Officer in the Commissariat Department: 1811–1815* (London, 1820), p.386.

23   Ibid, from W. Siborne, *Waterloo Letters*, letter no. 34.

24   Ibid.

25   Naylor, op. cit.

26   Dawson 2015, op. cit., p.72.

27   Mann, op. cit, pp.17–18.

28   Mercer, op. cit.

29   William Siborne, *The Waterloo Campaign* (London, 1848), p.266.

30   Dawson 2015, op. cit., p.73, and Mann 1984, op. cit., p.19.

31   Siborne, op. cit., p.269.

32   Barlow, op. cit., letter dated 4 July 1815.

33   Siborne, op. cit., pp.277–80.

34   Page, op. cit.

35   Cannon, op. cit., p.96.

36   1st Queen's Dragoon Guards' website, www.qdg.org.uk.

37   Barlow, op. cit., letter dated 4 July 1815.

38   QDG website, op. cit.

Chapter 11

1   Elton, op. cit.

2   Luckley, op. cit., p.17.

3   Naylor, op. cit.

4   *Two Generations, John Derry*, op. cit.

5   Hibbert, op. cit., letter dated 13 July 1815.

6   The 1st Cuirassiers was France's senior cuirassier regiment and one of the oldest regiments in the French Army, having entered service in 1635. It was known as *Le Régiment de Fer*.

7   The 2nd Cuirassiers, founded in 1643, was known as *La Reine-Mère* as it had been the regiment of French queens Maria Theresa and Marie-Antoinette.

8   Octave Levavasseur, *Souvenirs Militaires de Octave Levavasseur* (Paris, 1914), p.298.

9   Sir Morgan Crofton, 'Household Cavalry and the Waterloo Campaign', *Household Brigade Magazine*, 1911.

10   Email from Pierre de Wit to author, 16 November 2015, which quoted Le Comte Milhaud's letter reproduced in *Revue Bourguignonne, Vol. 15* (Dijon, 1905), p.133. De Wit also pointed out in this email that whilst Milhaud had claimed twenty of d'Erlon's cannons had been rescued by Delort's men,

there were, in fact, only sixteen cannons on the intermediate ridge captured by the British. The four missing cannons may be explained by the fact that in Letter No. 12 in Gareth Glover's *Waterloo Archive Volume IV*, Private Thomas Playford of the 2nd Life Guards claimed his regiment had also, 'captured several pieces of cannon; but being pressed on all sides by superior numbers, and the regiment having to fight its way back, it was unable to retain possession of the guns'.

11   Ibid.

12   Paul Dawson, *Charge the Guns!* (Stockton-on-Tees, 2015), p.125, from SHDDT C15 fol.1510.

13   Ibid, p.126.

14   François de Bas and Le Comte Jacques de t'Serclaes de Wommerson, *La Campagne de 1818 aux Pas-Bas d'après les rapports officiels néerlandais* (Brussels, 1908). pp.196–7. This listed the last official return of the French troops before the Battle of Waterloo on 9 June 1815 and showed the 5th and 10th Cuirassiers to have been in Farine's 1st Brigade of the 14th Cavalry Division, and the 6th and 9th Cuirassiers to have comprised Vial's 1st Brigade of the same division.

15   Henri Houssaye, *Revue des Deux Mondes* (Paris, 1898), p.613.

16   Lot, op. cit., p.91.

17   The 7th and 12th Cuirassiers were recorded to have taken on the Union Brigade in the histories of the following French cuirassiers regiments: 4th, 6th, 7th and 12th.

18   Hyacinthe-Hippolyte de Mauduit, *Histoire des derniers jours de la Grande armée* (Paris, 1854). Mauduit (1794–1862) fought in 1815 in the 1st Regiment of Foot Grenadiers of the Imperial Guard. He went on to write a history of the French Army of the time of Waterloo and included a detailed section on Waterloo based on eyewitness accounts.

19   According to Craan's and Siborne's maps, Delort's division was placed to the west of Watier's. Historian Andrew Field pointed out to the author that Mauduit, in a map in his *Des derniers jours de la Grande armée*, showed a different configuration for Milhaud's cuirassiers, deployed into two lines of division. He portrayed Watier's men in the front rank and Delort's in the second line. Presumably this portrayal of these troops was to show where they were later in the day after they had shaken out into a battle formation. Interestingly, Mauduit's placement corresponded with what was recorded in the regimental histories of the 1st Cuirassiers, which stated they were placed 'in the first line of Milhuad's corps on the right', and that of the 12th Cuirassiers, that stated that they were placed 'in the first line on the left of the corps'.

20   Willem Benjamin Craan, *Plan du champ de bataille de Waterloo, avec notice historique*. Craan interviewed Allied and French wounded in Brussels at the time

of Waterloo and used it to publish a detailed map of the battle in September 1816, with an explanatory note.

21   Lot, op. cit., note 2, pp.92–3.

22   Lot, op. cit., note 2, p.95.

23   Barlow op. cit., letter dated 4 July 1815.

24   Elton, op. cit.

25   Pierre de Wit, in an email to the author dated 25 February 2016.

26   *Two Generations, John Derry*, op. cit.

27   Elton, op. cit.

28   Hibbert, op. cit., letter dated 13 July 1815.

29   Dawson, op. cit., p.122.

30   Berton, op. cit., p.152.

31   Subsequent mentions of the Red Lancers fighting the heavy brigades are to be found in: *Correspondance de Napoleon 1er Tome XXXI Ouevres de Napoleon 1er a Sainte Helene* (Paris, 1869), p.234; Le General Baron Auguste Petiet, *Souvenirs Militaire* (Tours, 1844), p.220; Ferdinand de Cornot baron de Cussy, comte Marc de Germiny, *Souvenirs du chevalier de Cussy, garde du corps, diplomate et consul général, 1795–1866, Volume 1* (Paris, 1898), p.13; Edouard Prampain, *Précis d'histoire contemporaine: de 1789 à 1889* (Paris, 1898), p.238; and *Revue du Monde Cathlolique Tome 14* (Paris, 1866), p.800.

32   Gareth Glover, *Waterloo Archive VI* (Barnsley, 2014), p.68.

33   Siborne, op. cit., Letter No. 19 from Lt Waymouth, 2nd Life Guards, p.43.

34   Craan map, op. cit.

35   Siborne, op. cit., Letter No. 20 from Lt Waymouth, 2nd Life Guards, p.46.

36   Andrew Field in email to the author, 30 July 2015.

37   Ronald Pawly, *The Red Lancers* (Marlborough, 1998), p.107.

38   Antoine Fortuné de Brack, *Avant-Postes de cavalerie legère* (Paris, 1834), p.255.

39   Adkin, op. cit., p.357, see 5th and 6th Lancers' location on Map 29.

40   Levavasseur, op. cit., p.300.

41   Edgar Quinet, *Histoire de la campagne de 1815* (Paris, 1862), p.215.

42   Mauduit, op. cit., p.299.

43   Elton, op. cit.

44   Siborne, op. cit., p.47, Letter No. 21.

45   Fortuné de Brack, 'Reponse d'un Militaire a M. de Saint-Aulaire', in *Biblioteque Historique, Tome Premier* (Paris, 1818), pp.240–1.

46   Adkin, op. cit., p.246.

47   Emir Bukhari, *Napoleon's Dragooons and Lancers* (London, 1976), p.10.

48   Adkin, op. cit., p.58.

Chapter 12

1   Siborne, op. cit., Letter No. 19 from Lt Waymouth, 2nd Life Guards, p.43.
2   Ibid, Letter No. 20 from Lt Waymouth, 2nd Life Guards, pp.44–6.
3   Ibid, Letter No. 21.
4   Ibid, Letter No. 38 from Capt. Clark Kennedy of the Royals, p.77.
5   Gen. Sir Evelyn Wood VC, *Cavalry in the Waterloo Campaign* (London, 1895), p.140.
6   Glover 2014, op. cit., p.69.
7   Col Gurwood, *The Dispatches of Field Marshal the Duke of Wellington, K.G, Volume VIII* (London, 1852), p.392, Appendix XIII, Strength of the British Army on the morning of the Battle of Waterloo, 18 June 1815.
8   Andrew Field, *Waterloo: The French Perspective* (Barnsley, 2015), from Martin, *Souvenirs d'un ex-officier, 1812–1815* (Paris and Geneva, 1867), p.288.
9   Siborne, op. cit., p.60.
10   Glover, op. cit., p.56.
11   Siborne, op. cit., p.58.
12   Siborne, op. cit., p.59. Yet Clark Kennedy reckoned it was only 2,000 prisoners in Siborne, p.69.
13   Siborne, op. cit., p.64.
14   Glover, op. cit., p.57.
15   Siborne, op. cit., p.73.
16   Siborne op. cit., p.79.

Chapter 13

1   Siborne, op. cit., Letter No. 5 from Lord Uxbridge, p.8.
2   Elton, op. cit.
3   Siborne, op. cit., Letter No. 21 from Lt Waymouth, p.46.
4   The National Archives, Kew, 1st Dragoon Guards 1815–16, WO 12/96. This contains probably the most accurate guide to other ranks who served in, 'The RETURN of all the *Men* of the First (or King's) Dn Guards who served in the *Battle of Waterloo*, or in any of the *Actions* which immediately preceded it; and *Pay List* of such of them as in consequence thereof have become entitled to *Additional Rates of Pay*, and have actually been settled for the same.' This is the 'Waterloo paylist' for all KDG other ranks who were entitled to the two years' extra pay for having served at or just before the battle. According to this document, other than the officers, there were 578 KDG other ranks paid as having been present at the fighting in the lead-up to Waterloo and in the battle itself. According to the Official Return and regimental records,

twenty-eight KDG officers were present at Waterloo. So the total all ranks before deductions present and thus entitled to the name 'Waterloo man' and its financial benefits and privileges was 606 men. From this, Lt Hibbert's servant Private Oliver must be deducted for absence, to have made 577 other ranks. *The Digest* stated 585 privates had crossed to Ostend, plus one man had subsequently joined the regiment, which was Battersby's servant. The Official Return (see Gurwood, op. cit.) for the KDG on 18 June 1815 showed the same total of 585 men, having already deducted Hibbert's servant from the regiment's strength for that day. We know this, as only twenty-four non-staff officers were listed, when there were twenty-five if Hibbert was included. The 'Waterloo pay list's' total of 578 other ranks was, thus, eight men short of the 586 men shown in both *The Digest* and the Official Return for 18 June 1815 (as it reflected Oliver's absence). The author has considered the 'Waterloo pay list' as the most precise source of which KDG other ranks fought at Waterloo. So in his opinion, the reason for the difference of eight privates was that the regiment, in *The Digest* and subsequent returns, double-counted the farriers. They appear to have listed the farriers separately whilst also having included their numbers in the total number of privates. This mistake was repeated in the return the KDG submitted for its official strength given for the regiment on the morning of 18 June 1815. This can be proved as the names of the individual farriers were shown amongst the list of privates in the Waterloo payroll. So to compute the numbers of KDG present at Waterloo, Hibbert's servant must be deducted to have given a total of 577 other ranks. The total officers in the official return was twenty-eight, having deducted Hibbert. If one is to be precise, Asst-Surgeon Macauley must also be deducted, as he was not on the battlefield because he was running the regiment's sick depot in Brussels. This would mean there would have been twenty-seven KDG officers present on the battlefield of Waterloo. From this total of 604 all ranks must be deducted the twelve sick KDGs, as shown on the regimental return of 18 June 1815. This showed that twelve privates had been sick and two privates and two sergeants had been 'on command' or serving elsewhere. This gave a total of 592 KDG all ranks who were present at Waterloo.

5   Gurwood, op. cit.

6   This was calculated on the basis of the number of horses available. Apart from the two surgeons present at Waterloo, the other twenty-five regimental officers would have been mounted and 537 other ranks' horses were reported to have been transported to Ostend in *The Digest*. From these 562 men must be deducted the eight farriers, who would have not charged, to make a maximum possible 554 mounted KDGs at Waterloo. The farriers would have stayed behind with the rear party. One of their jobs in battle would have been to escort enemy prisoners to the rear of their lines.

7   Siborne, op. cit., p.77.
8   Gurwood, op. cit. The gross total strength of the KDG according to the return of 18 June 1815 was 613 all ranks before deductions. This comprised: twenty-eight officers; forty-seven TSMs and sergeants; eight trumpeters; and 530 rank and file (corporals and privates). The nine-man difference with the author's total of 604 all ranks was found by deducting Macauley, who was in Brussels, and the eight farriers, who were double counted (see note 4).
9   Page, op. cit.
10   Col Edward Owen, *The Waterloo Papers* (Tavistock, 1998), pp12–13.
11   Elton, op. cit.
12   Siborne, op. cit., Letter No. 25 from Lt Waymouth, p.51.
13   Elton, op. cit.
14   Siborne, op. cit., Letter No. 20 and No. 21 from Lt Waymouth, p.46.
15   *Two Generations*, op. cit., p.5.
16   Mann, 1984, p.45.
17   Siborne, op. cit., p.38.
18   Siborne, op. cit., Letter No. 5 from Lord Uxbridge, p.8.
19   Luckley, op. cit., p.17–18.
20   Sgt-Maj. E. Cotton, *A Voice from Waterloo* (London, 1849), p.63.
21   Elton, op. cit.
22   Glover, op. cit., p37–8, National Army Museum, ref. 9102–163.
23   Siborne, op. cit., Letter No. 20 from Lt Waymouth, p.44.
24   *Two Generations*, op. cit., p.5, and Clive Morris's (Curator, 1st The Queen's Dragoon Guards Heritage Trust) records on KDG officers and soldiers at Waterloo.
25   Ibid.
26   Elton, op. cit.
27   Siborne, op. cit., Letter No. 28 from Sir Clement Hill, p.46.
28   Siborne, op. cit., Letter No. 21 from Lt Waymouth, p.47.
29   Page, op. cit.
30   Naylor, op. cit.
31   Ibid.
32   Mann 1984, op. cit., p.45.
33   Adkin, op. cit., p.59.
34   Siborne, op. cit., p.41, Letter No. 8 from Lord Edward Somerset.
35   Cotton, op. cit., p.63.
36   Pierre de Witt, *The Campaign of 1815, A Study*, www.waterloo-campaign. nl. This website is a meticulously researched study of the Battle of Waterloo using only primary sources from many different countries. It is a remarkable historical work and will hopefully be turned into a book one day.
37   Col M.E. Janin, *Campagne de Waterloo* (Paris, 1820), p.35.

38   Pierre de Witt, www.waterloo-campaign.nl, from Francois Marcq, *Déscription des campagnes de guerre faites par moi, Marcq Francois etc.* (Paris, 1901).

39   Hibbert, op. cit., letter dated 13 July 1815.

40   De Witt, op. cit., from Lt-Col Muter: British Library, Add.ms.34.707, pp.60–2.

41   Luckley, op. cit., p.18.

Chapter 14

1   Page, op. cit.

2   Siborne, op. cit., Letter No. 5 from Uxbridge, p.9.

3   QDG website., op. cit. In a letter from the Duke of Richmond to the Marquis of Breadalbane dated 10 May 1849, Richmond informed Breadalbane that: 'The widow of Major Sweney [*sic*] of the King's Dragoon Guards – who save his Colonel (Lt Colonel William Fuller – killed in the battle) – broke through the French line at Waterloo, of who's [*sic*] party only himself and another survived, he being dreadfully wounded and made prisoner, has applied to me for admission for her and her friend Mrs Green to witness the arrival of the ladies at the Palace.'

4   *United Service Gazette*, 2 December 1865. Apparently, when playing chess with Lieutenant Mark Sweny RN, Napoleon had remarked that he was sure he had met him before but he had been wearing the dress of a British Army officer. Once they had discovered their connection, Bonaparte was reported to have commented, 'Such are the vicissitudes of life, your brother was my prisoner, and I am now yours.'

5   Siborne, op. cit., Letter No. 21 from Lt Waymouth, p.47.

6   Barlow, op. cit., Letter of 4 July 1815.

7   Elton, op. cit.

8   Mauduit, op. cit.

9   White-Spunner, op. cit., p.251.

10   Lot, op. cit., p.95.

11   Hibbert, op. cit., 13 July 1815.

12   Barlowe, op. cit., 4 July 1815.

13   Siborne, op. cit., Letter No. 38, p.77, from Capt. Clark Kennedy of the Royals.

14   Luckley, op. cit., p.18.

15   Siborne, op. cit., Letter No. 29 from Capt. Robert Wallace KDG, p.57.

16   Luckley, op. cit., p.18.

17   Cotton, op. cit., Appendix, No. IV, p.234.

18   Page, op. cit.

19   Glover, op.cit., Letter No. 105 from the Honourable Henry Lowther, p.238. This murder was also mentioned by John Edgecombe Daniel in his *Journal of an Officer in the Commissariat Department of the Army* (London, 1820) p.421.

20 White-Spunner, op. cit., p.251.

21 Charles Dalton, *The Waterloo Roll Call*, footnote to p.53.

22 Barlow, op. cit., 4 July 1815 to his wife Betsy.

23 Cotton, op. cit., p.63.

24 Glover, op. cit., Letter No.9 dated 23 June 1815 from Lord Edward Somerset, p.19.

25 Elton, op. cit.

26 Siborne, op. cit., Letter No. 26, from Maj. Marten of the Royals (Sub-Lieutenant, 2nd Life Guards at Waterloo), p.73.

27 White Spunner, op. cit., p.255, suggested 800 were killed or missing out of 2,500 in both Household and Union brigades. However, Barbero has suggested, on Clark Kennedy's evidence, the initial number was more like 1,000 sabres in the Union Brigade, as non-combatants and those who did not charge made up about 10 per cent of the total.

28 Hibbert, op. cit., 13 July 1815. This is a pretty rough estimate based on Hibbert stating that only 'about half the regiment' returned from the French lines and of this force, 'about a troop were killed or taken prisoners'.

29 Barlow, op. cit., letter of 4 July 1815.

30 Naylor, op. cit.

31 White-Spunner, op. cit., p.256. However, Pierre de Witt, in an email to the author of 25 February 2016, stated that from his research the number of prisoners was more like 1,900.

32 Anglesey, op. cit., p.142. However, the guns were not spiked and some gun crews were replaced by infantry and thus became effective again, according to Mark Adkin in a telephone conversation with the author on 8 February 2016.

Chapter 15

1 Naylor, op. cit.

2 Siborne, op. cit., Letter No. 18 from Lord Edward Somerset, p.41.

3 White-Spunner, op. cit., p.296.

4 Mann 1984, op. cit., p62–4.

5 Siborne, op. cit., Letter No. 9 from Lord Uxbridge, p.9.

6 Letter to author from Philip Haythornthwaite, 28 December 2015, from *The Army Quarterly*, July 1935, pp.292–6.

7 Ibid. Haythornthwaite argued that it was unlikely Churchill would have been in a position to have overheard Uxbridge make these comments on 18 June 1815. He felt they more likely referred to his dissatisfaction with his light cavalry at Genappe.

8 Siborne, op. cit., p.20.

9   Siborne, op. cit., Letter No. 76 from Lt Col the Hon. H. Murray, p.179.

10   Ibid.

11   Adkin, op. cit., p.355.

12   Siborne, op. cit., Letter No. 70 from Sir Hussey Vivian, p.149.

13   Dawson 2015, op. cit., p.231, from British Library ADD MS 34703 folio 231.

14   Capt. Battersby's memory is kept alive in his descendant regiment by his Waterloo
     medal, which was passed down his family to Dorothy Michelin (née Battersby)
     of Jamaica, who donated it to the 1st Queen's Dragoon Guards in 1994.

15   Taken from www.uptongreyparishcouncil.co.uk. The Three Horseshoes is
     now called the Hoddington Arms. Thomas Woodman's widow Anne was built
     a house in the grounds of Upton Grey House, which was called Waterloo
     Cottage.

16   Dawson 2015, op. cit., p.232, from Lt A.J. Hamilton of Scots Greys, Edward
     Almack, *History of the Second Dragoons*, pp.450–1.

17   Barlow, op. cit., letter dated 4 July 1815.

18   According to the official rolls there were 2,651 sabres in the two heavy
     brigades, but Barbero reckoned that the number was more like 2,000. This
     view was based on comments made by Clark Kennedy in Siborne, Letter
     No. 39, p77–8, in which he estimated there were only 950, and at the most
     1,000 sabres in the Union Brigade. The reason for this was that the Duke's
     Dispatches included 120–130 non-combatants or around 10 per cent of the
     brigade strength.

19   Barlow, op. cit., letter dated 23 June.

20   Barlow, op. cit., letter dated 4 July.

Chapter 16

1   Mann 1984, op. cit., p.67, from the letters of John Stubbings, then in the pos-
     session of Ernest Shead, Stubbings's direct descendant.

2   *Two Generations*, op. cit., p.5.

3   Barlow, op. cit, letter dated 4 July 1815.

4   Barlow op. cit, letter dated 23 June 1815.

5   Mann 1894, op. cit., p.73.

6   Burnham and McGuigan, op. cit., pp.261–3.

7   Elton letter, op.cit. Elton gave slightly different statistics for the KDG casual-
     ties, which were probably based on the first numbers to have emerged after
     the battle, as this letter of his to Sir Henry Fane was dated 15 July 1815. On
     a sheet of paper entitled, 'Return of killed, wounded and missing of the
     British Cavalry on 17th & 18th June', Elton listed the KDG losses as – Men:
     killed 43; wounded 104; missing 128, making a total of 275 casualties. Horses:

killed 55; wounded 13; missing 243, making a total of 311 equine casualties. The casualties of the other British heavy cavalry regiments listed were: 1st Life Guards: men 65, horses 85; 2nd Life Guards: men 155, horses 173; Blues: men 98, horses 103; Royals: men 196, horses 196; Greys: men 199, horses 228; and Inniskillings: men 217, horses 207.

8   Mann 1984, op. cit., p.73. He cited eleven different sources for his information, which have all been listed in his sources section.

9   The numbers for those killed listed in *The Digest* and other sources tallied exactly with the KDG Waterloo Return. However, there were some anomalies which have been addressed in the notes to the regimental roll in Appendix I.

10   KDG Waterloo Return, op. cit.

11   John Booth (ed.), *The Battle of Waterloo by a Near Observer* (London, 1817), p.274. The mortality rates for the other heavy brigade regiments were: Inniskillings, 34 per cent; 1st Life Guards, 31 per cent; Blues, 19 per cent; and 2nd Life Guards, 11 per cent.

12   Source for all casualty rates, Burnham & McGuigan, op. cit., pp.261–3. This source listed the KDG's strength at 595 men and casualties at 275 men. However, according to the Pay Return of the KDG at Waterloo, they fielded 606 men. Casualties according to *The Digest* were 263 men.

13   John Booth (ed.), op. cit.

14   Hibbert, op. cit., letter dated 13 July 1815.

15   Ibid.

16   Gareth Glover, *Waterloo Archives Volume I*, Letter No. 5 from Private Joseph Lord in Oldham Archives, 2006–046.

17   Hibbert, op. cit., letter dated 13 July 1815.

18   Barbero, op. cit., p.165.

19   Hibbert, op. cit., letter dated 13 July 1815.

20   Ibid.

21   Luckley, op. cit., p.19.

22   Hibbert, op. cit., letter dated 13 July 1815.

23   Luckley, op. cit., pp.18–19.

24   Ibid.

25   Siborne, op. cit., Letter No. 29 from Lt Col Robert Wallace, p.57.

26   Barbero, op. cit., p.163.

27   Dawson, op. cit., pp.225–6, from National Army Museum 9102–163.

28   Naylor, op. cit.

29   White-Spunner, op. cit., p.367.

30   *The KDG Waterloo payroll*, op. cit.

31   Glover 2014, op. cit., Letter No. 9 from Lord Somerset to his mother, p.21. From the Household Cavalry Archive, ref. AB 2997 (37).

32 Stubbings, op. cit.
33 Barlow, op. cit., letter dated 4 July 1815.

Chapter 17

1   Barlow, op. cit., letter dated 4 July 1815.
2   *The Digest*, op. cit.
3   Ibid.
4   Hibbert, op. cit., letter dated 26 July 1815.
5   Hibbert, op. cit., letter dated 29 June 1815.
6   Hibbert, op. cit., letter dated 15 July 1815.
7   Mann 1984, op. cit., p.82.
8   *The Digest*, op. cit.
9   Barlow, op. cit., letter dated 4 July 1815.
10 *The Digest*, op. cit.
11 Gen. Cavalié Mercer, *Journal of the Waterloo Campaign, Volume 2* (London, 2001), p.196.
12 *The Digest*, op. cit.
13 Naylor, op. cit.
14 Hibbert, op. cit., letter dated 26 July 1815.
15 Hibbert, op. cit., letter dated 15 July 1815.
16 Barlow, op. cit., letter dated 11 July 1815.
17 Hibbert, op. cit., letter dated 15 October 1815.
18 Barlow, op. cit., 30 August 1815.
19 Barlow, op. cit., 18 July 1815.
20 Booth (ed.), op.cit., p.286.
21 Mann 1993, op. cit., pp.200–1, from records held by the QDG Heritage Trust.
22 This was either an exaggeration or this was an Allied force.
23 Page, op.cit.
24 Hibbert, op. cit., letter dated 15 October 1815.
25 Barlow, op. cit., 3 August 1815.
26 *The Digest*, op. cit.
27 Hibbert, op. cit., letter dated 2 December 1815.
28 Sgt John Adams KDG, letter dated 17 January 1816, held by the QDG Heritage Trust.
29 Hibbert, op. cit.
30 Adams, op. cit.
31 Mann, op. cit., p.106.
32 *The Digest*, op. cit.

Chapter 18

1   *A List of the Officers of the Army and of the Corps of Royal Marines*, published by the War Office (London, 1821). According to this document, the following nine officers who were present at Waterloo had left the KDG by 1821: Naylor, Stirling, Hawley, D'Arcy Irvine, Middleton, Huntley, Going, Macauley and Pearson.

2   Clive Morris, Curator of 1st The Queen's Dragoon Guards Heritage Trust's analysis of the records of KDG officers and soldiers who fought at Waterloo.

3   *The Inverness Courier*, 8 May 1819.

4   Siborne, op. cit., Letter No. 29, p.56.

5   *Parliamentary Papers: 1780–1849, Volume 12* (London, 1816), p.61.

Chapter 19

1   These statistics were derived from QDG Curator Clive Morris's records, drawn from the Waterloo KDG men's discharge papers. This analysis was taken from as many men whose records indicated both their places of origin and their deaths. In this case it involved 107 KDG other ranks who had fought at Waterloo and had left the regiment between 1816–42.

2   Information on Thomas Barlow has been provided by Jill Birtwistle. She is his great-great-great-granddaughter through his first wife Elizabeth's daughter Margaret Rose, who married the son of a Methodist minister.

3   Ibid.

4   *Two Generations*, op. cit., p.5.

5   Ibid, p.6.

6   Ibid, p.7.

7   Ibid, p.8.

8   The other men who had made TSM before Page, who achieved this rank in 1814, were Fairclough, who achieved the rank in 1801, Wright in 1812 and Linton in 1813.

9   T.J.C. Cooke, *Sergeant Stubbings and the One-Eared Horse,* a private paper in the possession of Stubbings's great-grandson Ernest Shead.

10 Roderick Floud, Donald N. McCloskey and Deirdre N. McCloskey, *The Economic History of Britain Since 1700: 1700–1860* (Cambridge, 1994), p.363.

11 These average ages of death are based on a very rudimentary analysis of eleven of the officers and 106 men for whom there are records of their ages on death, as collected by Clive Morris. These men were amongst those who left the KDG from 1815–20.

Chapter 20

1   Mann 1993, op. cit., p.203.
2   It appeared from the records of the KDG soldiers that only thirty-three 'Waterloo Men' were still serving in the regiment after 1833.
3   J. Hope Grant, 'Commander of the Forces', in *The Illustrated London News*, December 1860, p.583.
4   Mann, op. cit., p.275.
5   Mann, op. cit., p.287–8.
6   The British cavalry regiment next purest to its roots is presently the Royal Scots Dragoon Guards, which is a product of two amalgamations and a blend of three regiments: 3rd Dragoon Guards, 6th Dragoon Guards and 2nd Dragoons (Scots Greys).

Chapter 21

1   Mark Adkin in an email to the author, dated 9 February 2016.
2   Col Edward Owen, *The Waterloo Papers* (Tavistock, 1998), pp.47–8. Napoleon's intention had been to destroy Wellington rather than take territory, or to bypass him and take Brussels. This was outlined in an anonymous eyewitness's log kept by one of Napoleon's captors on HMS *Northumberland*, who was probably Admiral Sir George Cockburn. The captured emperor had, 'said that on the morning of 18th June he did not entertain the remotest idea that the Duke of Wellington would have allowed him to have brought the English army to a decisive battle and he therefore had been more anxious to push on and if possible to force it as he considered nothing else could offer a chance of surmounting the difficulties with which he was surrounded.' Napoleon was reported to have then stated that with Wellington eliminated, the Prussians would likely have dispersed and then he could have gone on to have destroyed the Austrians before they could have joined up with the Russians.
3   Sir James Shaw Kennedy, *Notes on the Battle of Waterloo* (London, 1865), p.127.
4   The late Lt-Gen. Sir Christopher Wallace KBE, DL, in telephone conversation with the author.
5   Philip Haythornthwaite, letter to the author dated 14 December 2015.
6   Adkin, op. cit., pp.408–9.
7   Anglesey, op. cit., p.146.
8   Capt. Rees Howell Gronow, *The Reminiscences and Recollections of Captain Gronow, 1810–1860*, (London, 1900), pp.79–80.
9   See Chapter fifteen note 8, which referred to detrimental remarks and quotations made about the British cavalry by 1st Foot Guards officers Churchill and Stanhope.

10   White-Spunner, op. cit., pp.393–4.

11   Anglesey, op. cit., p.135, *Memorandum from Uxbridge* [n.d.], The Plas Newyd Papers.

12   Glover, op. cit., p.21, letter from Somerset to his mother dated 23 June 1815, from the Household Cavalry Archive, ref. AB 2997 (37).

13   Anglesey, op. cit., p.141.

14   Duke of Wellington, 'Wellington's Waterloo Dispatch'. Field Marshal the Duke of Wellington, official dispatch after Waterloo, 19 June 1815, in John Keegan, *The Penguin Book of War* (London, 1999), p.181. The only other regiment mentioned for actions on 18 June was the KGL, but it was not singled out for praise.

15   Sir Charles Oman, *Wellington's Army 1809–1814* (London, 1912), pp.111–12. This book gave a summary of Wellington's General Orders concerning the instructions to cavalry. The first of the five points was to maintain a reserve of at least half the total number of sabres in the unit charging to help the first line exploit its successes or to cover it in the event of failure. The second point was that a force of cavalry should be formed in three lines. When the first and the second lines were fielded, the reserve was to be formed in column. The third point concerned actions against cavalry, where the second line was to be 400–500 yards from the first and the reserve to be the same distance behind the second line. The fourth point stipulated the second line should only be 200 yards behind the first when charging infantry, so as to exploit an enemy just having recovered from an attack by the first line and probably still in the process of trying to reload its weapons. The fifth point maintained that whilst the first line was to attack at the gallop, the second line was to follow at the walk so they would not get 'mingled with the front line at the outset'.

16   Siborne, op. cit., Letter No. 7 from Lord Greenock, pp.13–14.

17   Glover, op. cit., pp.18–19.

18   Anglesey, op. cit., p.141.

19   Andrew Roberts, *Waterloo: Napoleon's Last Gamble* (London, 2005), p.57.

20   Adkin, op. cit., p.342.

21   Barbero, op. cit., pp.228–9.

22   Baron Friedrich Carl Ferdinand von Müffling, *A Sketch of the Battle of Waterloo: To Which are Added Official Despatches of Field Marshal the Duke of Wellington, Field Marshal Prince Blücher, and Reflections on the Battles of Ligny and Waterloo by General Müffling* (Brussels, 1833), p.cv.

23   Adkin, op. cit., p.409.

24   Shaw Kennedy, op. cit., p.106.

25   Ibid.

26   Quotation from email of 12 December 2015 to author from Gen. Sir Rupert Smith KCB, DSO, OBE, QGM.

27   'A General Officer', *Colburn's United Service Magazine and Military Journal*, quoted by Philip Haythornthwaite in *The Hand of History: An Anthology of History Quotations and Commentaries*, Michael Leventhal (ed.) (Elstree, 2011), p.57.

28   The senior British officers who were consulted and a consensus of whose two opinions has been outlined were Gen. Sir Rupert Smith and the late Lt-Gen. Sir Christopher Wallace.

29   White-Spunner, op. cit., pp.443–4.

30   Adkin, op. cit., Map 27, is entitled D'Erlon's I Corps Attack: Phase 3, the Crisis of the Entire Battle (1.45–2.15 p.m.), p.348.

31   Author's conversation with Mark Adkin, 18 December 2015.

32   Alessandro Barbero email to author, 17 March 2015.

33   Anglesey, op. cit., p.135, from Memorandum by Uxbridge [n.d.], PNP.

34   All net proceeds from this book will be put towards the creation and erection of a memorial to all the KDGs who fought at Waterloo. It is hoped to locate this monument somewhere appropriate to the regiment on or in the vicinity of the battlefield of Waterloo.

BIBLIOGRAPHY

A List of the Officers of the Army and of the Corps of Royal Marines, published by the War Office (London, 1821).

Adkin, Mark, *The Waterloo Companion* (London, 2001).

Anglesey, the Marquess of, *One Leg: The Life and Letters of Henry William Paget, First Marquess of Anglesey* (London, 1961).

Barbero, Alessandro, *The Battle: A New History of the Battle of Waterloo* (London, 2003).

Beamish, N.L., *History of the King's German Legion, Vol. II.* (London, 1837).

Berton, Le Maréchal de camp, *Precis, Historique, Militaire et Critique des Batailles de Fleurus et Waterloo* (Paris, 1818).

Bonaparte, Napoleon, *Correspondance de Napoleon 1er Tome XXXI Ouevres de Napoleon 1er à Sainte Helene* (Paris, 1869).

Booth, John (ed.), *The Battle of Waterloo by Near Observer* (London, 1817).

Bukhari, Emir, *Napoleon's Dragoons and Lancers* (London, 1976).

Burnham, Bob and McGuigan, Ron, *The British Army Against Napoleon, Facts, Lists and Trivia 1805–1815* (Barnsley, 2010).

Cannon, Richard, *Historical Records of the British Army, 1st Dragoon Guards* (London, 1837).

Cookson, J.E., *The British Armed Nation 1793–1815* (Oxford, 1997).

Corrigan, Gordon, *Waterloo: A New History* (London, 1992).

Cotton, Sgt-Maj. Edward, *A Voice from Waterloo* (London, 1849).

Craan, Willem Benjamin, *Plan du champ de bataille de Waterloo, avec notice Historique* (Brussels, 1816).

Crofton, Sir Morgan, 'Household Cavalry and the Waterloo Campaign', *Household Brigade Magazine*, 1911.

Dalton, Charles, *The Waterloo Roll Call* (London, 1904).

Daniel, John Edgecombe, *Journal of an Officer in the Commissariat Department: 1811–1815* (London, 1820).

Dawson, Paul, *Boots and Saddles* (Stockton-on-Tees, 2014).

Dawson, Paul. L, *Charge the Guns!* (Stockton-on-Tees, 2015).

de Bas Francois and de t'Serclaes de Wommerson, Le Comte Jacques, *La Campagne de 1818 aux Pas-Bas d'après les rapports officiels néerlandais* (Brussels, 1908).

de Brack, Antoine Fortune, *Avant-Postes de cavalerie légère* (Paris, 1834).

de Brack, Fortune, 'Reponse d'un Militaire a M. de Saint-Aulaire', *Biblioteque Historique Tome Premier* (Paris, 1818).

de Cornot, Ferdinand, baron de Cussy, de Germiny, comte Marc de Germiny, *Souvenirs du chevalier de Cussy, garde du corps, diplomate et consul général, 1795–1866, Volume 1* (Paris, 1898).

de Mauduit, Hyacinthe-Hippolyte, *Histoire des derniers jours de la Grande armée* (Paris, 1854).

Dundas, General Sir David, *Instructions and Regulations for the Formation and Movements of the Cavalry* (London, 1796).

Elton, Margaret, *Annals of the Elton Family* (Stroud, 1994).

Field, Andrew, *Waterloo: The French Perspective* (Barnsley, 2015).

Fletcher, Ian, *Galloping at Everything, The British Cavalry in the Peninsular War and at Waterloo 1808–15* (Staplehurst, 1999).

Floud, Roderick and McCloskey Donald, *The Economic History of Britain Since 1700, Volume I: 1700–1860* (Cambridge, 1994).

Fortescue, Sir John, *British Campaigns in Flanders 1690–1794 (Extracts from Volume 4 of A History of the British Army)* (London, 1918).

Fosten, Bryan, *Wellington's Heavy Cavalry* (London, 1982).

Fremont-Barnes, Gregory, *Waterloo 1815: Britain's Day of Destiny* (Stroud, 2014).

General Standing Orders for Third, Or Prince of Wales's Dragoon Guards (Edinburgh, 1803).

Glover, Gareth, *Waterloo Archives Volume I: British Sources* (Barnsley, 2010).

Glover, Gareth, *Waterloo Archive, Volume IV: British Sources* (Barnsley, 2012).

Glover, Gareth, *Waterloo Archive, Volume VI: British Sources* (Barnsley, 2014).

Gronow, Rees Howell, *Reminiscences of Captain Gronow* (London, 1862).

Gurwood, Lt-Col John, *The Dispatches of Field Marshal the Duke of Wellington: During His Various Campaigns, Volumes II and VIII* (London, 1852).

Haythornthwaite, Philip, *British Cavalryman 1793–1815* (London, 1994).

Haythornthwaite, Philip and Hook, Adam, *Napoleonic Heavy Cavalry & Dragoon Tactics* (Oxford, 2013).

Houssaye, Henri, *Revue des Deux Mondes* (Paris, 1898).

Jan Luiten van Zanden, *Wages and the Cost of Living in Southern England 1450–1700* (International Institute of Social History), www.iisg.nl/hpw/dover.php.

Johnson, Col W. and Howell, Lt-Col H.A.L., *Roll of Commissioned Officers in the Medical Service of the British Army 20 June 1727 to 23 June 1898* (Aberdeen, 1917).

Levavasseur, Octave, *Souvenirs Militaires de Octave Levavasseur* (Paris, 1914).

Leventhal, Michael (ed.), *The Hand of History: An Anthology of History Quotations and Commentaries* (Elstree, 2011).

Haythornthwaite, Philip, from 'A General Officer', *Colburn's United Service Magazine and Military Journal*.

Longford, Elizabeth, *Wellington: The Years of the Sword* (London, 1971).

Lot, Henri, *Les deux généraux Ordener* (Paris, 1910).

Luckley, George, *The history of Thomas Hasker, soldier and Methodist: With his letters* (London, 1875).

Mann, Michael, *And They Rode On* (Salisbury, 1984).

Mann, Michael, *The Regimental History of 1st The Queen's Dragoon Guards* (Norwich, 1993).

Marcq, Francois, *Campagnes de guerre faites par moi, etc.* (Paris, 1901).

Martin, Jacques François, *Souvenirs d'un ex-officier, 1812–1815* (Paris & Geneva, 1867).

Martyn, Charles, *The British Cavalry Sword From 1600* (Barnsley, 2004).

Maxwell, Sir Herbert, *The Life of Wellington: The Restoration of the Martial Power of Great Britain* (London, 1899).

Mercer, Gen. Alexander Cavalié, *Journal of the Waterloo Campaign, Volumes I & II* (London, 1870).

Müffling, Baron Friedrich Carl Ferdinand von, *A sketch of the Battle of Waterloo: To Which are Added Official Despatches of Field Marshal the Duke of Wellington, Field Marshal Prince Blücher, and Reflections on the Battles of Ligny and Waterloo by General Müffling* (Brussels, 1833).

Oman, Sir Charles, *Wellington's Army 1809–1814* (London, 1912).

Pawly, Ronald, *The Red Lancers* (Marlborough, 1998).

Petiet, Le general Baron Auguste, *Souvenirs Militaire* (Tours, 1844).

Prampain, Edouard, *Précis d'histoire contemporaine: de 1789 à 1889* (Paris, 1898).

Quinet, Edgar, *Histoire de la campagne de 1815* (Paris, 1862).

Ramsay, David, *Military Memoirs of Great Britain: Or a History of the War, 1755–1763* (Edinburgh, 1779).

Revue du Monde Catholique Tome 14 (Paris, 1866).

Roberts, Andrew, *Waterloo: Napoleon's Last Gamble* (London, 2005).

Rogers, Col H.C.B., *Wellington's Army* (London, 1979).

Shaw Kennedy, Sir James, *Notes on the Battle of Waterloo* (London, 1865).

Siborne, William, *History of the War in France and Belgium, in 1815: Containing Minute Details* (Cambridge, 2012).

Siborne, William, *The Waterloo Campaign* (London, 1848).

Siborne, Maj.-Gen. H.T., *Waterloo Letters* (London, 1891).

Skrine, Sir Francis, *Fontenoy and Great Britain's Share in the War of the Austrian Succession 1741–48* (London and Edinburgh, 1906).

Stouff, Louis, *Le lieutenant général Delort: d'après ses archives et les archives du ministre de la guerre, 1792–1815* (Paris, 1906).

Sweetman, John, *Raglan from the Peninsula to the Crimea* (Barnsley, 2010).

The Standing Orders King's Dragoon Guards, published 1819.

Two Generations, John Derry (1792–1869) and John Derry Junior (1817–1838), private papers held by the Derry family.

White-Spunner, Sir Barney, *Horse Guards* (London, 2006).

White-Spunner, Sir Barney, *Of Living Valour* (London, 2015).

Wilson, John Harold, *Court Satires of the Restoration* (Ohio, 1976).

Wood, General Sir Evelyn VC, *Cavalry in the Waterloo Campaign* (London, 1895).

INDEX